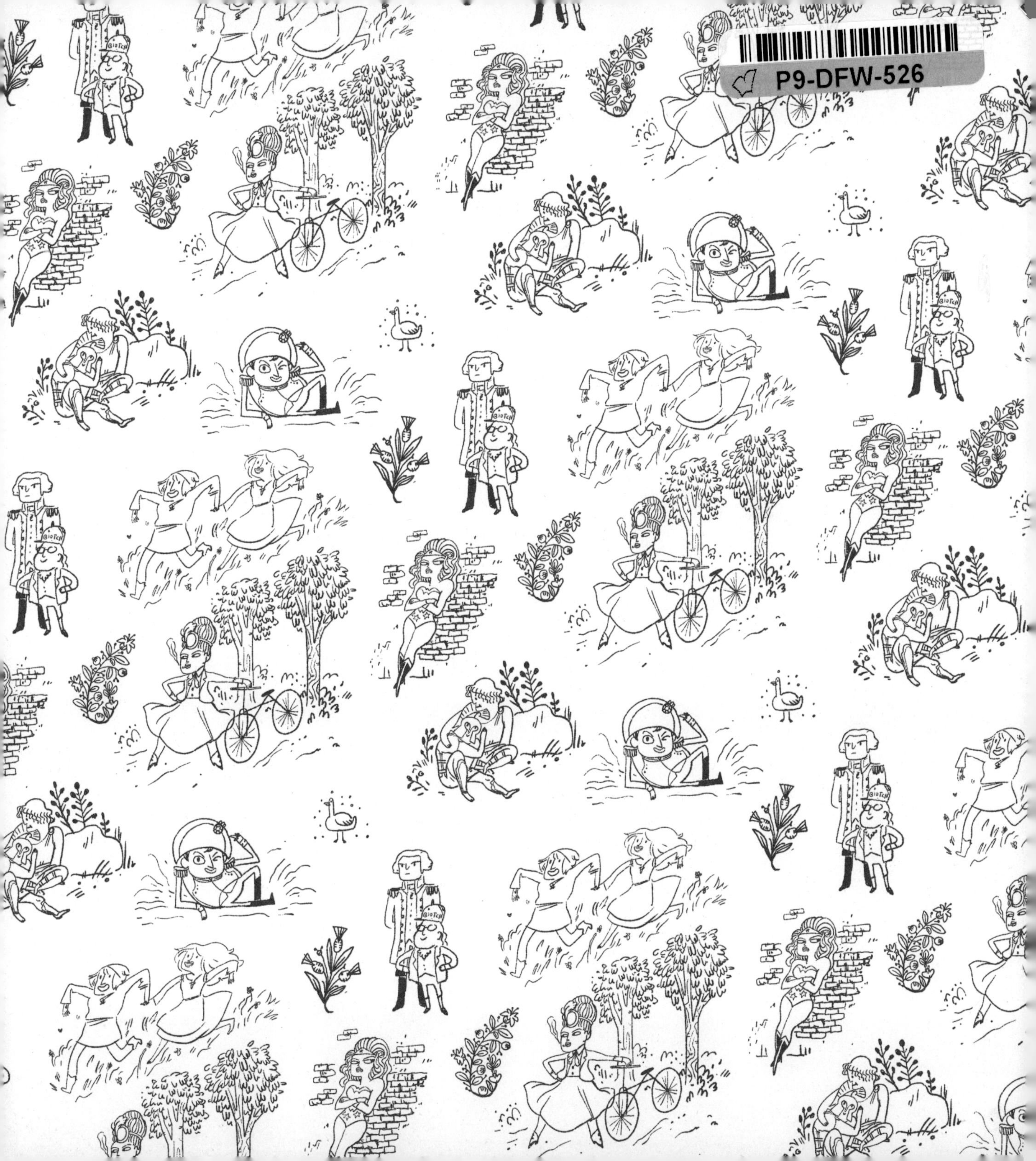
BIOTCH

STEP ASIDE, POPS

Thank you to Chris, Peggy, Tom, Julia, and Tracy at Drawn & Quarterly,
who brought this book to you.

To Laureen, for talking humour with me.

To Becky and Maura for endless support.

To Mom and Dad, forever.

And to the readers who have been with me this whole time.
Thank you! You're the reason I'm here.

 Comics first published at *harkavagrant.com*. First hardcover edition: September 2015. Printed in China. 10 9 8 7 6 5 4 3 2 1

drawnandquarterly.com

Library and Archives Canada Cataloguing in Publication: Beaton, Kate, 1983–[*Hark! A Vagrant.* Selections] *Step Aside, Pops: A Hark! A Vagrant Collection*/Kate Beaton. ISBN 978-1-77046-208-3 (bound) 1. Graphic novels. I. Title. PN6733.B42S74 2015 741.5'971 C2015-902359-9

Drawn & Quarterly acknowledges the financial contribution of the Government of Canada through the Canada Book Fund and the Canada Council for the Arts for our publishing activities and for support of this edition.

Published in the USA by Drawn & Quarterly, a client publisher of Farrar, Straus and Giroux. Orders: 888.330.8477. Published in Canada by Drawn & Quarterly, a client publisher of Raincoast Books. Orders: 800.663.5714.

STEP ASIDE, POPS

A HARK! A VAGRANT COLLECTION

KATE BEATON

DRAWN AND QUARTERLY

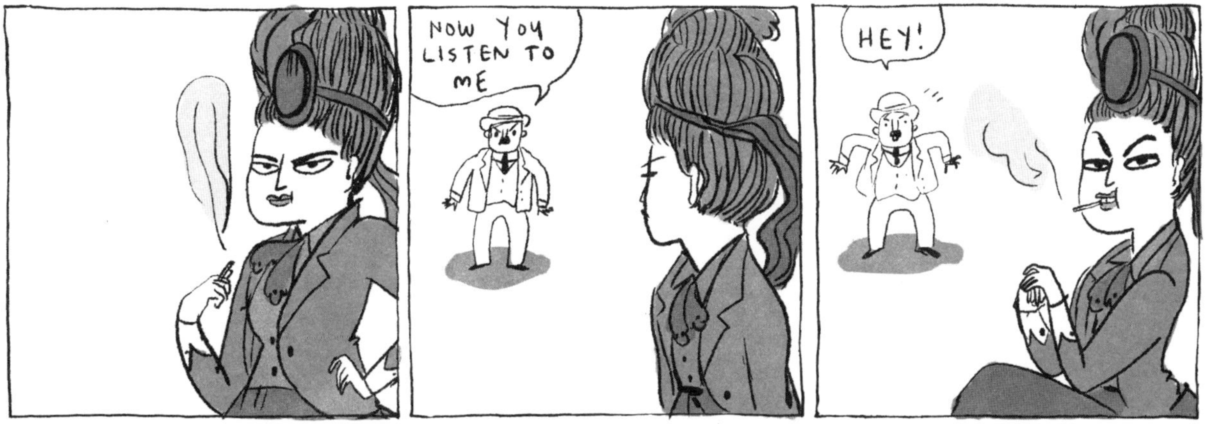
NOW YOU LISTEN TO ME
HEY!

I named my comic *Hark! A Vagrant* a long time ago in an effort to title it nothing in particular but also something that sounded vaguely old-timey and absurd. Related: my advice to young artists would be to name their comic something that doesn't require them to repeat themselves several times when someone asks for it. But it's a good thing that *Hark! A Vagrant* doesn't mean anything. When I get asked to describe my comics, the easiest thing to say is that it is historical or literary or pop-culture parodies. But really the comics are just a reflection of whatever I find interesting or whatever I'm reading or thinking about. Some things are a predictable fit, some things repeat themselves, and some come out of left field. If it were about one thing all the time, eventually I think I'd be dipping into an empty well. I like doing focused projects, but *Hark!* will always be a mixed bag. In the end, I just try to come up with something funny. Hopefully, we are on the same page.

CHOPIN AND LISZT

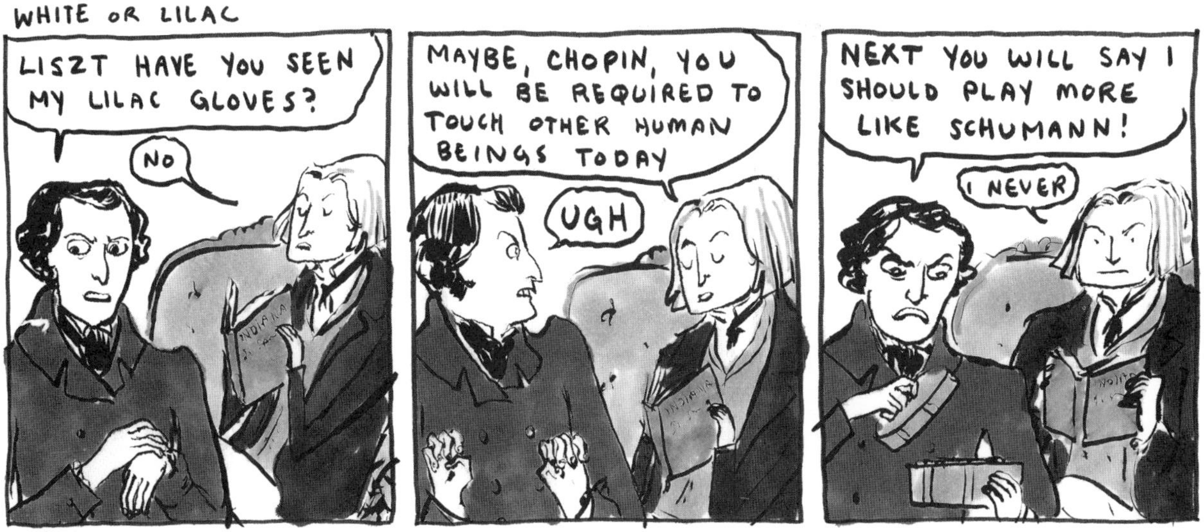
WHITE OR LILAC
LISZT HAVE YOU SEEN MY LILAC GLOVES?
NO
MAYBE, CHOPIN, YOU WILL BE REQUIRED TO TOUCH OTHER HUMAN BEINGS TODAY
UGH
NEXT YOU WILL SAY I SHOULD PLAY MORE LIKE SCHUMANN!
I NEVER

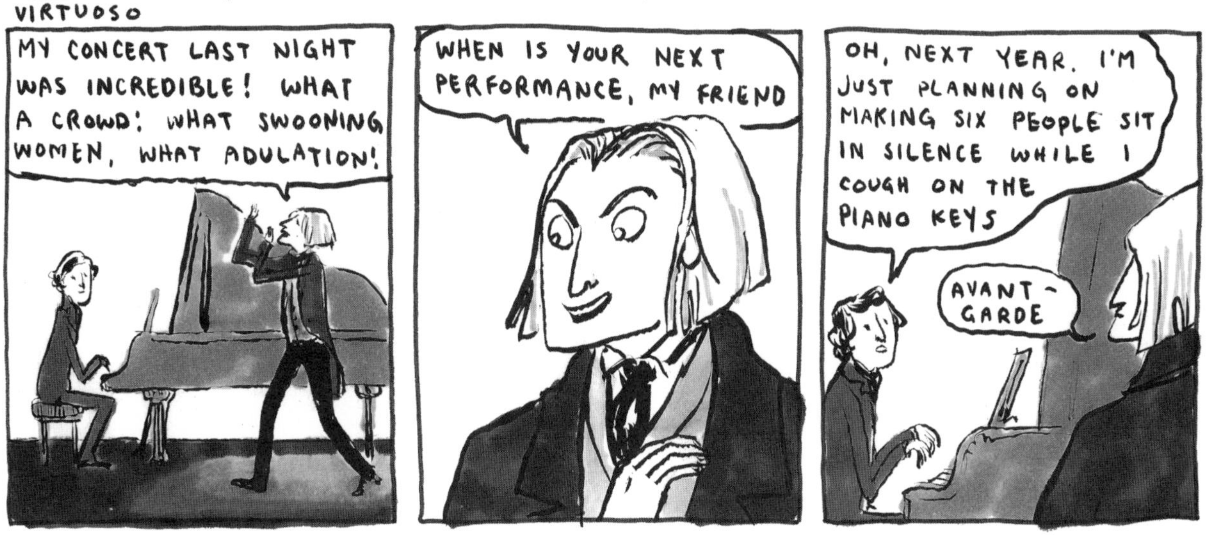
VIRTUOSO
MY CONCERT LAST NIGHT WAS INCREDIBLE! WHAT A CROWD! WHAT SWOONING WOMEN, WHAT ADULATION!
WHEN IS YOUR NEXT PERFORMANCE, MY FRIEND
OH, NEXT YEAR. I'M JUST PLANNING ON MAKING SIX PEOPLE SIT IN SILENCE WHILE I COUGH ON THE PIANO KEYS
AVANT-GARDE

Sometimes we get along with our friends. Sometimes we don't! Sometimes our friends are going all Jerry Lee Lewis on the keys and we just want some quiet time to cough into a handkerchief—is that too much to ask?

RAZZLE DAZZLE

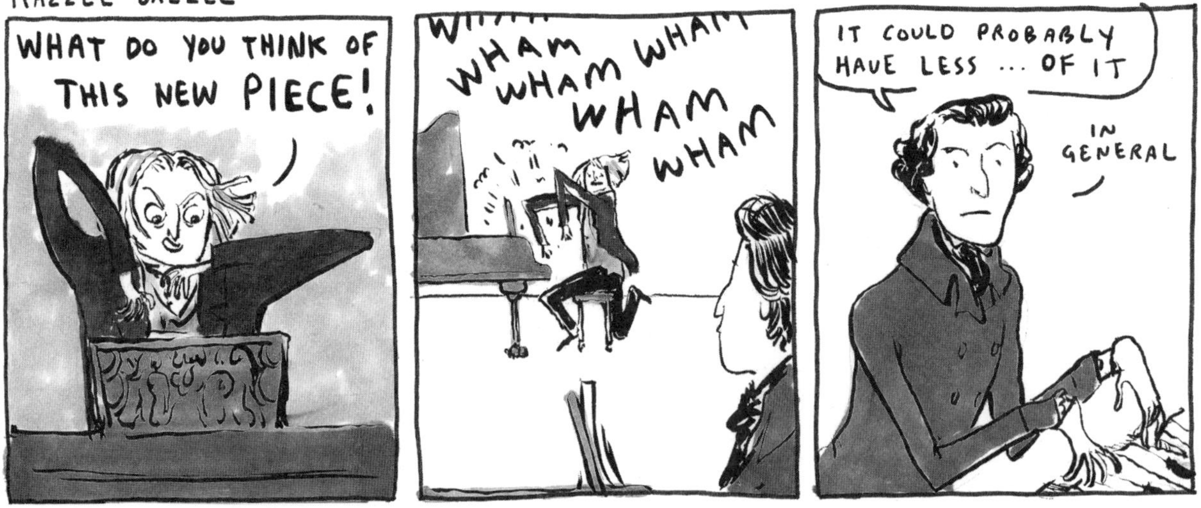
WHAT DO YOU THINK OF THIS NEW PIECE!
WHAM WHAM WHAM WHAM WHAM
IT COULD PROBABLY HAVE LESS ... OF IT
IN GENERAL

CLASSICAL IF YOU PLEASE

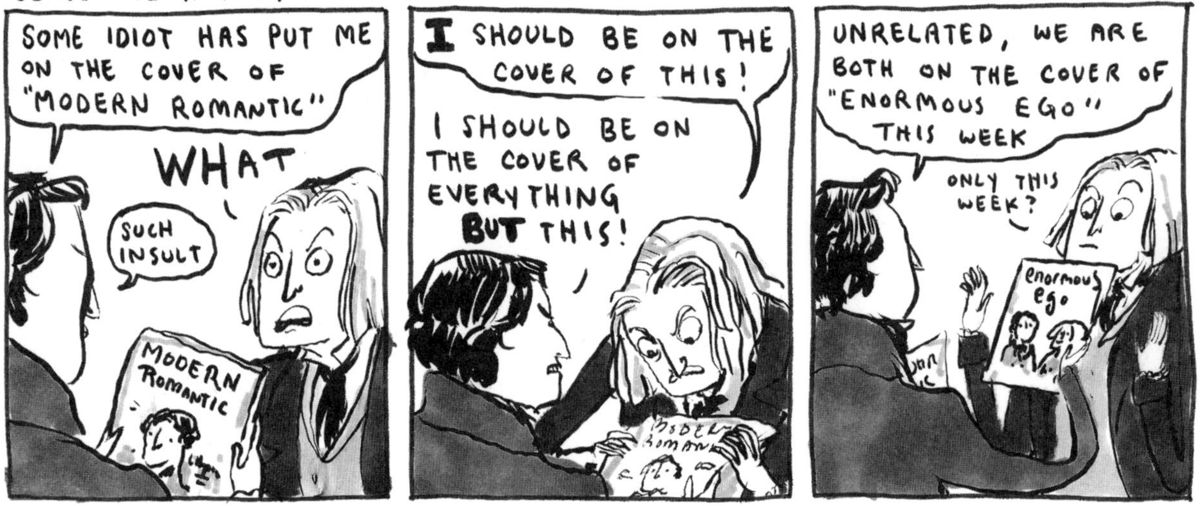
SOME IDIOT HAS PUT ME ON THE COVER OF "MODERN ROMANTIC"
WHAT
SUCH INSULT
MODERN ROMANTIC
I SHOULD BE ON THE COVER OF THIS!
I SHOULD BE ON THE COVER OF EVERYTHING BUT THIS!
UNRELATED, WE ARE BOTH ON THE COVER OF "ENORMOUS EGO" THIS WEEK
ONLY THIS WEEK?
enormous ego

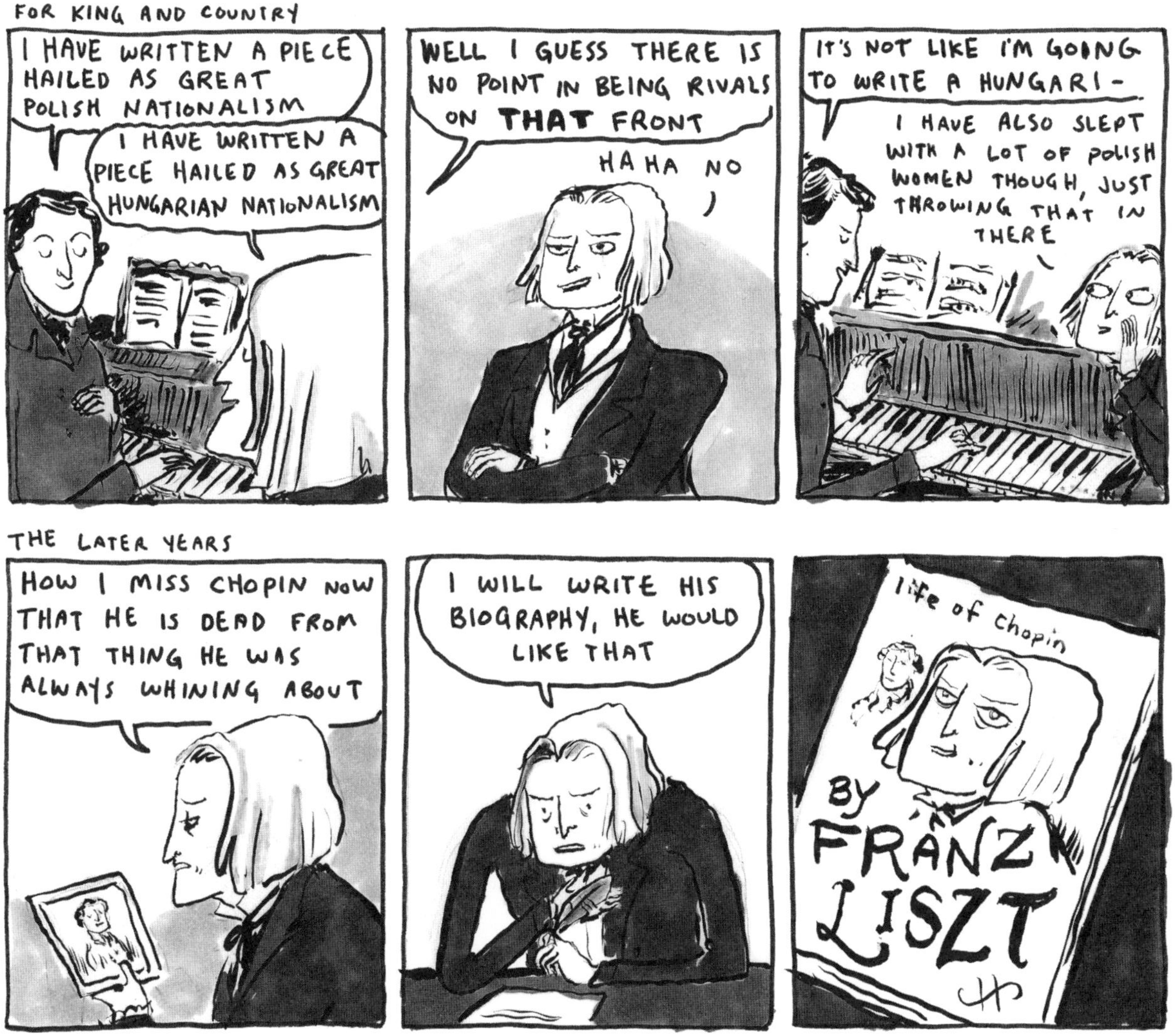
FOR KING AND COUNTRY
I HAVE WRITTEN A PIECE HAILED AS GREAT POLISH NATIONALISM
I HAVE WRITTEN A PIECE HAILED AS GREAT HUNGARIAN NATIONALISM
WELL I GUESS THERE IS NO POINT IN BEING RIVALS ON THAT FRONT
HA HA NO
IT'S NOT LIKE I'M GOING TO WRITE A HUNGARI-
I HAVE ALSO SLEPT WITH A LOT OF POLISH WOMEN THOUGH, JUST THROWING THAT IN THERE
THE LATER YEARS
HOW I MISS CHOPIN NOW THAT HE IS DEAD FROM THAT THING HE WAS ALWAYS WHINING ABOUT
I WILL WRITE HIS BIOGRAPHY, HE WOULD LIKE THAT
life of Chopin
BY FRANZ LISZT

JULIUS CAESAR

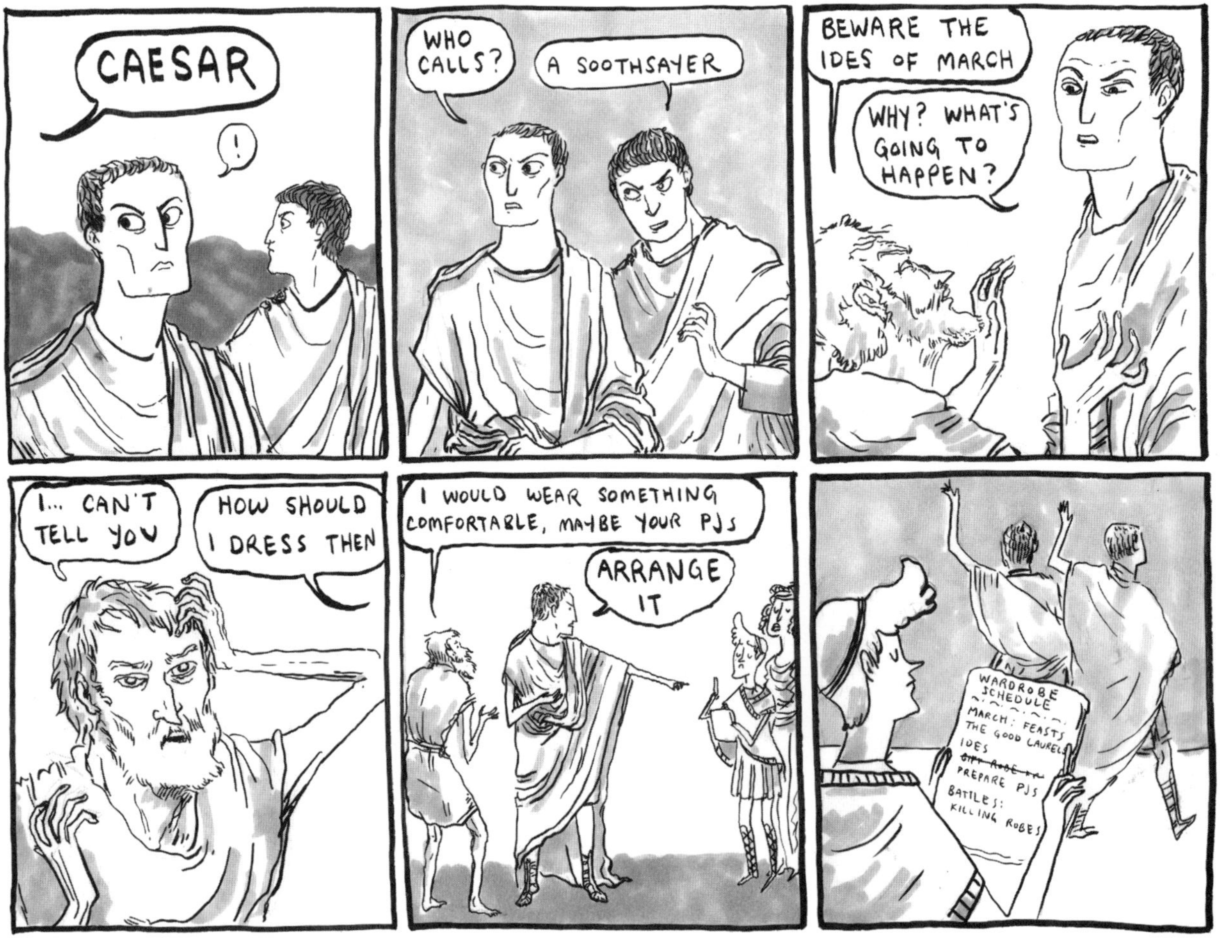
CAESAR
!
WHO CALLS?
A SOOTHSAYER
BEWARE THE IDES OF MARCH
WHY? WHAT'S GOING TO HAPPEN?
I... CAN'T TELL YOU
HOW SHOULD I DRESS THEN
I WOULD WEAR SOMETHING COMFORTABLE, MAYBE YOUR PJs
ARRANGE IT
WARDROBE SCHEDULE
MARCH: FEASTS
THE GOOD LAURELS
IDES
PREPARE PJS
BATTLES:
KILLING ROBES

It's the Ides of March and you know you should stay inside, but there's nothing in the fridge anyway, you know? These comics were written by my lovely sister, Laureen Beaton!

ET TU, BRUTE?
THEN FALL, CAESAR
ARE THOSE... GLADIATOR PYJAMAS?

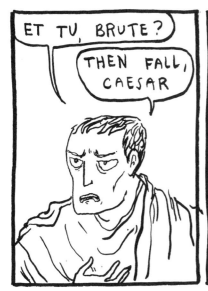

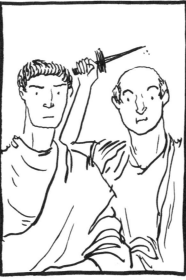

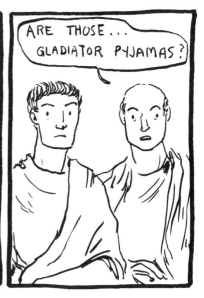

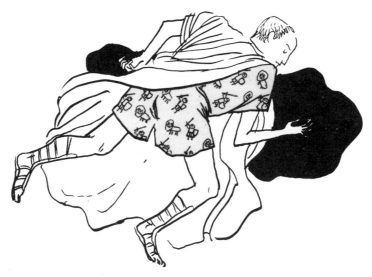

JULIUS CAESAR, PART TWO

CALPURNIA

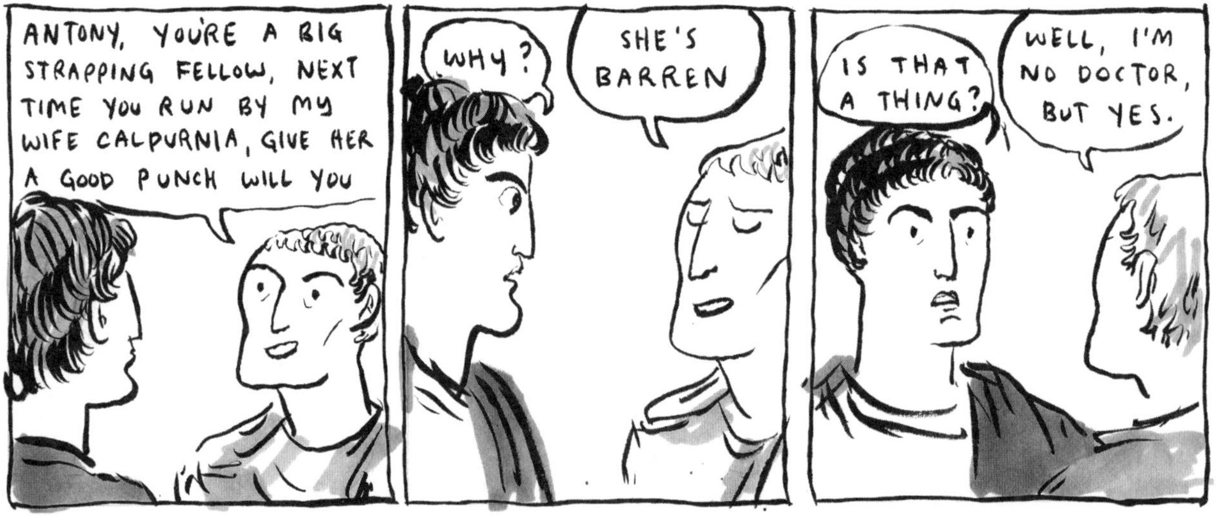
ANTONY, YOU'RE A BIG STRAPPING FELLOW, NEXT TIME YOU RUN BY MY WIFE CALPURNIA, GIVE HER A GOOD PUNCH WILL YOU
WHY?
SHE'S BARREN
IS THAT A THING?
WELL, I'M NO DOCTOR, BUT YES.

SUCH MEN ARE DANGEROUS

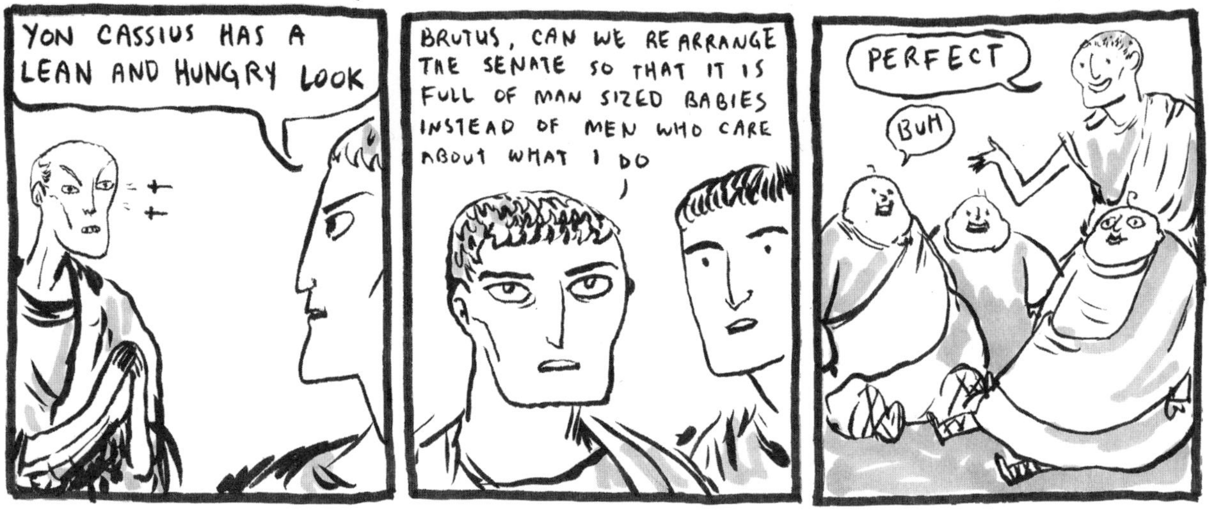
YON CASSIUS HAS A LEAN AND HUNGRY LOOK
BRUTUS, CAN WE REARRANGE THE SENATE SO THAT IT IS FULL OF MAN SIZED BABIES INSTEAD OF MEN WHO CARE ABOUT WHAT I DO
PERFECT
BUH

IDES OF MARCH

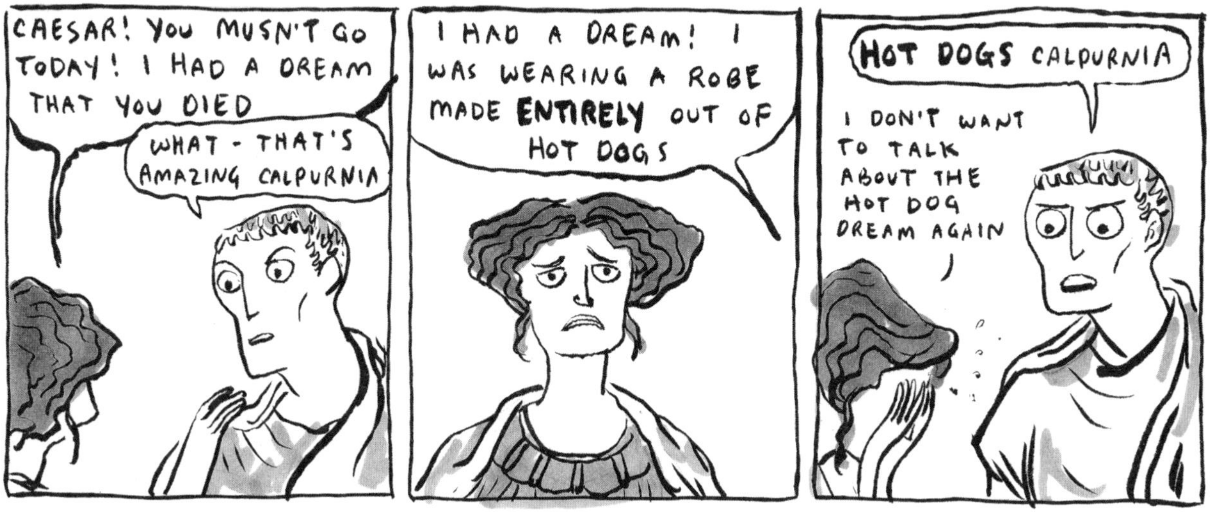
CAESAR! YOU MUSN'T GO TODAY! I HAD A DREAM THAT YOU DIED
WHAT - THAT'S AMAZING CALPURNIA
I HAD A DREAM! I WAS WEARING A ROBE MADE **ENTIRELY** OUT OF HOT DOGS
HOT DOGS CALPURNIA
I DON'T WANT TO TALK ABOUT THE HOT DOG DREAM AGAIN

I RUV YOU

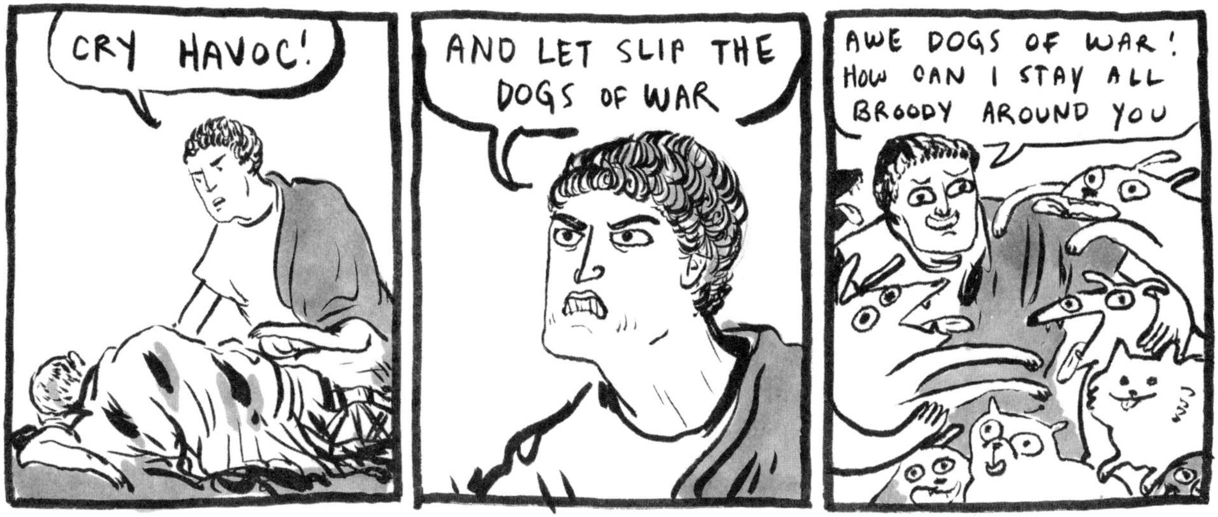
CRY HAVOC!
AND LET SLIP THE DOGS OF WAR
AWE DOGS OF WAR! HOW CAN I STAY ALL BROODY AROUND YOU

WRONG CINNA

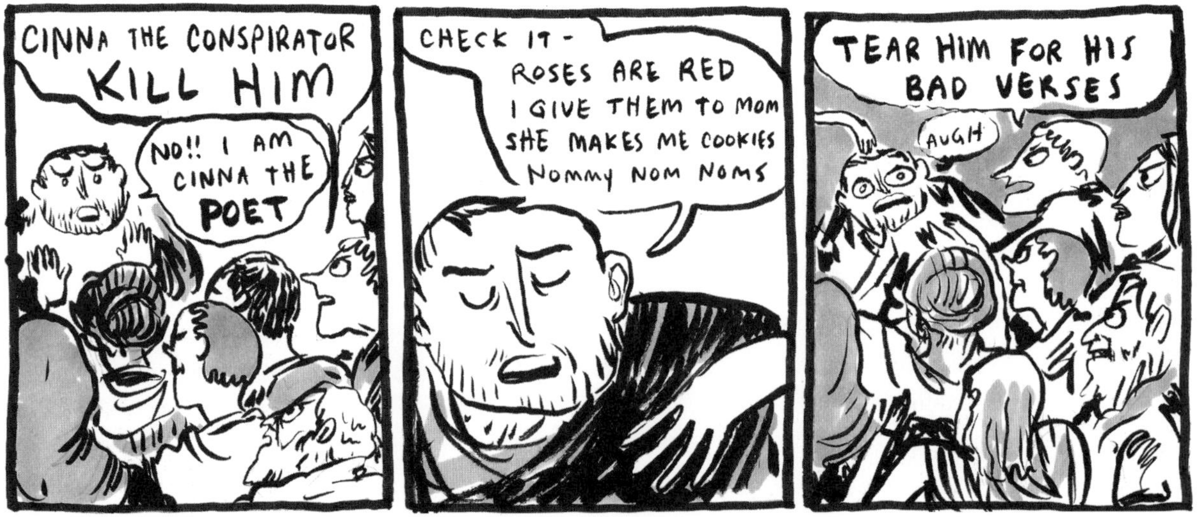
CINNA THE CONSPIRATOR
KILL HIM
NO!! I AM CINNA THE POET
CHECK IT -
ROSES ARE RED
I GIVE THEM TO MOM
SHE MAKES ME COOKIES
NOMMY NOM NOMS
TEAR HIM FOR HIS BAD VERSES
AUGH

GREAT CAESAR'S GHOST

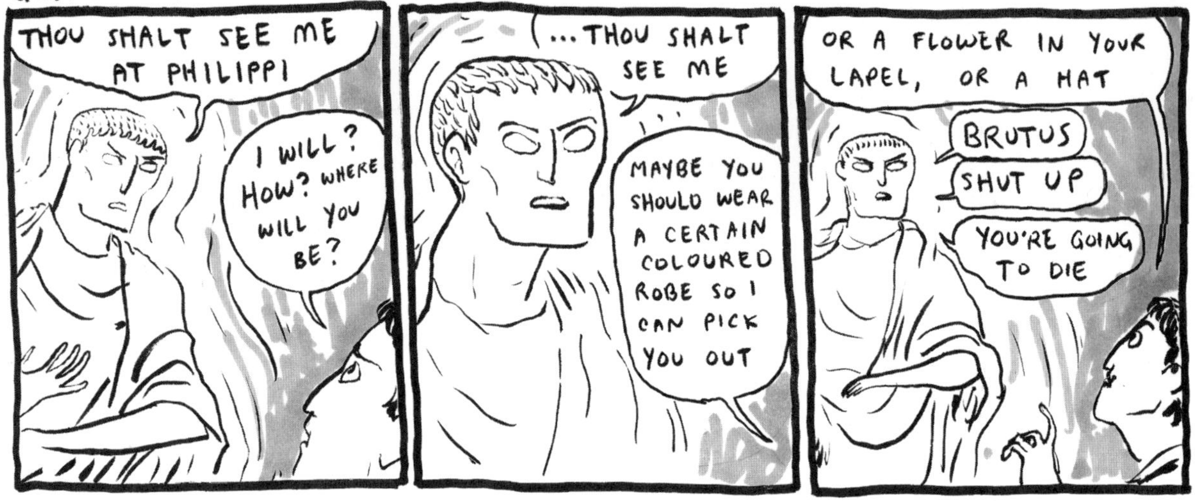
THOU SHALT SEE ME AT PHILIPPI
I WILL? HOW? WHERE WILL YOU BE?
...THOU SHALT SEE ME
...
MAYBE YOU SHOULD WEAR A CERTAIN COLOURED ROBE SO I CAN PICK YOU OUT
OR A FLOWER IN YOUR LAPEL, OR A HAT
BRUTUS
SHUT UP
YOU'RE GOING TO DIE

DEFEATED

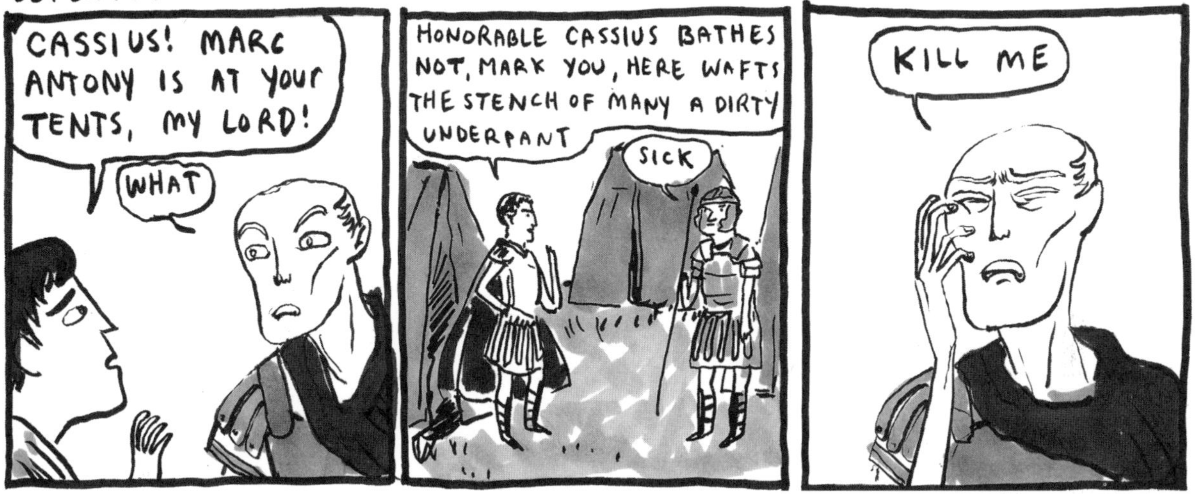
CASSIUS! MARC ANTONY IS AT YOUR TENTS, MY LORD!
WHAT
HONORABLE CASSIUS BATHES NOT, MARK YOU, HERE WAFTS THE STENCH OF MANY A DIRTY UNDERPANT
SICK
KILL ME

BRUTUS IS DEAD

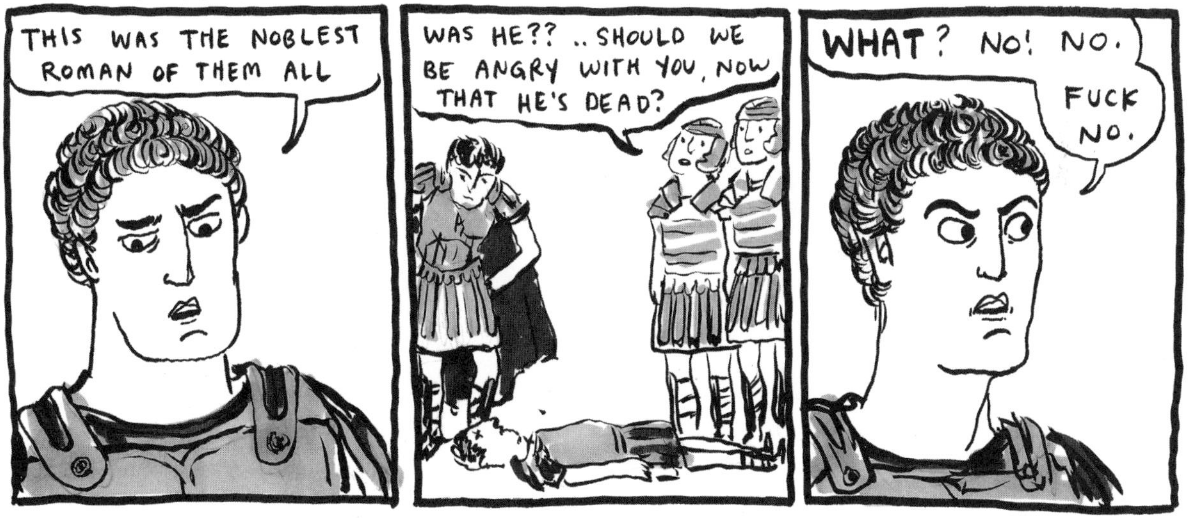
THIS WAS THE NOBLEST ROMAN OF THEM ALL
WAS HE?? ..SHOULD WE BE ANGRY WITH YOU, NOW THAT HE'S DEAD?
WHAT? NO! NO.
FUCK NO.

LOIS LANE, REPORTER

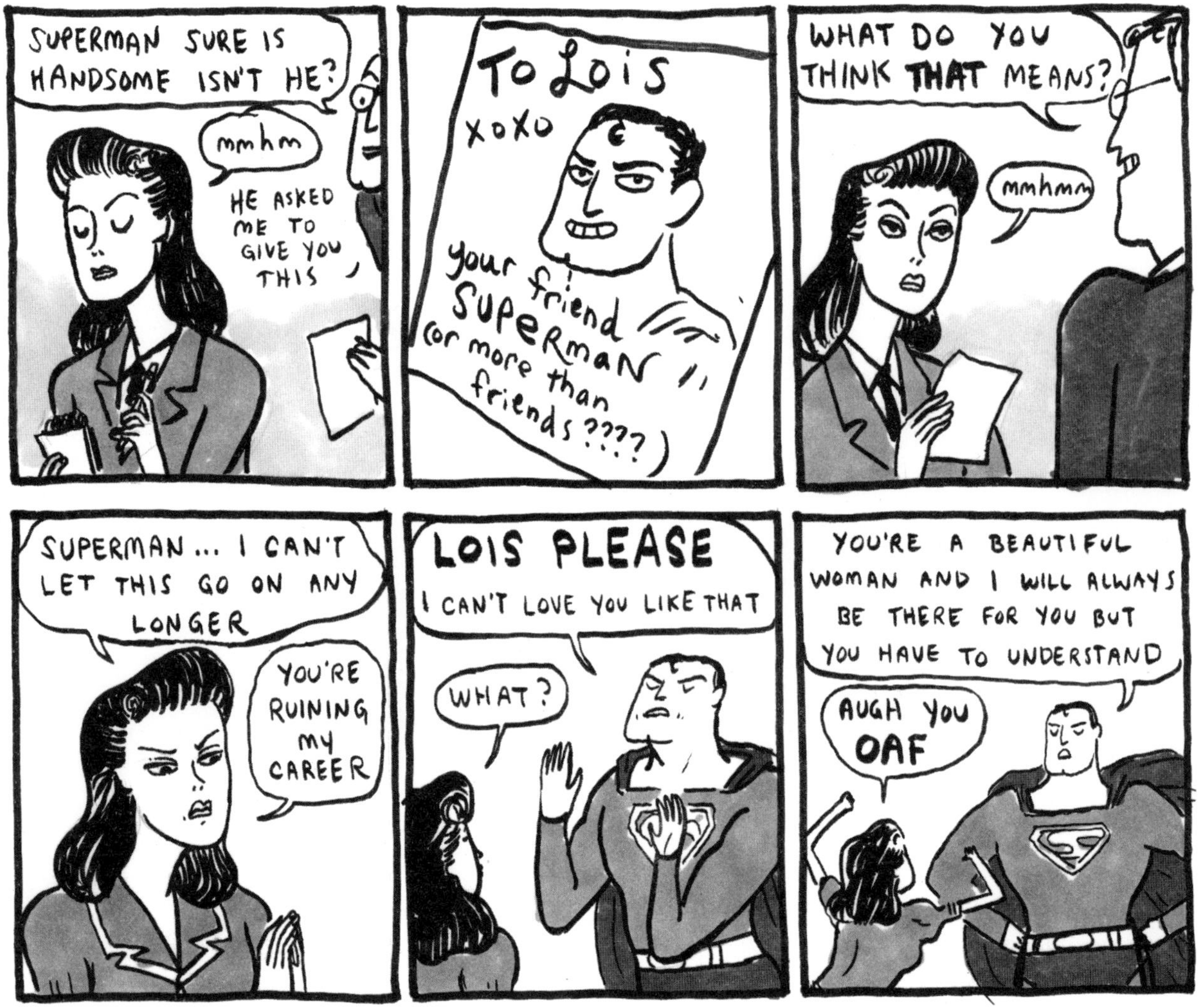
SUPERMAN SURE IS HANDSOME ISN'T HE?
mmhm
HE ASKED ME TO GIVE YOU THIS
TO LOIS
XOXO
your friend Superman (or more than friends????)
WHAT DO YOU THINK THAT MEANS?
mmhmm
SUPERMAN ... I CAN'T LET THIS GO ON ANY LONGER
YOU'RE RUINING MY CAREER
LOIS PLEASE
I CAN'T LOVE YOU LIKE THAT
WHAT?
YOU'RE A BEAUTIFUL WOMAN AND I WILL ALWAYS BE THERE FOR YOU BUT YOU HAVE TO UNDERSTAND
AUGH YOU OAF

Don't give me those comics where Lois is a wet blanket who can't figure out the man beside her is Superman. If Lois isn't kicking ass, taking names, and winning ten Pulitzer Prizes an issue, I don't even want to hear about it.

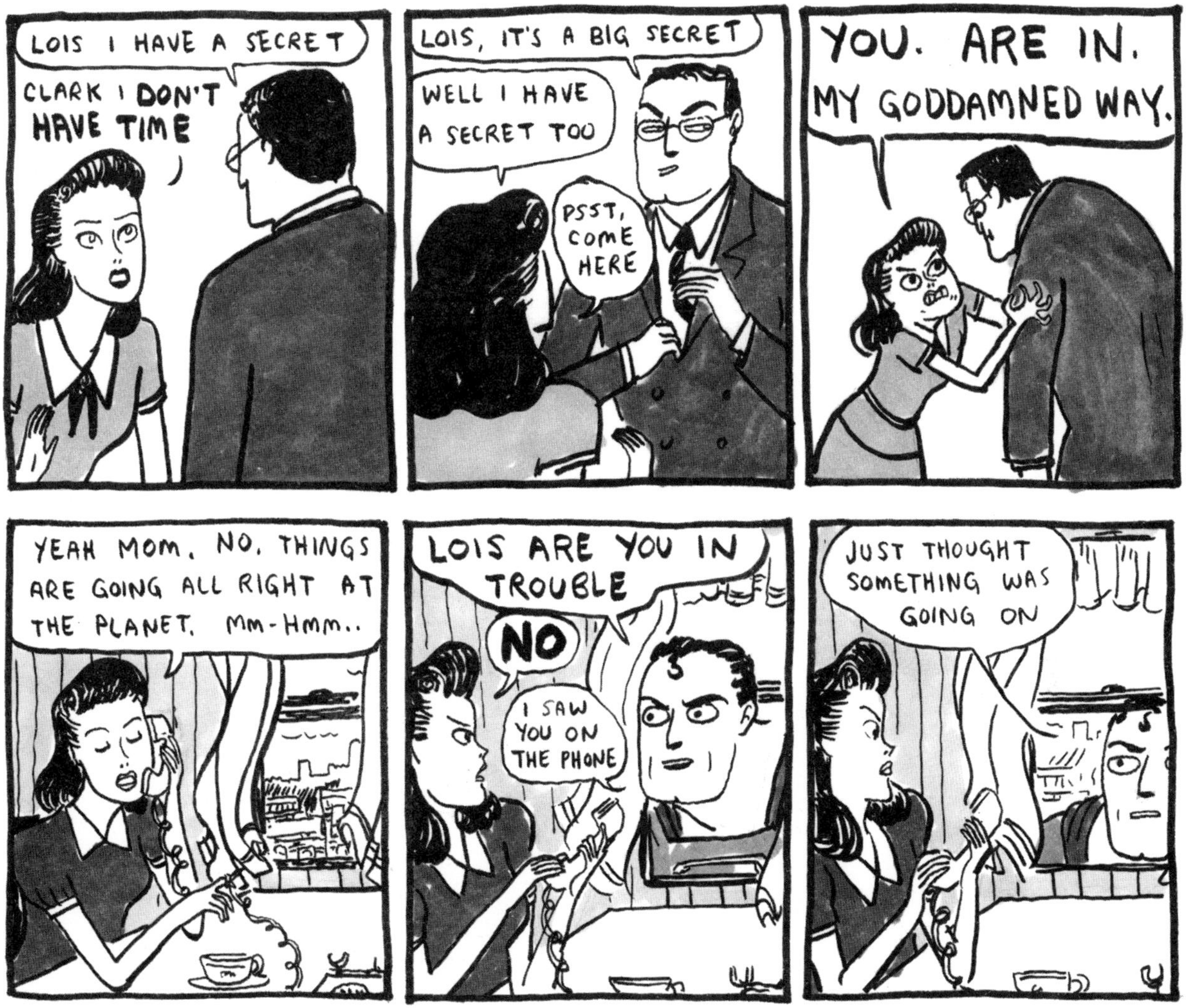
LOIS I HAVE A SECRET
CLARK I DON'T HAVE TIME
LOIS, IT'S A BIG SECRET
WELL I HAVE A SECRET TOO
PSST, COME HERE
YOU. ARE IN. MY GODDAMNED WAY.
YEAH MOM. NO. THINGS ARE GOING ALL RIGHT AT THE PLANET. MM-HMM..
LOIS ARE YOU IN TROUBLE
NO
I SAW YOU ON THE PHONE
JUST THOUGHT SOMETHING WAS GOING ON

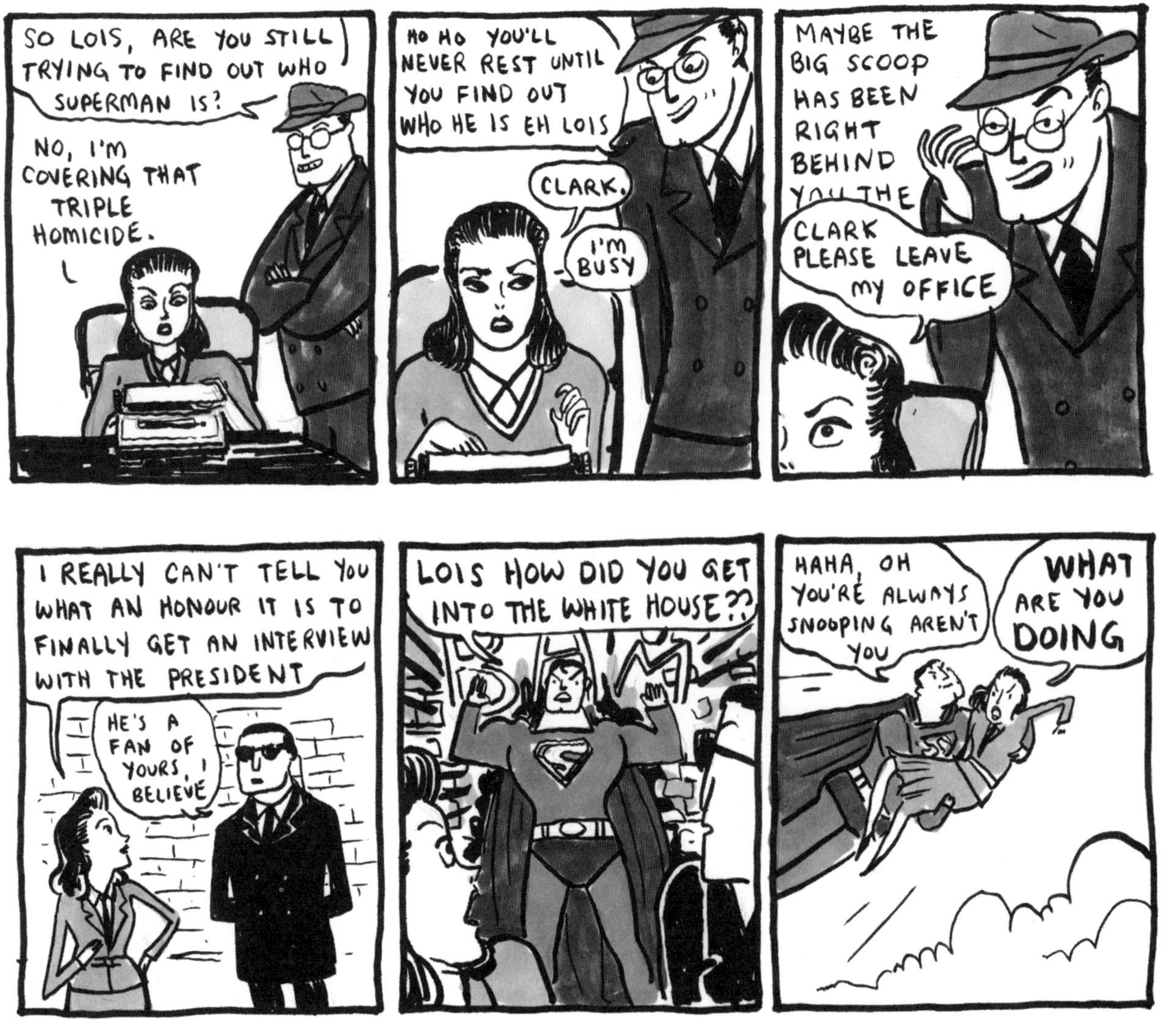
SO LOIS, ARE YOU STILL TRYING TO FIND OUT WHO SUPERMAN IS?
NO, I'M COVERING THAT TRIPLE HOMICIDE.
HO HO YOU'LL NEVER REST UNTIL YOU FIND OUT WHO HE IS EH LOIS
CLARK.
I'M BUSY
MAYBE THE BIG SCOOP HAS BEEN RIGHT BEHIND
CLARK PLEASE LEAVE MY OFFICE
I REALLY CAN'T TELL YOU WHAT AN HONOUR IT IS TO FINALLY GET AN INTERVIEW WITH THE PRESIDENT
HE'S A FAN OF YOURS, I BELIEVE
LOIS HOW DID YOU GET INTO THE WHITE HOUSE??
HAHA, OH YOU'RE ALWAYS SNOOPING AREN'T YOU
WHAT ARE YOU DOING

WITH GREAT POWER COMES GREAT RESPONSIBILITY

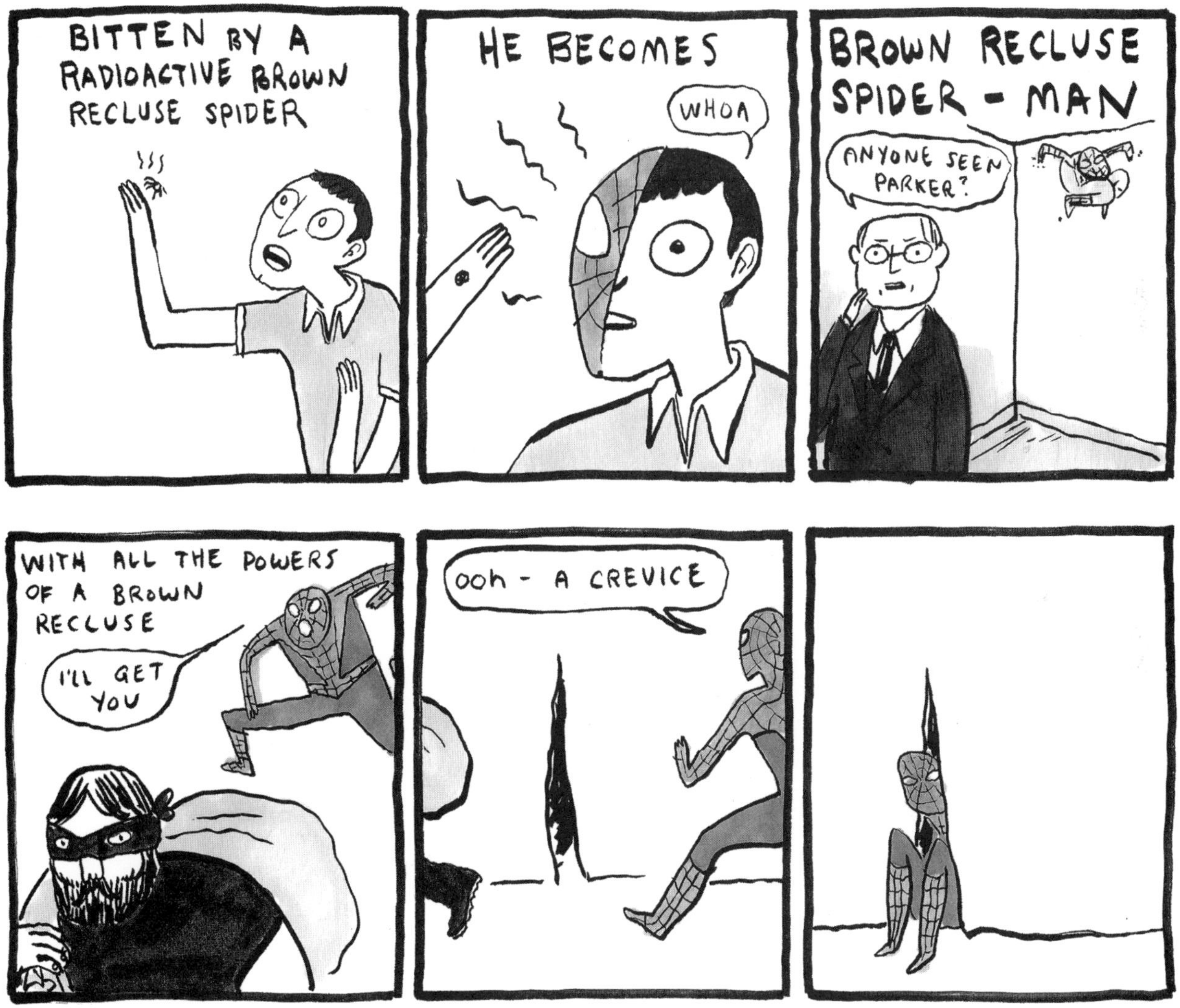
BITTEN BY A RADIOACTIVE BROWN RECLUSE SPIDER
HE BECOMES
WHOA
BROWN RECLUSE SPIDER-MAN
ANYONE SEEN PARKER?
WITH ALL THE POWERS OF A BROWN RECLUSE
I'LL GET YOU
OOH - A CREVICE

Did they specify what kind of spider it was? I feel like this is important. They probably did. Oh well.

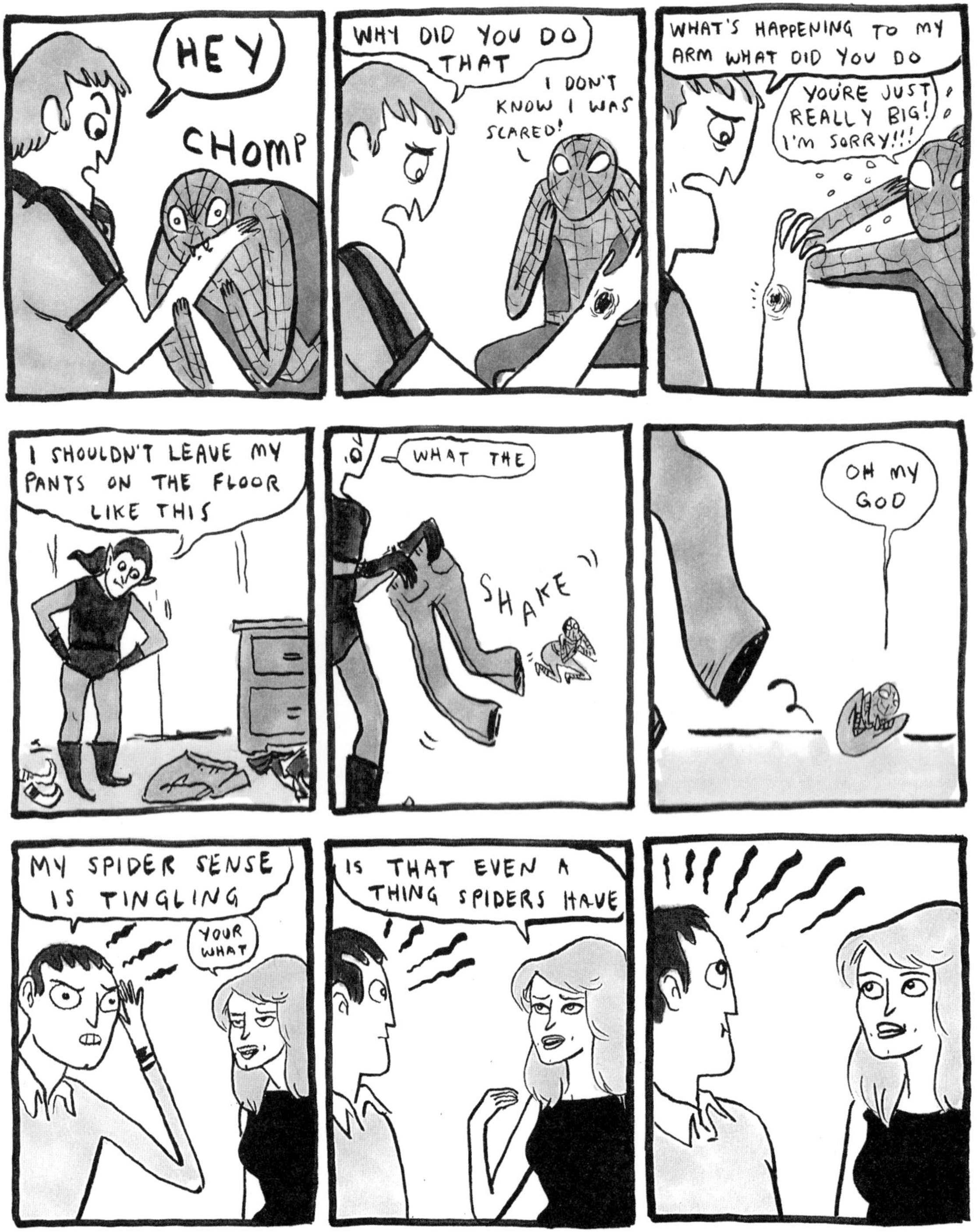
HEY
CHOMP
WHY DID YOU DO THAT
I DON'T KNOW I WAS SCARED!
WHAT'S HAPPENING TO MY ARM WHAT DID YOU DO
YOU'RE JUST REALLY BIG! I'M SORRY!!!
I SHOULDN'T LEAVE MY PANTS ON THE FLOOR LIKE THIS
WHAT THE
SHAKE
OH MY GOD
MY SPIDER SENSE IS TINGLING
YOUR WHAT
IS THAT EVEN A THING SPIDERS HAVE

JUÁREZ AND MAXIMILIAN

HAPSBURGS OF MEXICO

ALLOW ME TO INTRODUCE MYSELF, I AM ARCHDUKE FERDINAND MAXIMILIAN AND I AM HERE AS THE NEW EMPEROR OF MEXICO

I BELIEVE IN DECREASING THE POWER OF THE CHURCH, FEEDING THE HUNGRY, EDUCATING THE CHILDREN, GOOD GOVERNMENT.

THAT IS AMAZING

BUT THE WAY I SEE IT IS THAT I'M THE PRESIDENT OF MEXICO AND YOU'RE A **DUKE FROM AUSTRIA**

YOU WOUND ME MR. JUAREZ

Maximilian should be a bad guy since he was a puppet ruler. But he was too nice and too well meaning. I mean, no, Maximilian, you can't rule Mexico, but we feel really bad about having to execute you! Why do you have to make things so complicated? And Juárez probably had some fun in his life, but I suppose coming from poverty to president and trying to save your country from a European takeover will make a man a bit serious about the whole thing.

21

YOU'RE NOT IN OUR CLIQUE

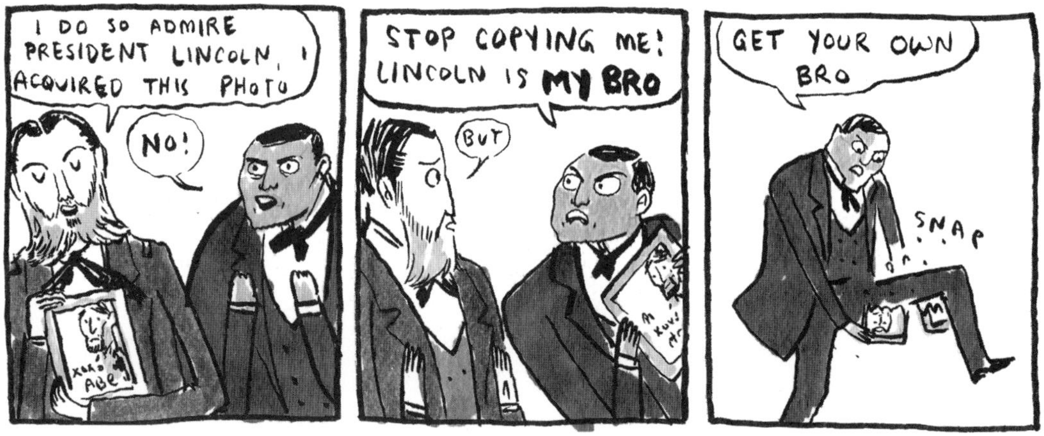
I DO SO ADMIRE PRESIDENT LINCOLN, I ACQUIRED THIS PHOTO
NO!
XOXO ABE
STOP COPYING ME! LINCOLN IS **MY BRO**
BUT
GET YOUR OWN BRO
SNAP

SERIOUS JUÁREZ

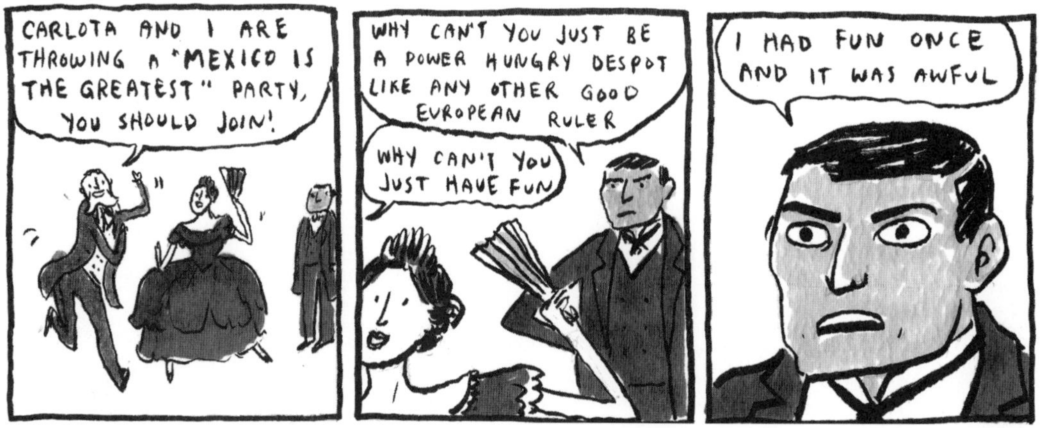
CARLOTA AND I ARE THROWING A "MEXICO IS THE GREATEST" PARTY, YOU SHOULD JOIN!
WHY CAN'T YOU JUST BE A POWER HUNGRY DESPOT LIKE ANY OTHER GOOD EUROPEAN RULER
WHY CAN'T YOU JUST HAVE FUN
I HAD FUN ONCE AND IT WAS AWFUL

FAUX PAS

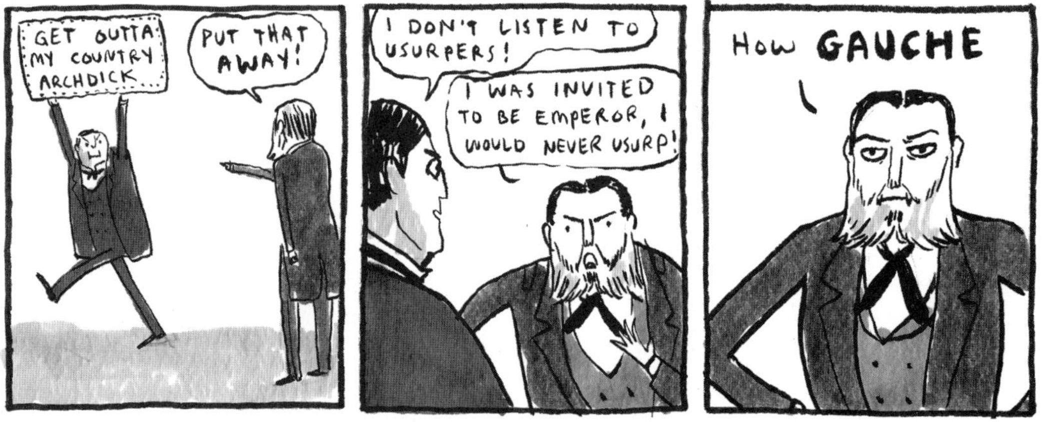
GET OUTTA MY COUNTRY ARCHDICK
PUT THAT AWAY!
I DON'T LISTEN TO USURPERS!
I WAS INVITED TO BE EMPEROR, I WOULD NEVER USURP!
HOW **GAUCHE**

DIPLOMATIC TACTICS

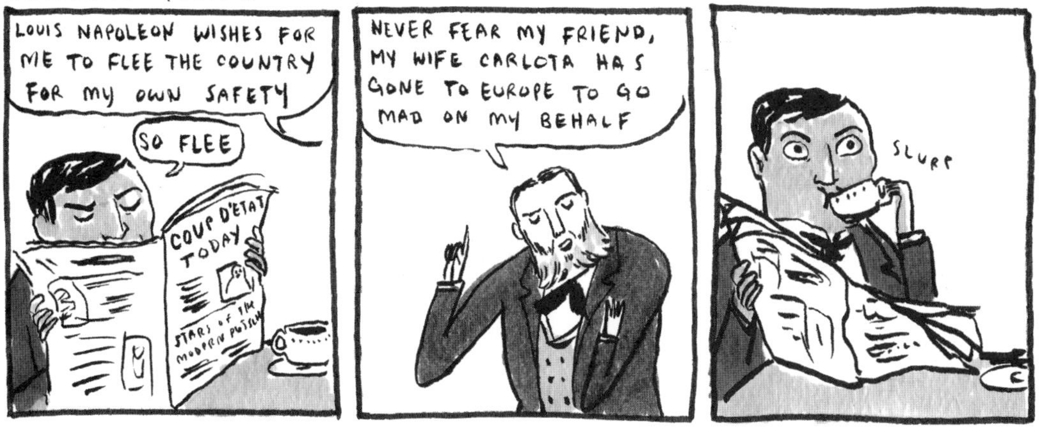
LOUIS NAPOLEON WISHES FOR ME TO FLEE THE COUNTRY FOR MY OWN SAFETY
SO FLEE
COUP D'ETAT TODAY
STARS OF THE MODERN PUTSCH
NEVER FEAR MY FRIEND, MY WIFE CARLOTA HAS GONE TO EUROPE TO GO MAD ON MY BEHALF
SLURP

THE FRENCH ARMY PULLS OUT

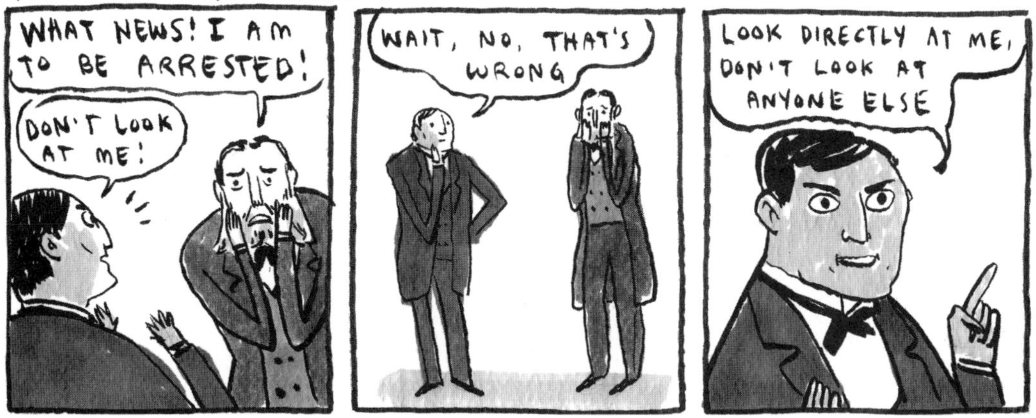
WHAT NEWS! I AM TO BE ARRESTED!
DON'T LOOK AT ME!
WAIT, NO, THAT'S WRONG
LOOK DIRECTLY AT ME, DON'T LOOK AT ANYONE ELSE

EXECUTE

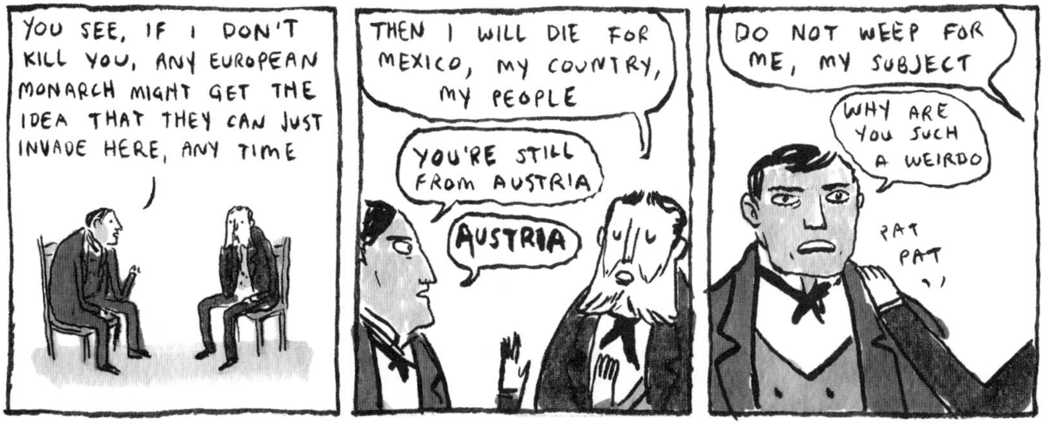
YOU SEE, IF I DON'T KILL YOU, ANY EUROPEAN MONARCH MIGHT GET THE IDEA THAT THEY CAN JUST INVADE HERE, ANY TIME
THEN I WILL DIE FOR MEXICO, MY COUNTRY, MY PEOPLE
YOU'RE STILL FROM AUSTRIA
AUSTRIA
DO NOT WEEP FOR ME, MY SUBJECT
WHY ARE YOU SUCH A WEIRDO
PAT PAT

STRONG FEMALE
CHARACTERS

This comic was conceived by Carly Monardo, Meredith Gran, and myself one night. We are professionals in the entertainment industry and we think we know what we are talking about when we say that there needs to be more strong female characters out there and we know just what to do about it. Just kidding! It was a contest to see who could create the worst character possible.

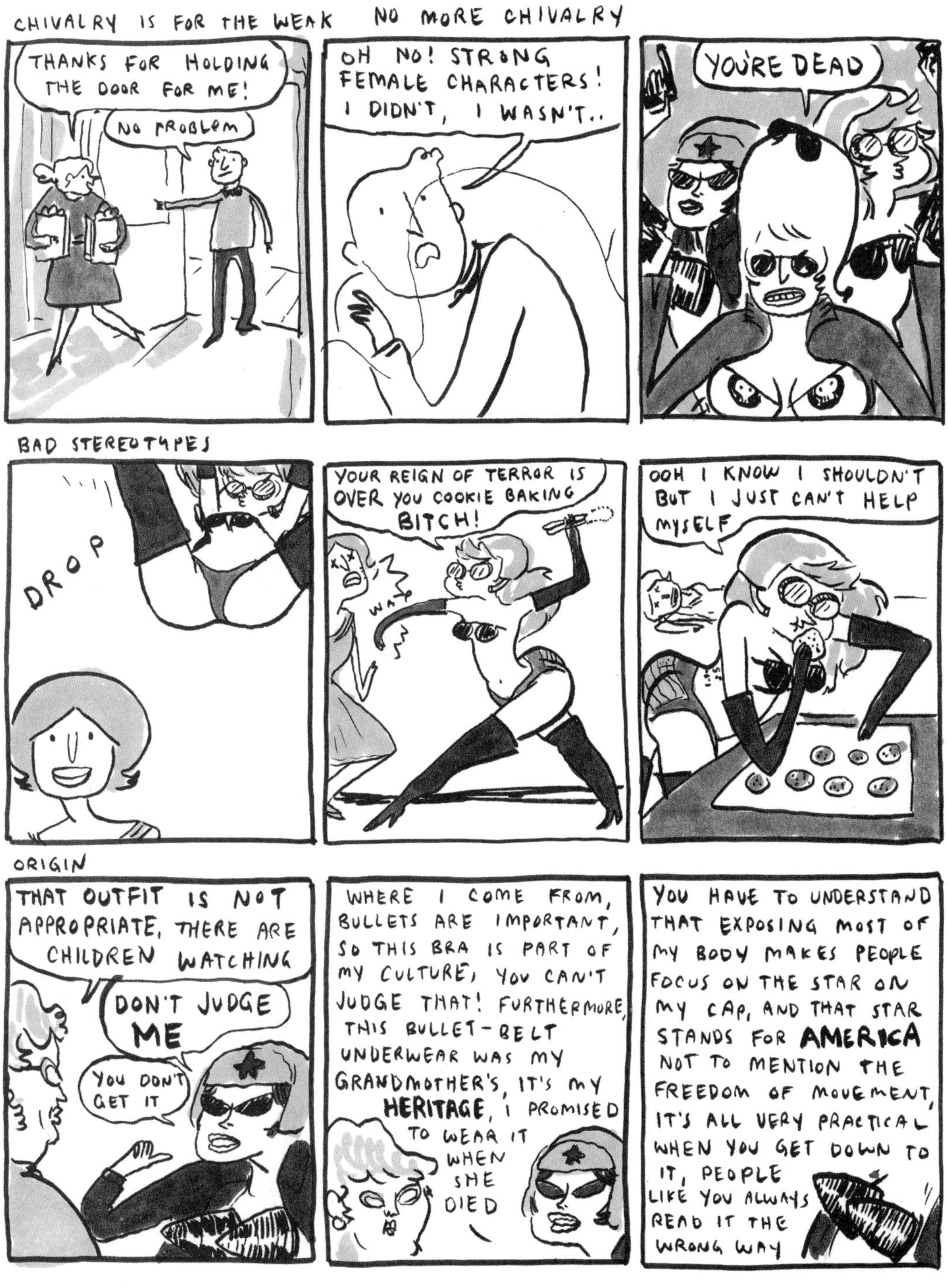
CHIVALRY IS FOR THE WEAK
THANKS FOR HOLDING THE DOOR FOR ME!
NO PROBLEM
NO MORE CHIVALRY
OH NO! STRONG FEMALE CHARACTERS! I DIDN'T, I WASN'T..
YOU'RE DEAD
BAD STEREOTYPES
DROP
YOUR REIGN OF TERROR IS OVER YOU COOKIE BAKING BITCH!
WAP
OOH I KNOW I SHOULDN'T BUT I JUST CAN'T HELP MYSELF
ORIGIN
THAT OUTFIT IS NOT APPROPRIATE, THERE ARE CHILDREN WATCHING
DON'T JUDGE ME
YOU DON'T GET IT
WHERE I COME FROM, BULLETS ARE IMPORTANT, SO THIS BRA IS PART OF MY CULTURE, YOU CAN'T JUDGE THAT! FURTHERMORE, THIS BULLET-BELT UNDERWEAR WAS MY GRANDMOTHER'S, IT'S MY HERITAGE, I PROMISED TO WEAR IT WHEN SHE DIED
YOU HAVE TO UNDERSTAND THAT EXPOSING MOST OF MY BODY MAKES PEOPLE FOCUS ON THE STAR ON MY CAP, AND THAT STAR STANDS FOR AMERICA NOT TO MENTION THE FREEDOM OF MOVEMENT, IT'S ALL VERY PRACTICAL WHEN YOU GET DOWN TO IT, PEOPLE LIKE YOU ALWAYS READ IT THE WRONG WAY

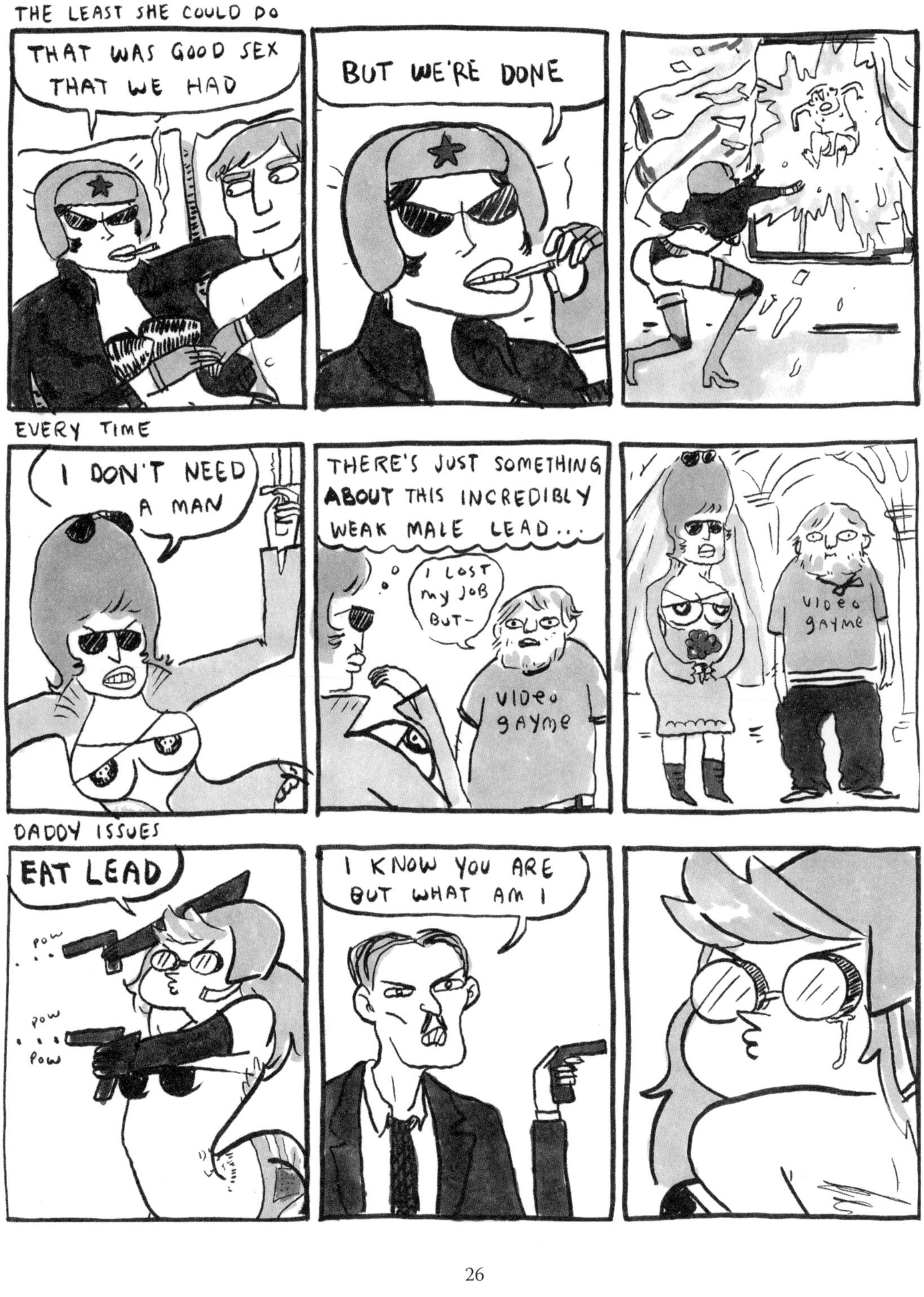
THE LEAST SHE COULD DO
THAT WAS GOOD SEX THAT WE HAD
BUT WE'RE DONE
EVERY TIME
I DON'T NEED A MAN
THERE'S JUST SOMETHING ABOUT THIS INCREDIBLY WEAK MALE LEAD...
I LOST my JOB BUT-
VIDEO GAYME
VIDEO GAYME
DADDY ISSUES
EAT LEAD
POW
POW
POW
I KNOW YOU ARE BUT WHAT AM I

TAKE BACK THE NIGHT

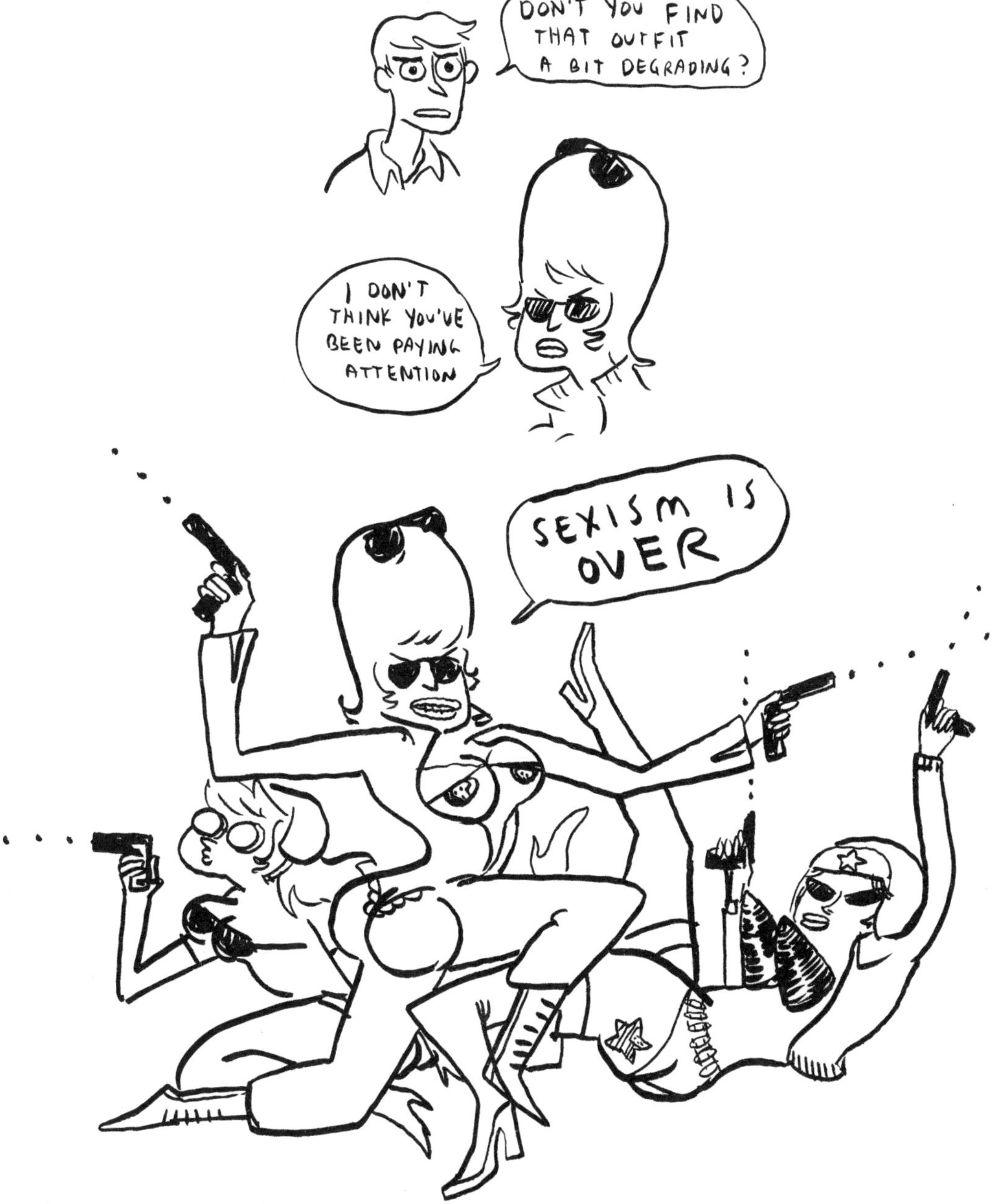
DON'T YOU FIND THAT OUTFIT A BIT DEGRADING?
I DON'T THINK YOU'VE BEEN PAYING ATTENTION
SEXISM IS OVER

I'M FEELING UNCOMFORTABLE WITH THIS DEVELOPMENT

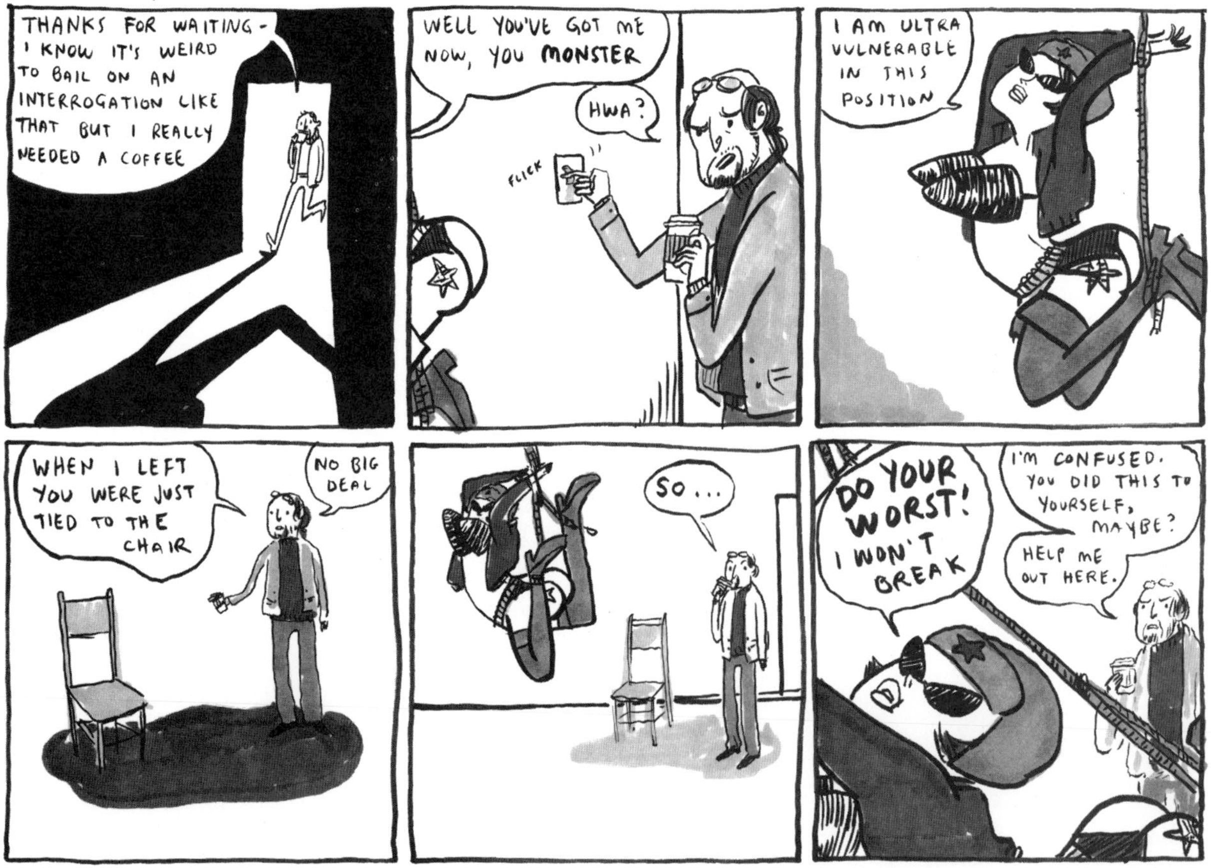
THANKS FOR WAITING - I KNOW IT'S WEIRD TO BAIL ON AN INTERROGATION LIKE THAT BUT I REALLY NEEDED A COFFEE
WELL YOU'VE GOT ME NOW, YOU MONSTER
HWA?
FLICK
I AM ULTRA VULNERABLE IN THIS POSITION
WHEN I LEFT YOU WERE JUST TIED TO THE CHAIR
NO BIG DEAL
SO...
DO YOUR WORST! I WON'T BREAK
I'M CONFUSED. YOU DID THIS TO YOURSELF, MAYBE?
HELP ME OUT HERE.

DEFENSE PROGRAM

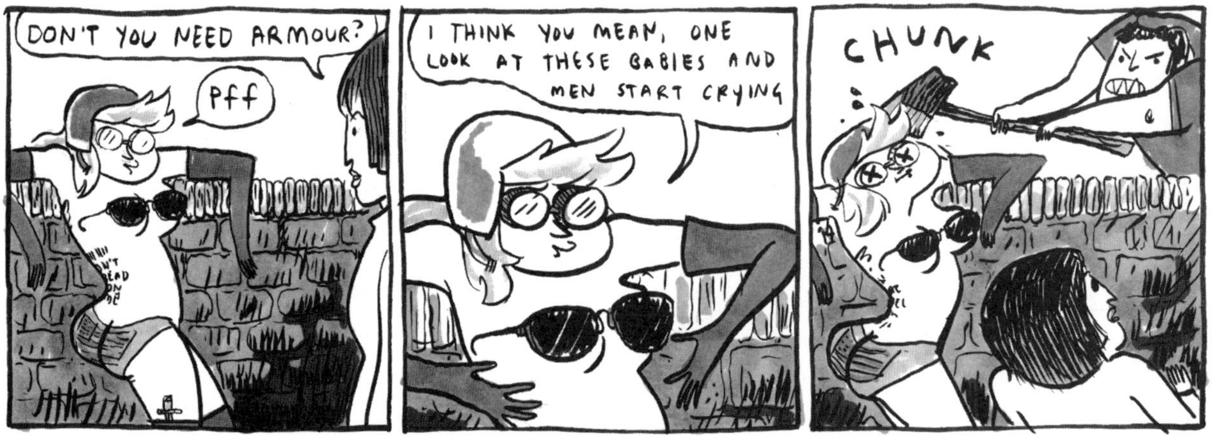
DON'T YOU NEED ARMOUR?
Pff
I THINK YOU MEAN, ONE LOOK AT THESE BABIES AND MEN START CRYING
CHUNK

WOMEN FUEL

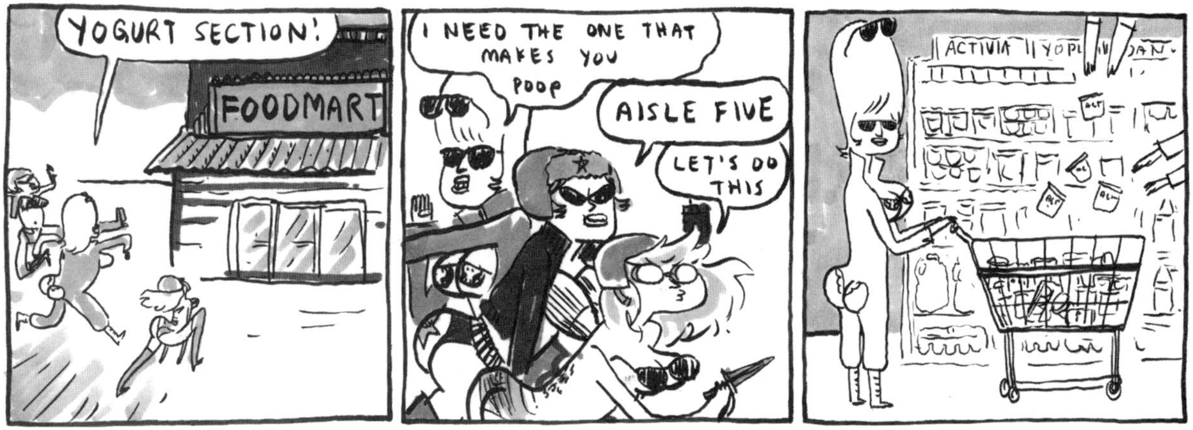
YOGURT SECTION!
FOODMART
I NEED THE ONE THAT MAKES YOU POOP
AISLE FIVE
LET'S DO THIS
ACTIVIA

SHOW OF STRENGTH

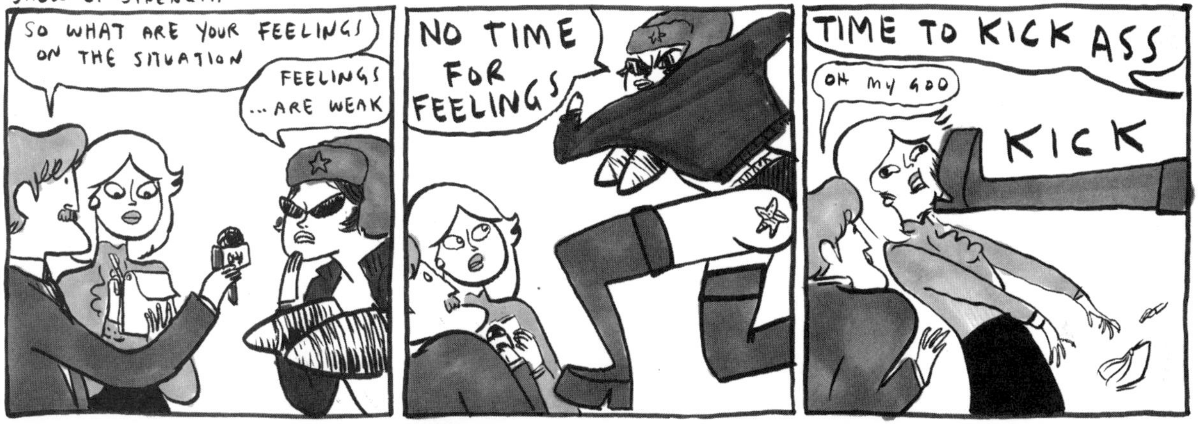
SO WHAT ARE YOUR FEELINGS ON THE SITUATION
FEELINGS ...ARE WEAK
NO TIME FOR FEELINGS
TIME TO KICK ASS
OH MY GOD
KICK

COOPERATING THE ONLY WAY I KNOW HOW

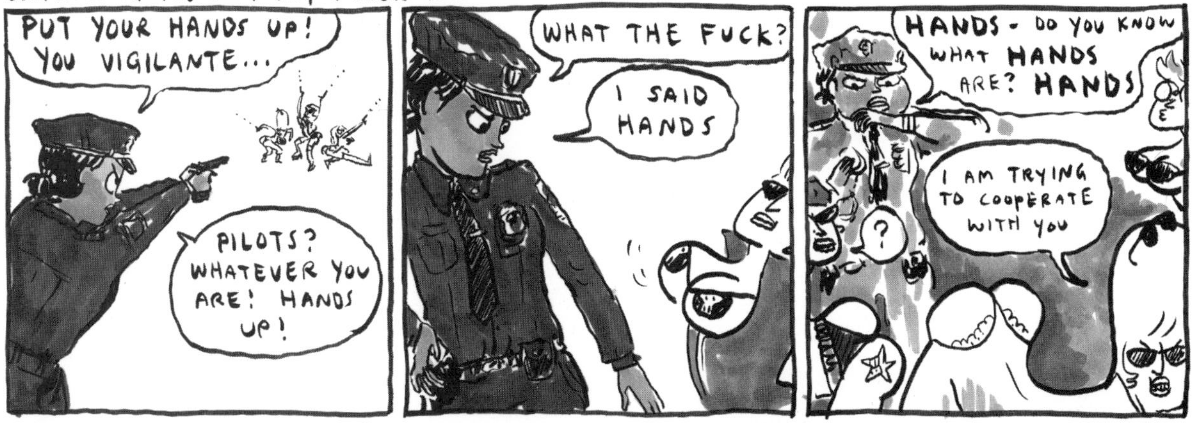
PUT YOUR HANDS UP! YOU VIGILANTE...
PILOTS? WHATEVER YOU ARE! HANDS UP!
WHAT THE FUCK?
I SAID HANDS
HANDS - DO YOU KNOW WHAT HANDS ARE? HANDS
?
I AM TRYING TO COOPERATE WITH YOU

THE RUM REBELLION

THAT BOUNTY BASTARD
WHAT WE NEED IS TO SEND A MAN WHO CAN WHIP NEW SOUTH WALES INTO SHAPE! THERE'S NO CONTROL OVER JOHN MACARTHUR AND HIS 'BUSINESS' FRIENDS
MACARTHUR? UGH, HE'S IMPOSSIBLE
QUITE. CAPTAIN BLIGH IS THE MAN FOR THE JOB
BLIGH?? UGH, HE'S INSUFFERABLE!
THAT'S VERY TRUE. MAYBE THEY'LL JUST KILL EACH OTHER
I'LL ARRANGE A SHIP
MACARTHUR INTRODUCES HIMSELF
!
WELCOME TO SYDNEY, GOVERNOR BLIGH! LET ME JUST TELL YOU HOW WE RUN THINGS HERE
YOU RUN THINGS?? THE DEVIL YOU DO! IT'S ME WHO RUNS THINGS HERE AND YOU'LL THANK ME FOR IT!
NOT THE FRIENDLIEST CHAP

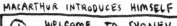

Here is our old friend William Bligh. I say old friend because you probably know him from *Mutiny on the Bounty* already, not because we are personal acquaintances (he is dead). It is easy to find Bligh in the history books—you just follow a breadcrumb trail of temper tantrums.

WOOL INDUSTRY

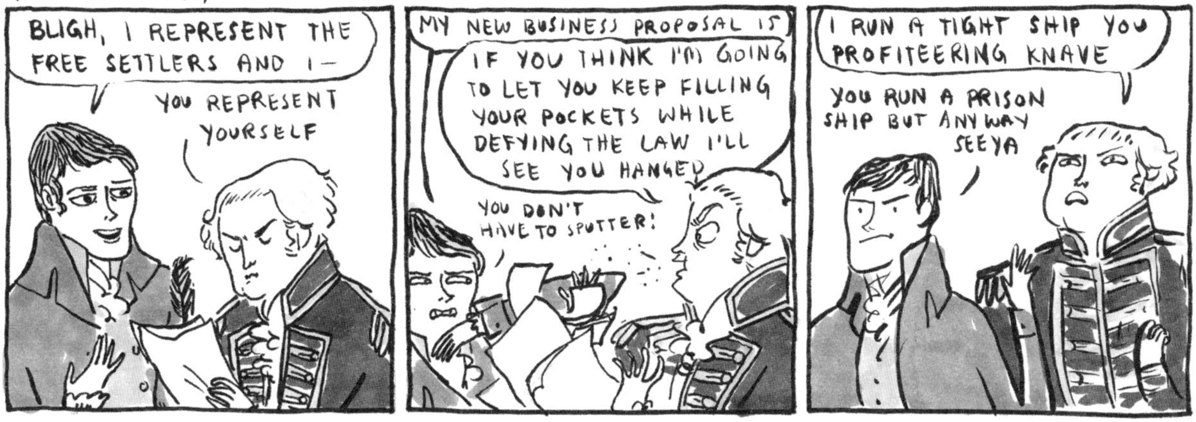
BLIGH, I REPRESENT THE FREE SETTLERS AND I—
YOU REPRESENT YOURSELF
MY NEW BUSINESS PROPOSAL IS
IF YOU THINK I'M GOING TO LET YOU KEEP FILLING YOUR POCKETS WHILE DEFYING THE LAW I'LL SEE YOU HANGED
YOU DON'T HAVE TO SPUTTER!
I RUN A TIGHT SHIP YOU PROFITEERING KNAVE
YOU RUN A PRISON SHIP BUT ANYWAY SEEYA

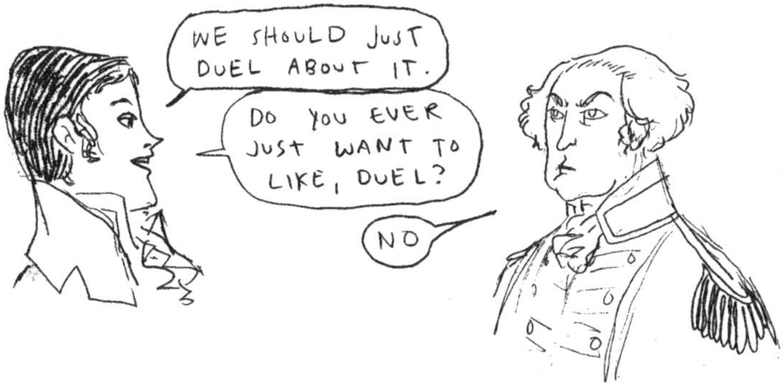
WE SHOULD JUST DUEL ABOUT IT.
DO YOU EVER JUST WANT TO LIKE, DUEL?
NO

BLIGH TAKES ACTION

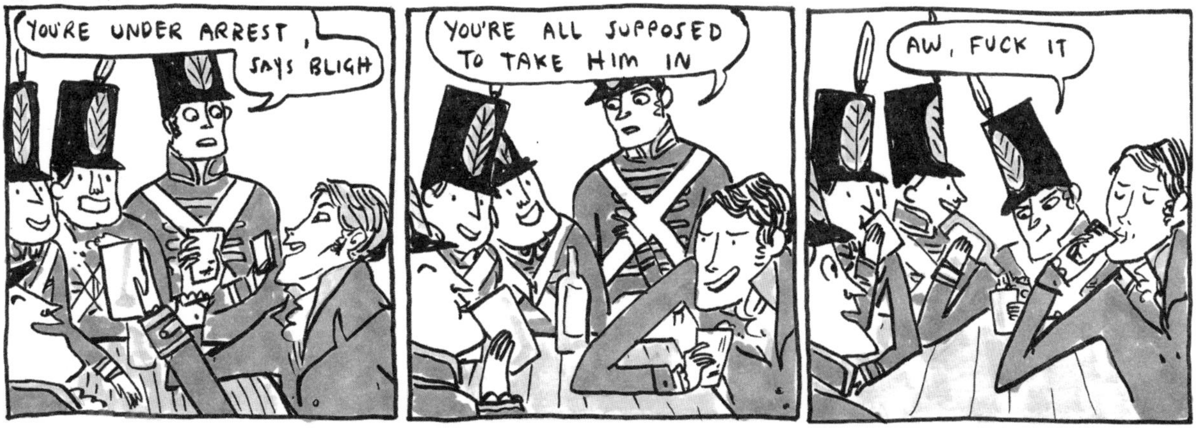
YOU'RE UNDER ARREST, SAYS BLIGH
YOU'RE ALL SUPPOSED TO TAKE HIM IN
AW, FUCK IT

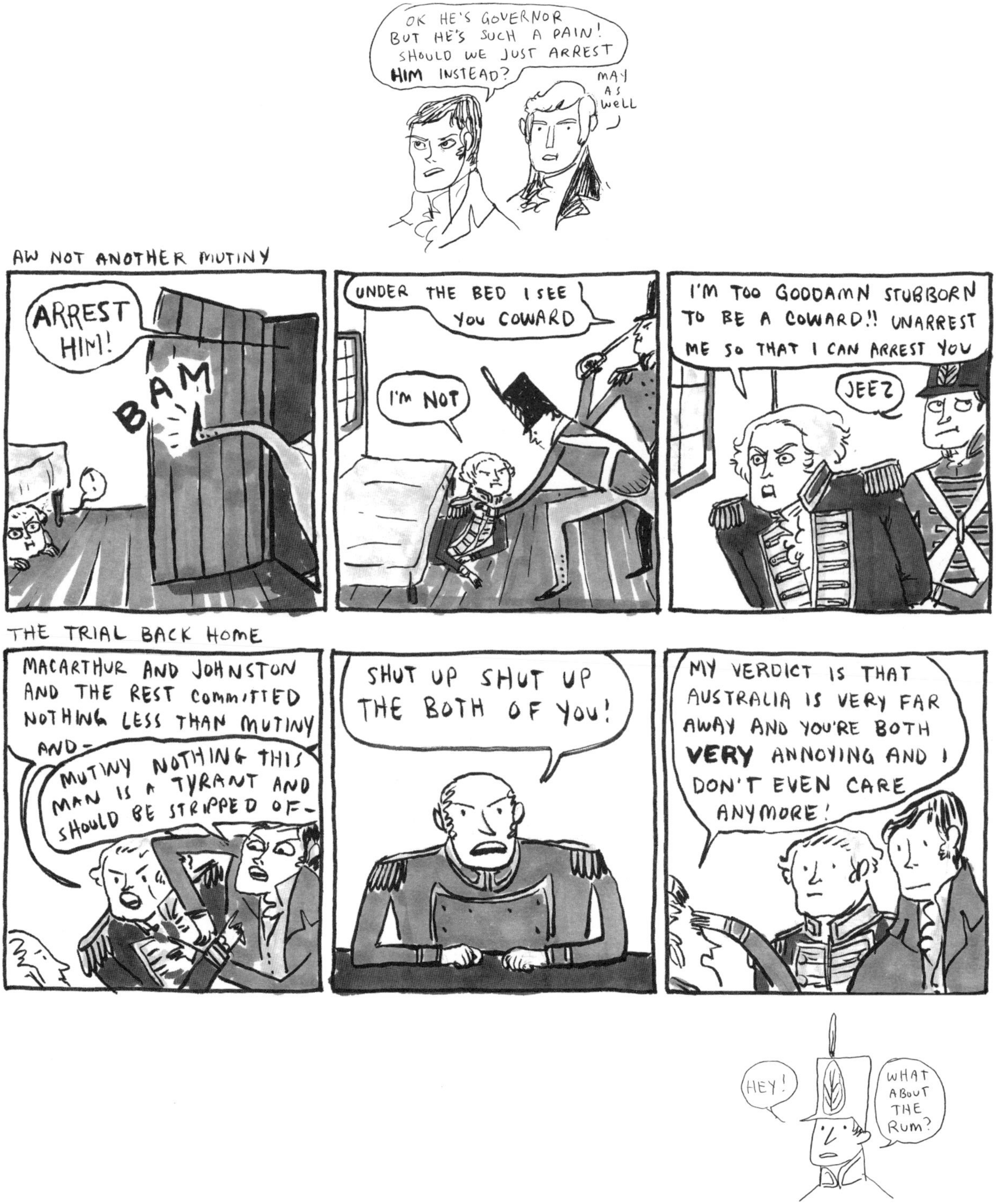
OK HE'S GOVERNOR BUT HE'S SUCH A PAIN! SHOULD WE JUST ARREST HIM INSTEAD?
MAY AS WELL
AW NOT ANOTHER MUTINY
ARREST HIM!
BAM
!
UNDER THE BED I SEE YOU COWARD
I'M NOT
I'M TOO GODDAMN STUBBORN TO BE A COWARD!! UNARREST ME SO THAT I CAN ARREST YOU
JEEZ
THE TRIAL BACK HOME
MACARTHUR AND JOHNSTON AND THE REST COMMITTED NOTHING LESS THAN MUTINY AND—
MUTINY NOTHING THIS MAN IS A TYRANT AND SHOULD BE STRIPPED OF—
SHUT UP SHUT UP THE BOTH OF YOU!
MY VERDICT IS THAT AUSTRALIA IS VERY FAR AWAY AND YOU'RE BOTH VERY ANNOYING AND I DON'T EVEN CARE ANYMORE!
HEY!
WHAT ABOUT THE RUM?

USURPERS OF THE REGENCY

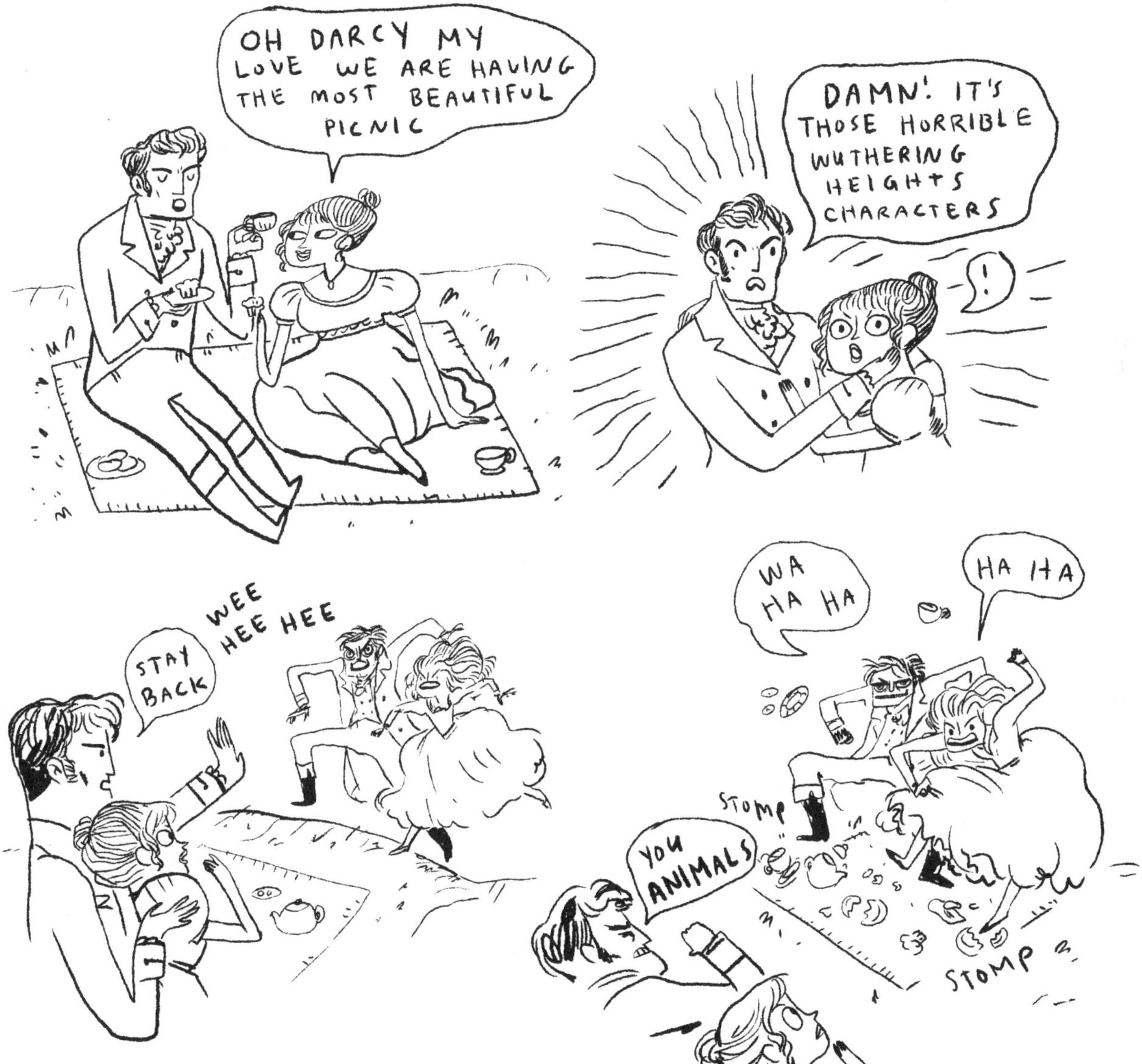

OH DARCY MY LOVE WE ARE HAVING THE MOST BEAUTIFUL PICNIC
DAMN! IT'S THOSE HORRIBLE WUTHERING HEIGHTS CHARACTERS
!
STAY BACK
WEE HEE HEE
WA HA HA
HA HA
STOMP
YOU ANIMALS
STOMP

They say Austenmania is dead, in which case, long live Brontëmania, and may we always have a mania to sustain us.

NANCYS

THE SKY PHANTOM
by CAROLYN KEENE
THERE'S THE PHANTOM
HEY YOU'RE NOT MY COPILOT, YOU'RE A **TEENAGE GIRL**

The Mystery at Lilac Inn
CAROLYN KEENE
I'VE TURNED INTO OLD YELLER
IT MUST BE THE RABIES DON'T LET THEM SHOOT ME IN THE END
I AGREE THAT WHAT'S HAPPENING RIGHT NOW IS CRAZY BUT I DON'T THINK IT HAS ANYTHING TO DO WITH THAT

The Clue of the
Whistling Bagpipes

by CAROLYN
KEENE

NANCY WHAT ARE YOU DOING?

WHAA WHAA .. WHAA WHAA WHAA

UH, BLENDING IN? DON'T YOU KNOW ANYTHING ABOUT SOLVING MYSTERIES?

WE'RE NOT IN SCOTLAND, WE... WE WERE NEVER IN SCOTLAND

WHAA WHAA WHA WAAA WHAA AA WH

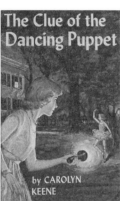

The Clue of the
Dancing Puppet

by CAROLYN
KEENE

THEY'LL NEVER KNOW

NANCY I - OH IT'S HER DECOY AGAIN

I'M NOT SURE WHY SHE ALWAYS THINKS THIS WILL WORK

I'M NANCY

THE MESSAGE IN
THE HOLLOW OAK
by CAROLYN KEENE

HOW COULD YOU LEAD ME ON THIS WILD GOOSE CHASE JANICE, THERE'S NOTHING IN THIS TREE! I THOUGHT WE WERE FRIENDS

DON'T GIVE ME THOSE PUPPY-DOG EYES, IT'S NOT GOING TO WORK THIS TIME

SHELLEY AND BYRON AND DREAMS

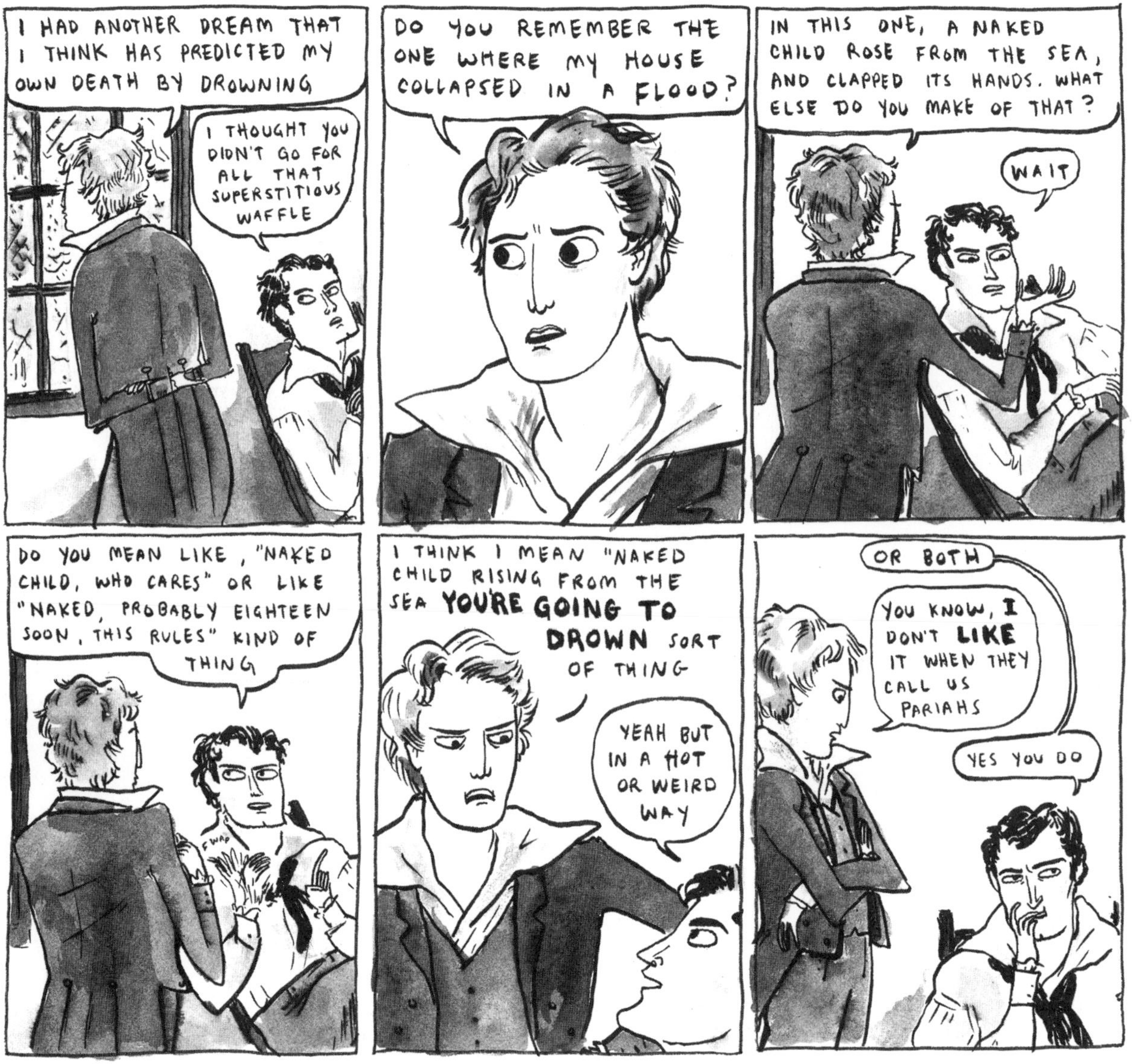
I HAD ANOTHER DREAM THAT I THINK HAS PREDICTED MY OWN DEATH BY DROWNING
I THOUGHT YOU DIDN'T GO FOR ALL THAT SUPERSTITIOUS WAFFLE
DO YOU REMEMBER THE ONE WHERE MY HOUSE COLLAPSED IN A FLOOD?
IN THIS ONE, A NAKED CHILD ROSE FROM THE SEA, AND CLAPPED ITS HANDS. WHAT ELSE DO YOU MAKE OF THAT?
WAIT
DO YOU MEAN LIKE, "NAKED CHILD, WHO CARES" OR LIKE "NAKED, PROBABLY EIGHTEEN SOON, THIS RULES" KIND OF THING
FWAP
I THINK I MEAN "NAKED CHILD RISING FROM THE SEA **YOU'RE GOING TO DROWN** SORT OF THING
YEAH BUT IN A HOT OR WEIRD WAY
OR BOTH
YOU KNOW, **I** DON'T **LIKE** IT WHEN THEY CALL US PARIAHS
YES YOU DO

"How long do you mean to be content?"—Lord B.

It's funny how when Shelley, the atheist, drowned, all the newspapers were like THAT SHOWED HIM, as if God himself just put his thumb on the boat and pushed down to prove a point. Take that, Shelley! That is not what this comic is about but I'm throwing it in there.

THE LAST DAYS OF GEORGES DANTON

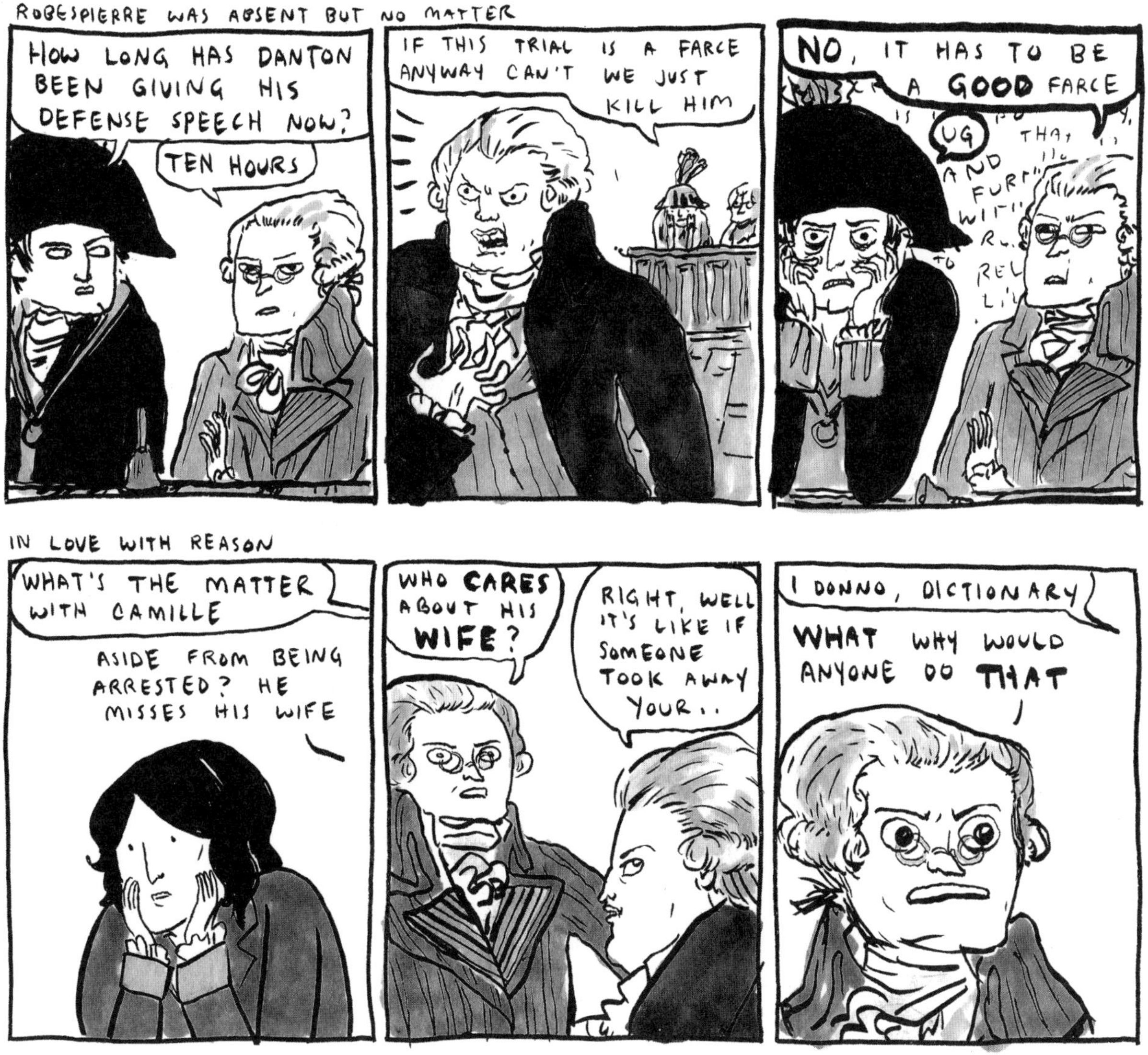
ROBESPIERRE WAS ABSENT BUT NO MATTER
HOW LONG HAS DANTON BEEN GIVING HIS DEFENSE SPEECH NOW?
TEN HOURS
IF THIS TRIAL IS A FARCE ANYWAY CAN'T WE JUST KILL HIM
NO, IT HAS TO BE A GOOD FARCE
UG
IN LOVE WITH REASON
WHAT'S THE MATTER WITH CAMILLE
ASIDE FROM BEING ARRESTED? HE MISSES HIS WIFE
WHO CARES ABOUT HIS WIFE?
RIGHT, WELL IT'S LIKE IF SOMEONE TOOK AWAY YOUR..
I DONNO, DICTIONARY
WHAT WHY WOULD ANYONE DO THAT

Quick! Who's your favorite revolutionary! Is it Danton? Mine too! How many people described as "lionesque" actually fit the bill in looks and character? Did you say Robespierre is your favorite? You're out of the fan club.

OPTIONS

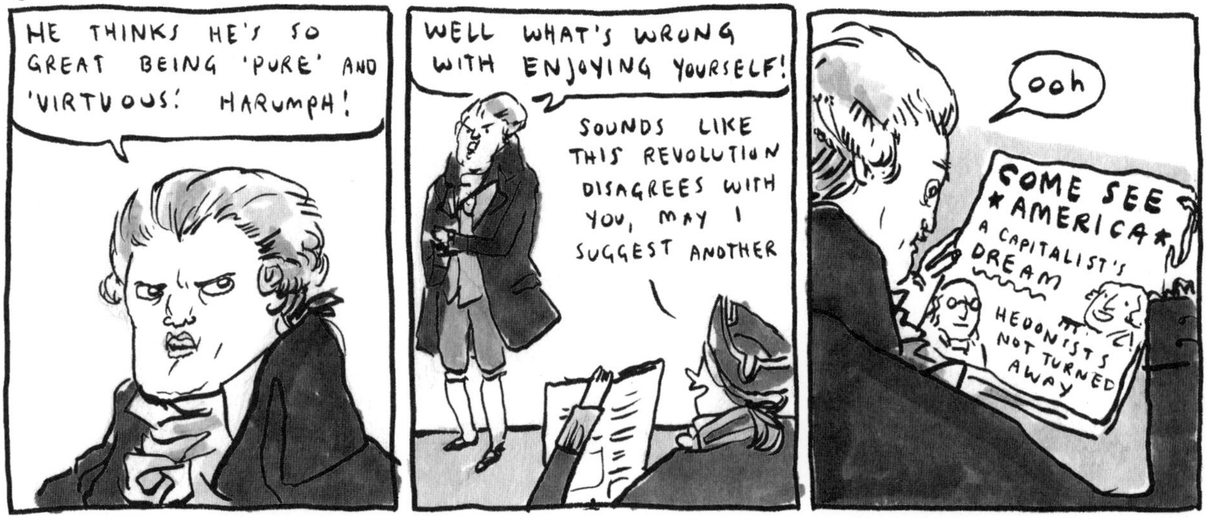
HE THINKS HE'S SO GREAT BEING 'PURE' AND 'VIRTUOUS!' HARUMPH!
WELL WHAT'S WRONG WITH ENJOYING YOURSELF!
SOUNDS LIKE THIS REVOLUTION DISAGREES WITH YOU, MAY I SUGGEST ANOTHER
ooh
COME SEE ★AMERICA★
A CAPITALIST'S DREAM
HEDONISTS NOT TURNED AWAY

DARE AND DARE AGAIN

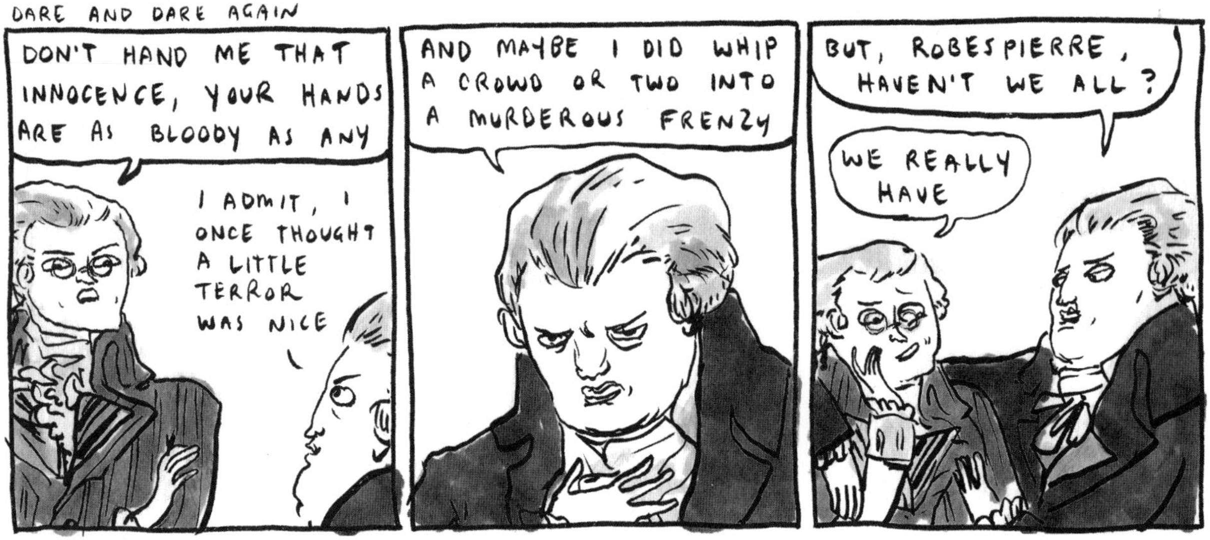
DON'T HAND ME THAT INNOCENCE, YOUR HANDS ARE AS BLOODY AS ANY
I ADMIT, I ONCE THOUGHT A LITTLE TERROR WAS NICE
AND MAYBE I DID WHIP A CROWD OR TWO INTO A MURDEROUS FRENZY
BUT, ROBESPIERRE, HAVEN'T WE ALL?
WE REALLY HAVE

THEY'RE TERROR-IFIC

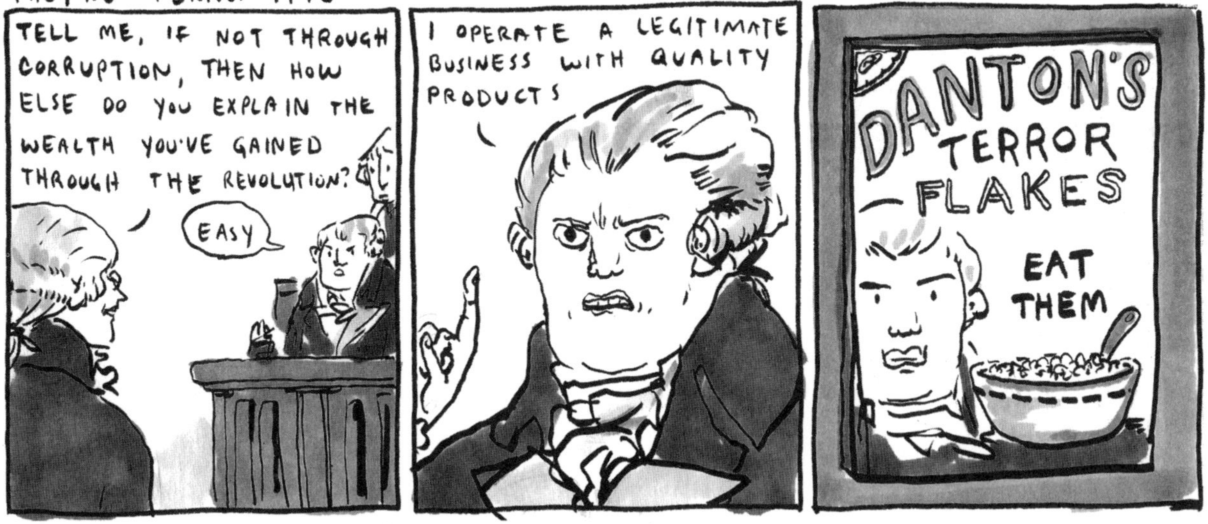
TELL ME, IF NOT THROUGH CORRUPTION, THEN HOW ELSE DO YOU EXPLAIN THE WEALTH YOU'VE GAINED THROUGH THE REVOLUTION?
EASY
I OPERATE A LEGITIMATE BUSINESS WITH QUALITY PRODUCTS
DANTON'S
TERROR FLAKES
EAT THEM

SHOW MY HEAD TO THE PEOPLE, IT'S WORTH SEEING

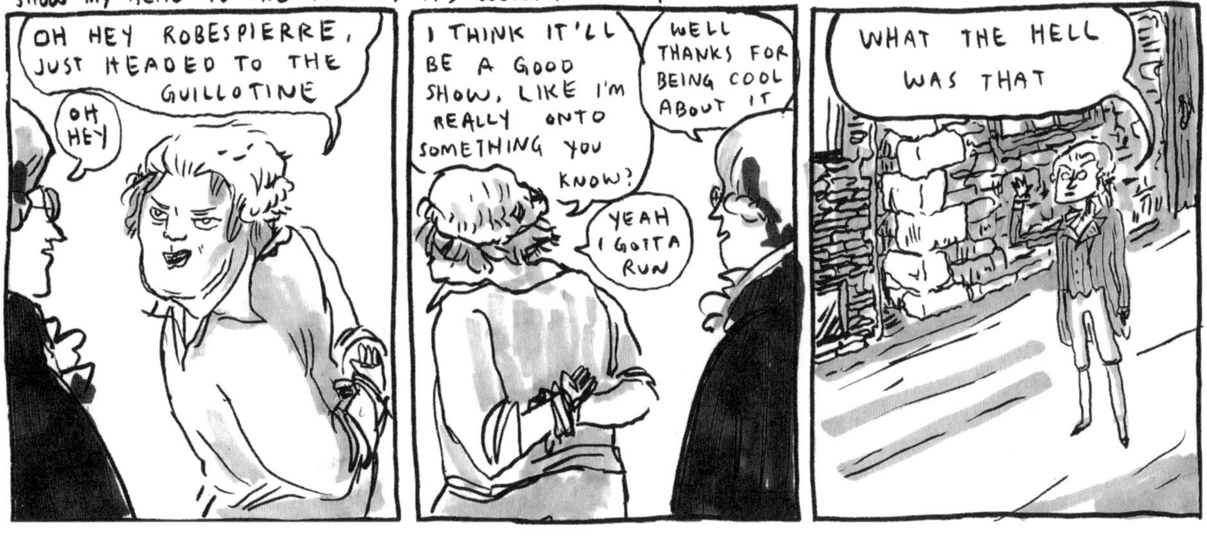
OH HEY ROBESPIERRE, JUST HEADED TO THE GUILLOTINE
OH HEY
I THINK IT'LL BE A GOOD SHOW, LIKE I'M REALLY ONTO SOMETHING YOU KNOW?
WELL THANKS FOR BEING COOL ABOUT IT
YEAH I GOTTA RUN
WHAT THE HELL WAS THAT

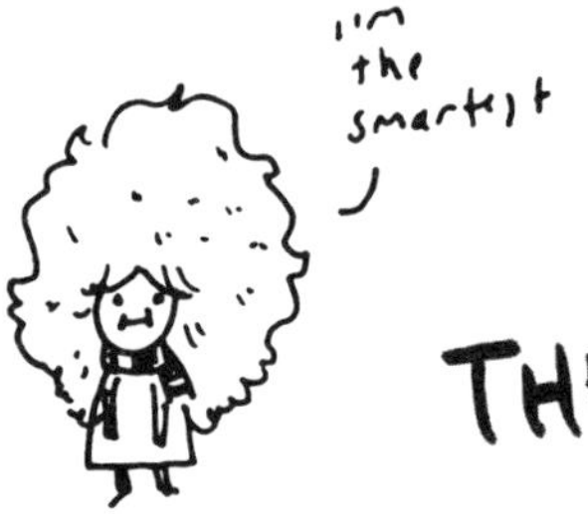
i'm the smartest

THE ADVENTURES OF TINY HERMIONE

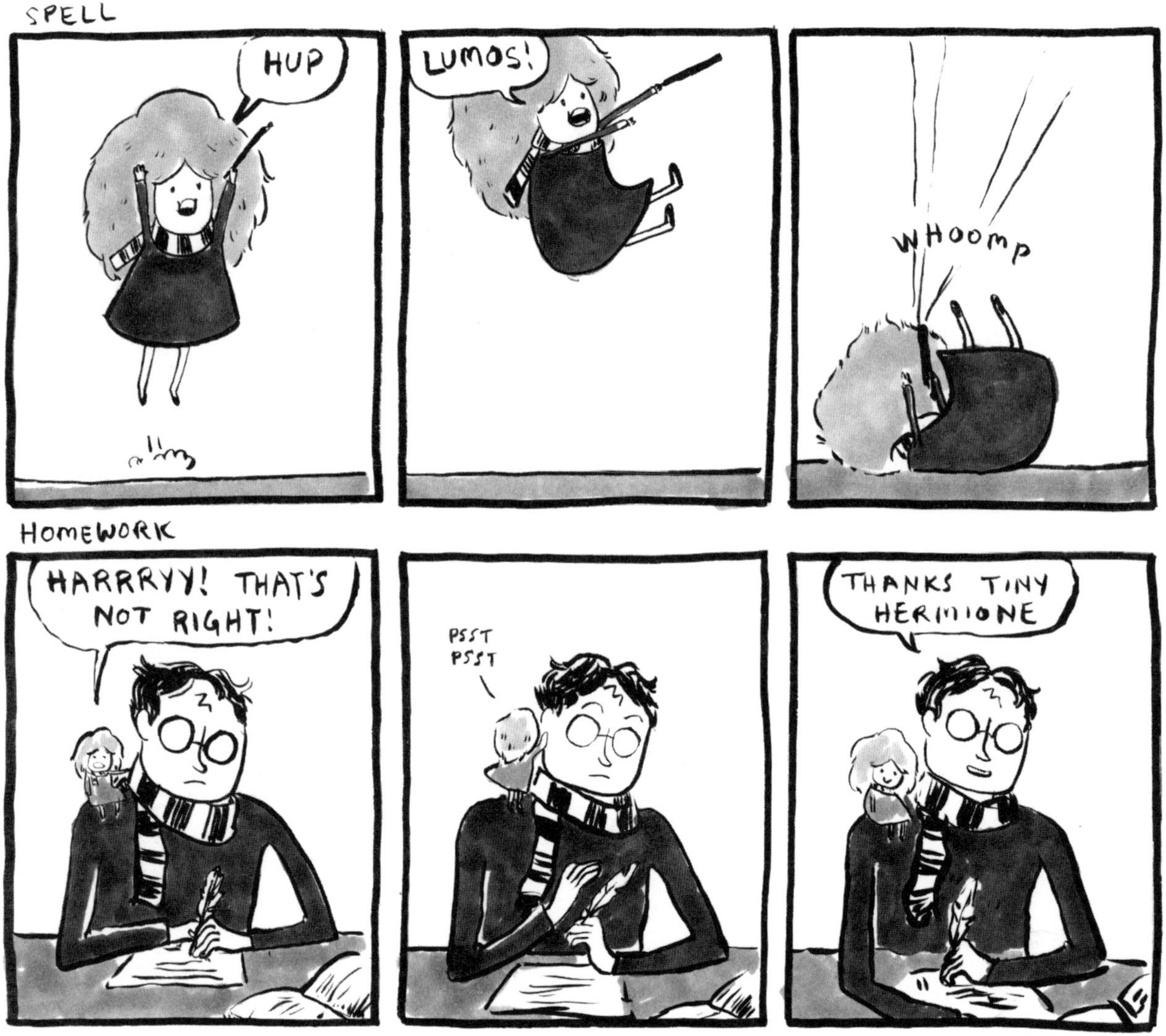
SPELL
HUP
LUMOS!
WHOOMP
HOMEWORK
HARRRYY! THAT'S NOT RIGHT!
PSST PSST
THANKS TINY HERMIONE

Hermione, she's a tiny genius that live in your pocket. You can trust me. I read the books.

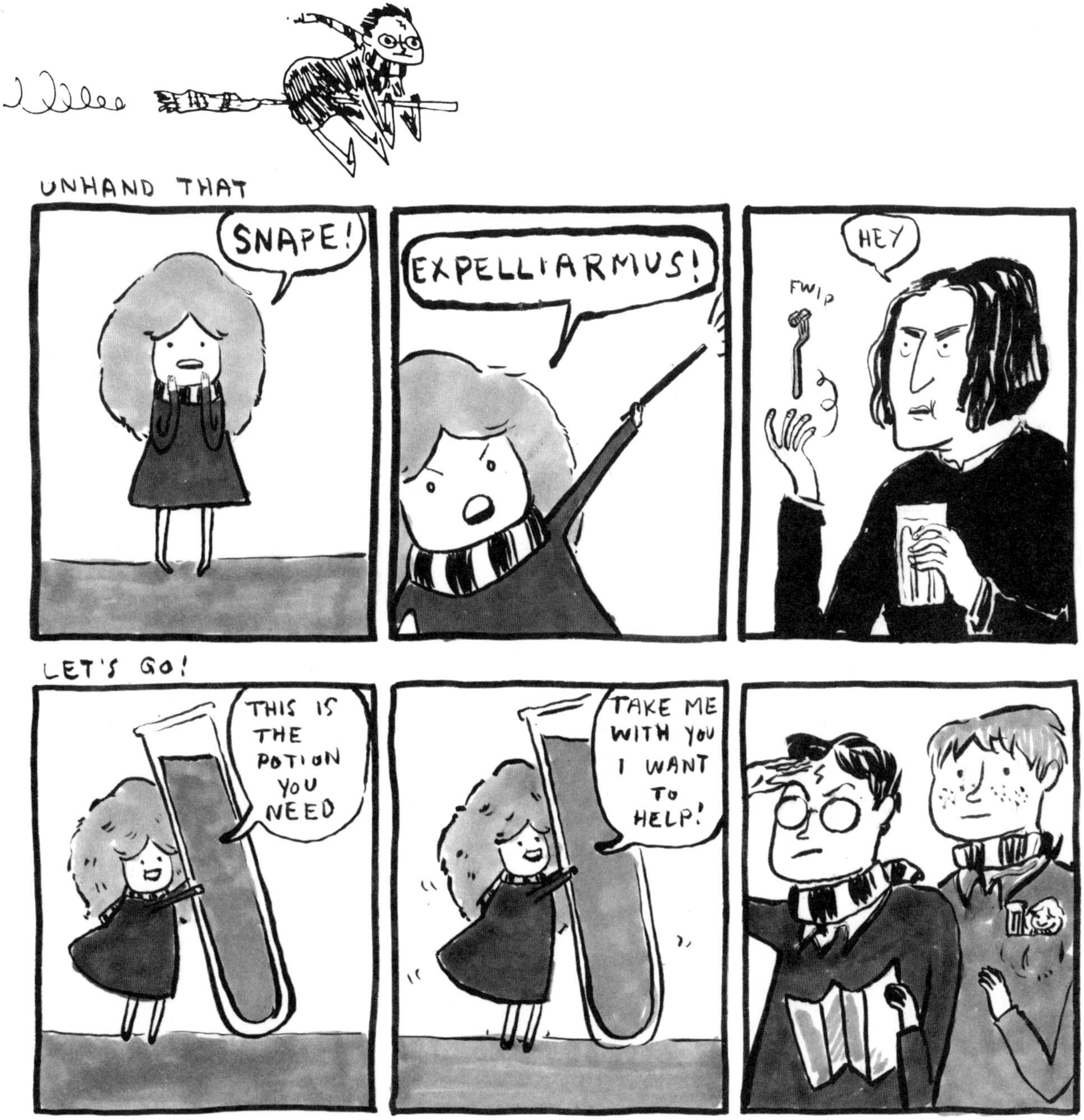
UNHAND THAT
SNAPE!
EXPELLIARMUS!
FWIP
HEY
LET'S GO!
THIS IS THE POTION YOU NEED
TAKE ME WITH YOU I WANT TO HELP!

WUTHERING HEIGHTS

PART ONE: MR. LOCKWOOD ARRIVES

WRONG ADDRESS

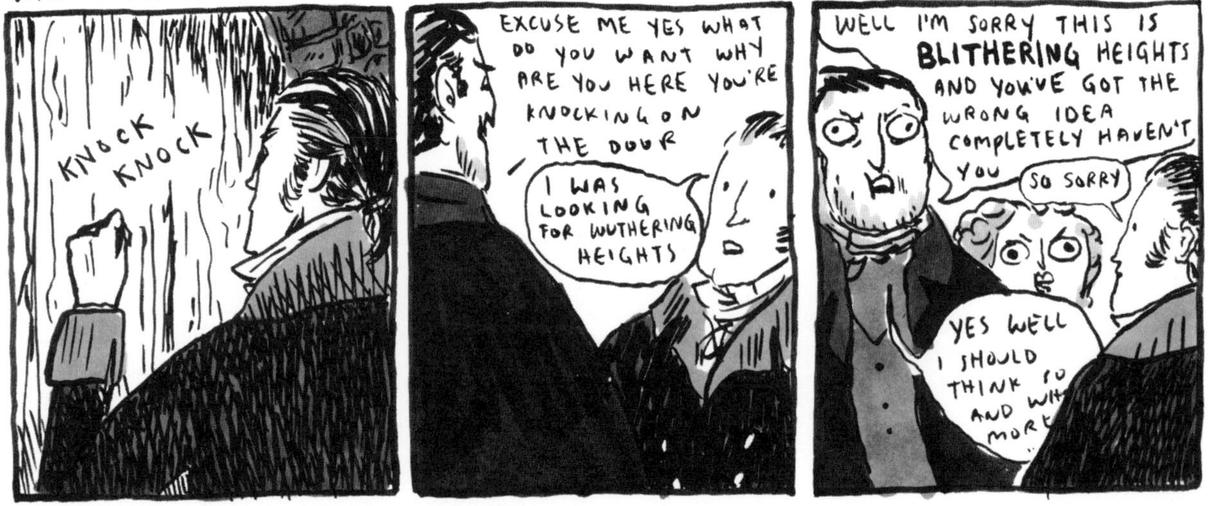

KNOCK KNOCK
EXCUSE ME YES WHAT DO YOU WANT WHY ARE YOU HERE YOU'RE KNOCKING ON THE DOOR
I WAS LOOKING FOR WUTHERING HEIGHTS
WELL I'M SORRY THIS IS **BLITHERING** HEIGHTS AND YOU'VE GOT THE WRONG IDEA COMPLETELY HAVEN'T YOU
SO SORRY
YES WELL I SHOULD THINK

YOU MIGHT SAY IT WASN'T A WELCOMING PLACE

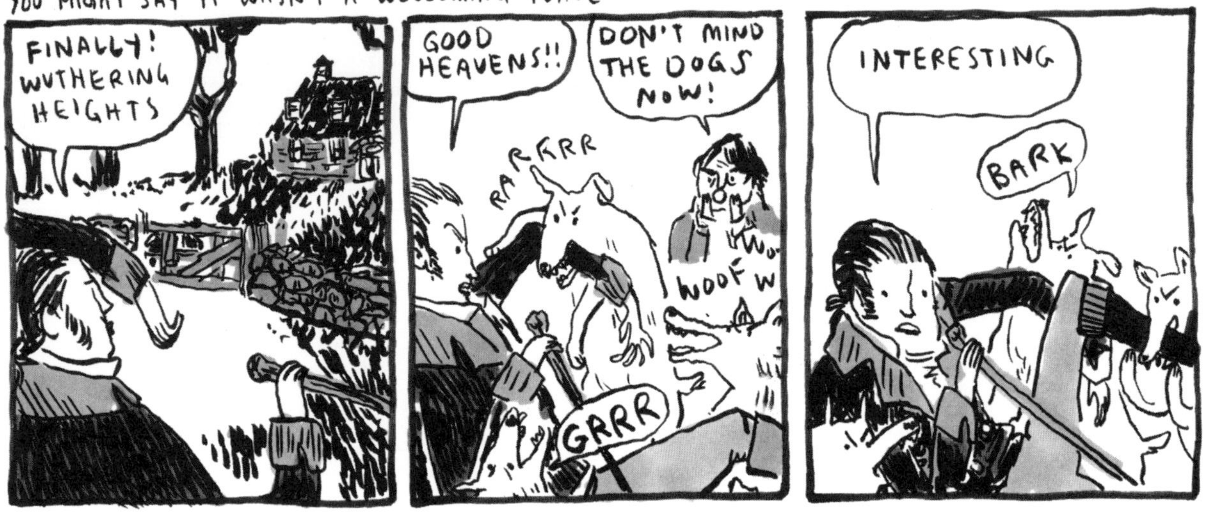

FINALLY! WUTHERING HEIGHTS
GOOD HEAVENS!!
DON'T MIND THE DOGS NOW!
WOOF
GRRR
INTERESTING
BARK

IT'S ME, I'M CATHY, I'VE COME HOME

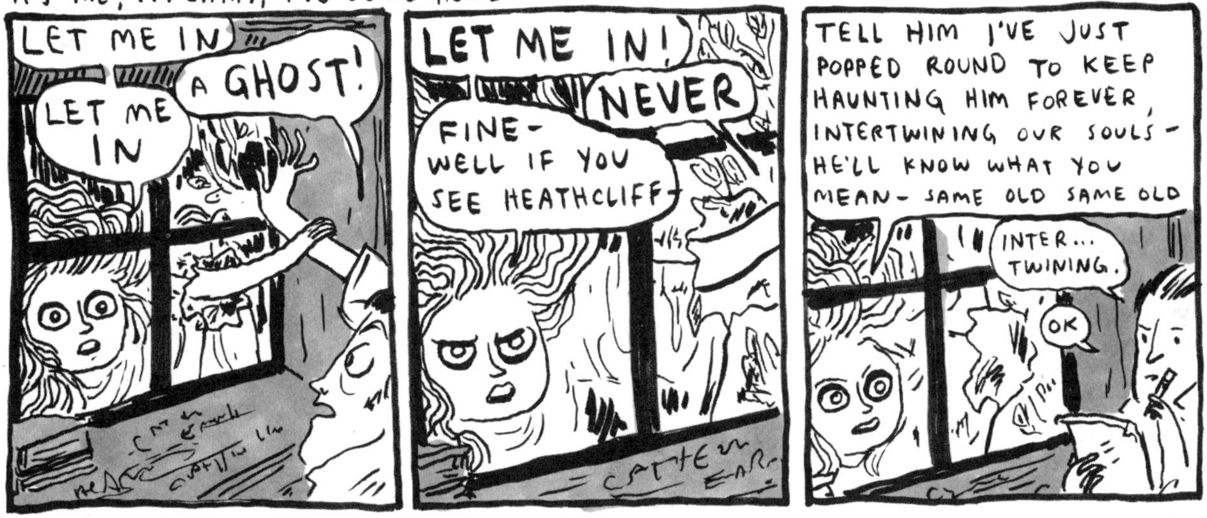
LET ME IN
LET ME IN
A GHOST!
LET ME IN!
NEVER
FINE- WELL IF YOU SEE HEATHCLIFF-
TELL HIM I'VE JUST POPPED ROUND TO KEEP HAUNTING HIM FOREVER, INTERTWINING OUR SOULS - HE'LL KNOW WHAT YOU MEAN - SAME OLD SAME OLD
INTER... TWINING.
OK

SORRY I RUINED NELLY DEAN

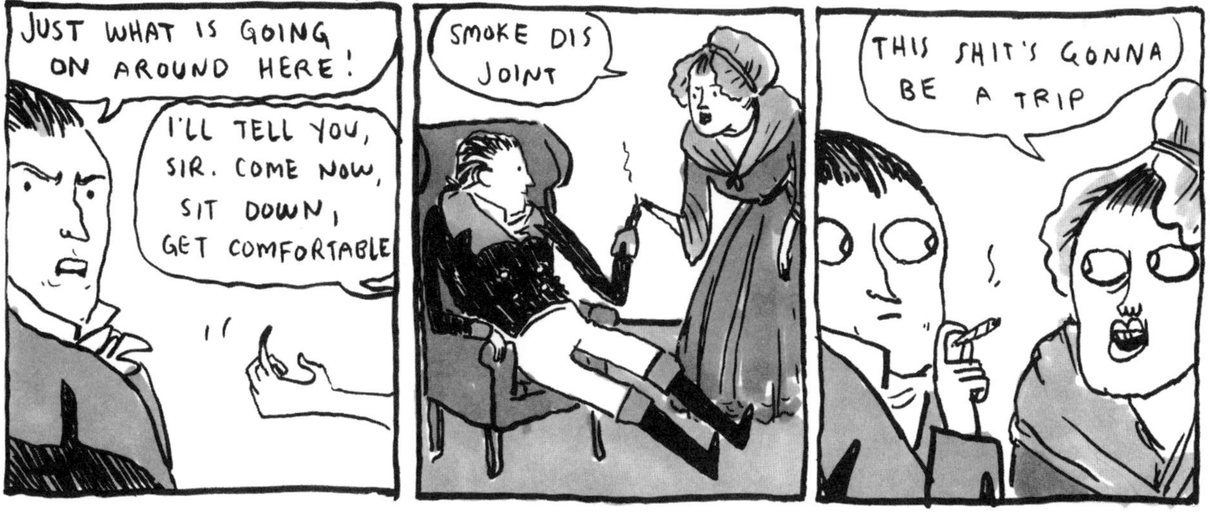
JUST WHAT IS GOING ON AROUND HERE!
I'LL TELL YOU, SIR. COME NOW, SIT DOWN, GET COMFORTABLE
SMOKE DIS JOINT
THIS SHIT'S GONNA BE A TRIP

WUTHERING HEIGHTS

PART TWO: CHILDHOOD OF HEATHCLIFF

NEW ADDITION

CHILDREN, WOULD YOU LIKE THE PRESENT I BROUGHT BACK FROM THE CITY?

IT'S NOT WHAT YOU ASKED FOR **AT ALL**! IT'S AN ANGRY BOY I PICKED UP IN A GUTTER

HE'S A GHASTLY LITTLE FELLOW BUT MAYBE YOU'LL GET USED TO IT

SNARL

I NEEDED TO POSSESS YOU

WHY DO YOU LIKE HEATHCLIFF SO MUCH, CATHY? EVEN FATHER PREFERS HIM TO ME

I DON'T "LIKE" HIM, HINDLEY, YOU SILLY GOOSE, WE ARE JUST OBSESSED WITH ONE ANOTHER

WELL... AS LONG AS YOU DON'T LIKE HIM

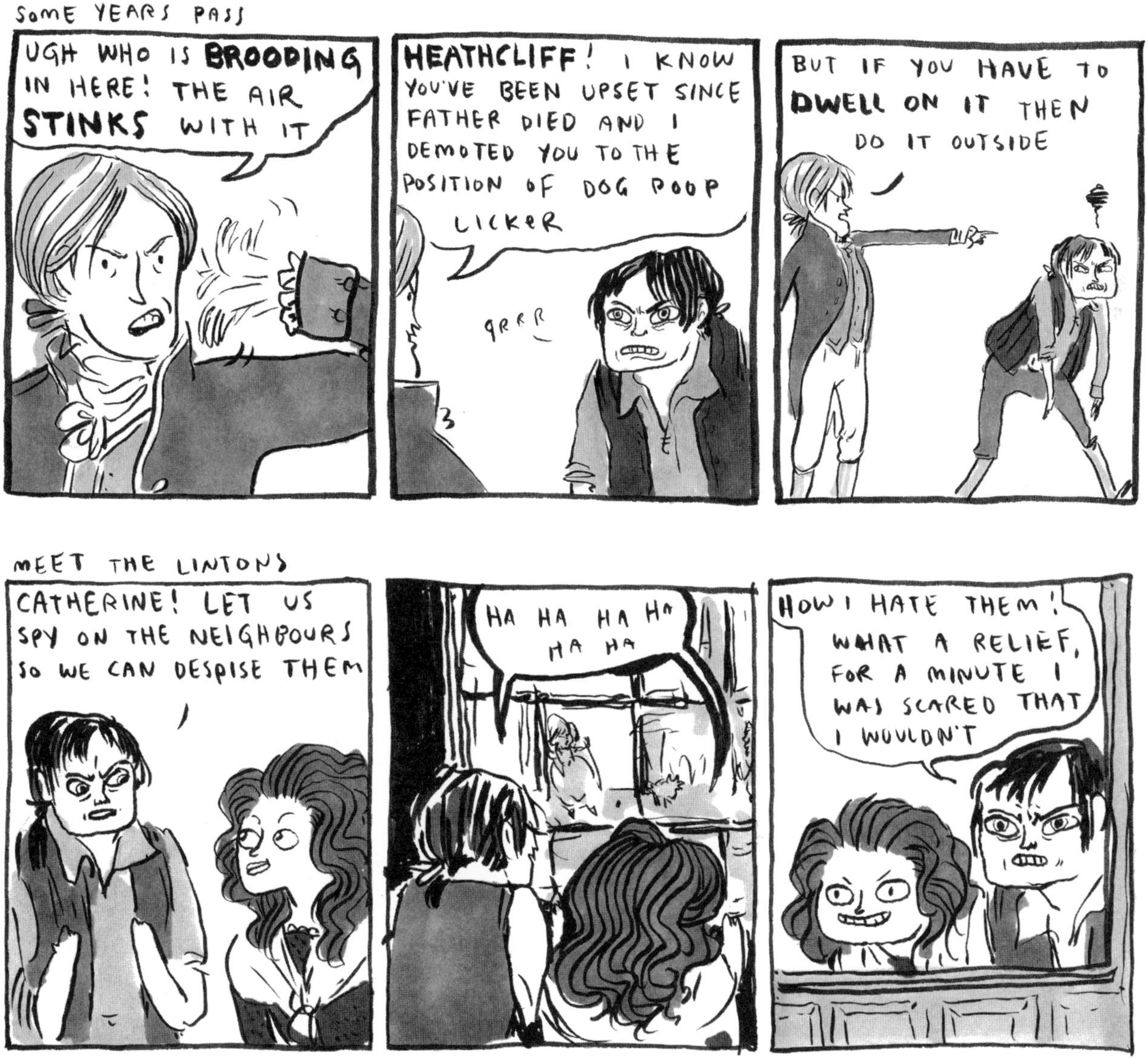
SOME YEARS PASS
UGH WHO IS BROODING IN HERE! THE AIR STINKS WITH IT
HEATHCLIFF! I KNOW YOU'VE BEEN UPSET SINCE FATHER DIED AND I DEMOTED YOU TO THE POSITION OF DOG POOP LICKER
GRRR
BUT IF YOU HAVE TO DWELL ON IT THEN DO IT OUTSIDE
MEET THE LINTONS
CATHERINE! LET US SPY ON THE NEIGHBOURS SO WE CAN DESPISE THEM
HA HA HA HA HA HA
HOW I HATE THEM! WHAT A RELIEF, FOR A MINUTE I WAS SCARED THAT I WOULDN'T

OUT-AND-OUTER

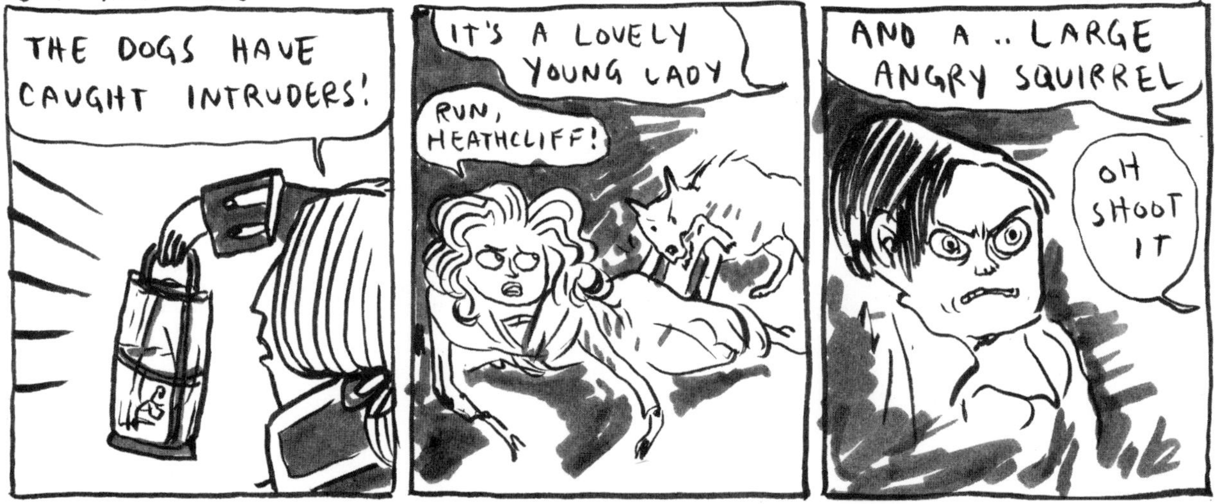
THE DOGS HAVE CAUGHT INTRUDERS!
IT'S A LOVELY YOUNG LADY
RUN, HEATHCLIFF!
AND A .. LARGE ANGRY SQUIRREL
OH SHOOT IT

THAT'S OUR HEATHCLIFF

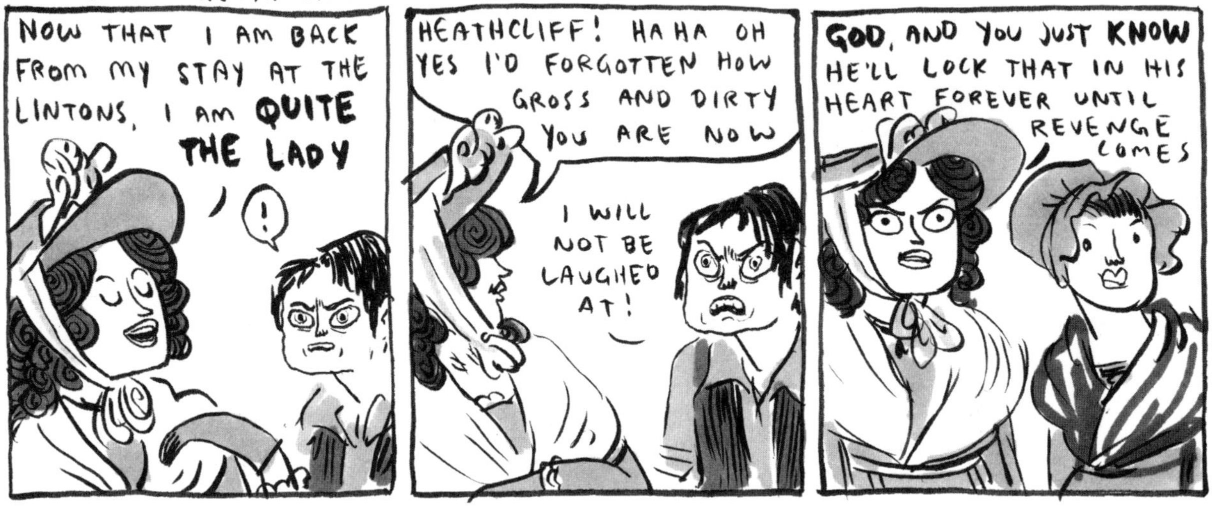
NOW THAT I AM BACK FROM MY STAY AT THE LINTONS, I AM **QUITE THE LADY**
!
HEATHCLIFF! HAHA OH YES I'D FORGOTTEN HOW GROSS AND DIRTY YOU ARE NOW
I WILL NOT BE LAUGHED AT!
GOD, AND YOU JUST **KNOW** HE'LL LOCK THAT IN HIS HEART FOREVER UNTIL REVENGE COMES

WUTHERING HEIGHTS

PART THREE: HEATHCLIFF AND CATHY GROW UP

WHAT DRIVES HEATHCLIFF

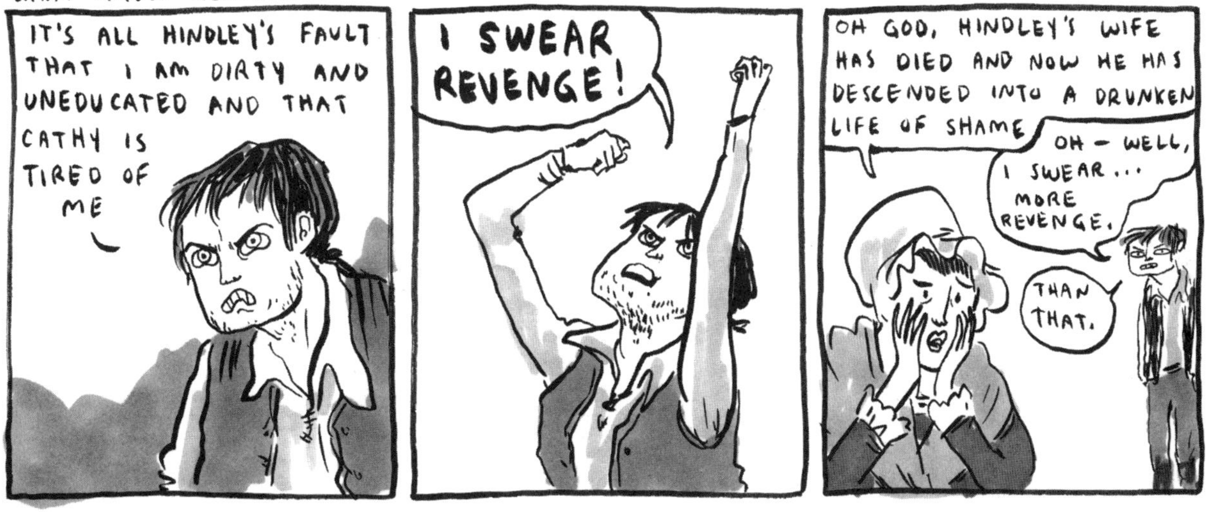
IT'S ALL HINDLEY'S FAULT THAT I AM DIRTY AND UNEDUCATED AND THAT CATHY IS TIRED OF ME
I SWEAR REVENGE!
OH GOD, HINDLEY'S WIFE HAS DIED AND NOW HE HAS DESCENDED INTO A DRUNKEN LIFE OF SHAME
OH - WELL, I SWEAR... MORE REVENGE.
THAN THAT.

EDGAR FALLS IN LOVE

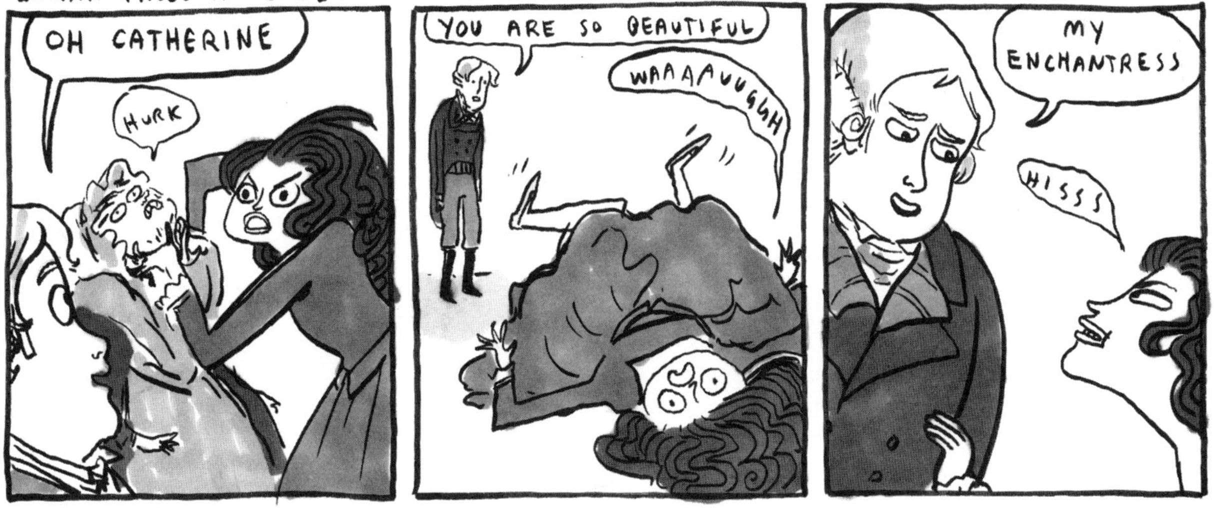
OH CATHERINE
HURK
YOU ARE SO BEAUTIFUL
WAAAAAUUGGH
MY ENCHANTRESS
HISSS

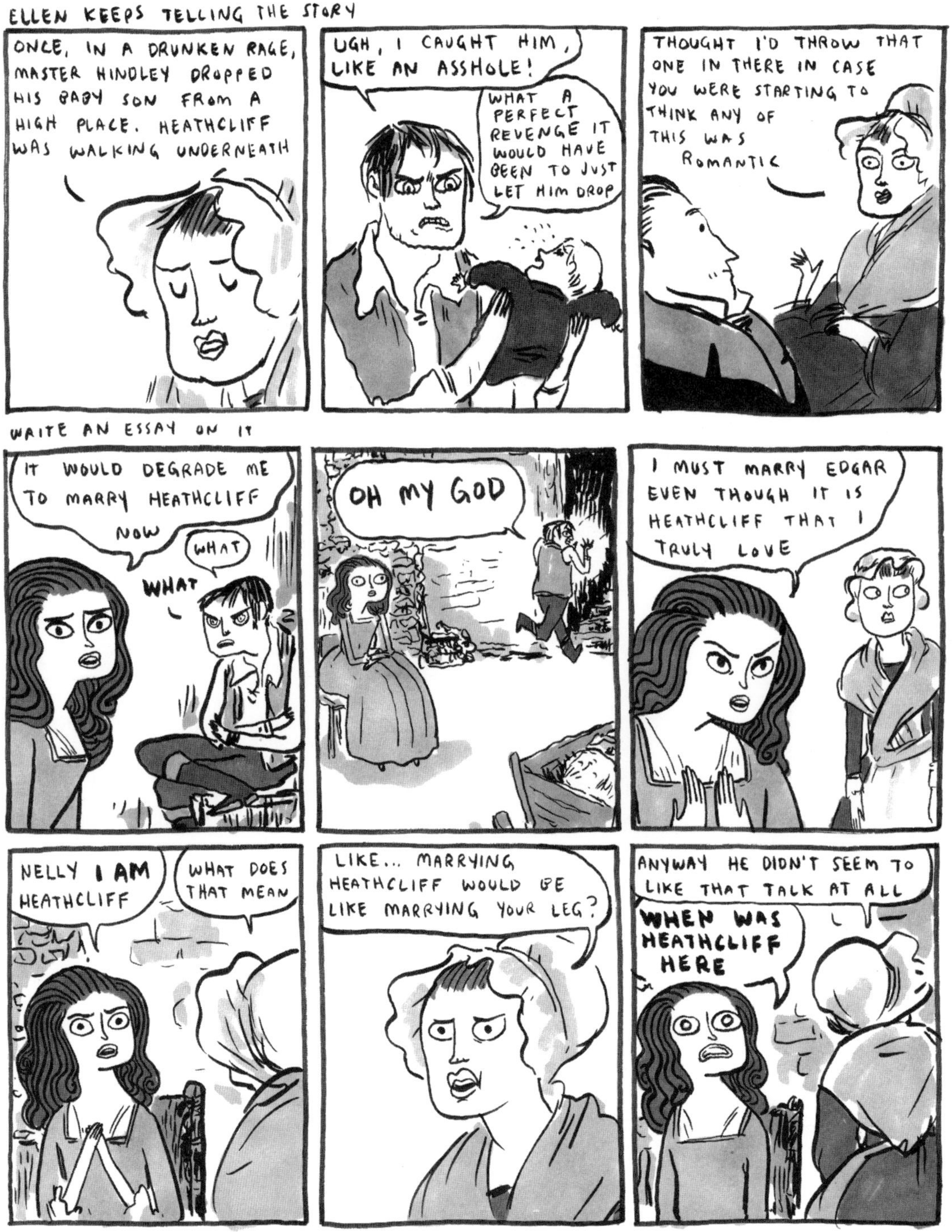
ELLEN KEEPS TELLING THE STORY
ONCE, IN A DRUNKEN RAGE, MASTER HINDLEY DROPPED HIS BABY SON FROM A HIGH PLACE. HEATHCLIFF WAS WALKING UNDERNEATH
UGH, I CAUGHT HIM, LIKE AN ASSHOLE!
WHAT A PERFECT REVENGE IT WOULD HAVE BEEN TO JUST LET HIM DROP
THOUGHT I'D THROW THAT ONE IN THERE IN CASE YOU WERE STARTING TO THINK ANY OF THIS WAS ROMANTIC
WRITE AN ESSAY ON IT
IT WOULD DEGRADE ME TO MARRY HEATHCLIFF NOW
WHAT
WHAT
OH MY GOD
I MUST MARRY EDGAR EVEN THOUGH IT IS HEATHCLIFF THAT I TRULY LOVE
NELLY I AM HEATHCLIFF
WHAT DOES THAT MEAN
LIKE... MARRYING HEATHCLIFF WOULD BE LIKE MARRYING YOUR LEG?
ANYWAY HE DIDN'T SEEM TO LIKE THAT TALK AT ALL
WHEN WAS HEATHCLIFF HERE

EXIT HEATHCLIFF

I'M LEAVING, I'M LEAVING! I'M GOING TO TURN THIS THING AROUND. CATHY WILL UNDERSTAND WHY I'M GONE, WE KNOW EACH OTHER SO WELL

eh?

NEXT TIME ON WUTHERING HEIGHTS

NO ONE IS LONELY IN A GRAVEYARD!

CATHY!

C.L.

Author's note: If we kept going with these, they'd be half of the book. And so, another time, my friends

COMPLEX

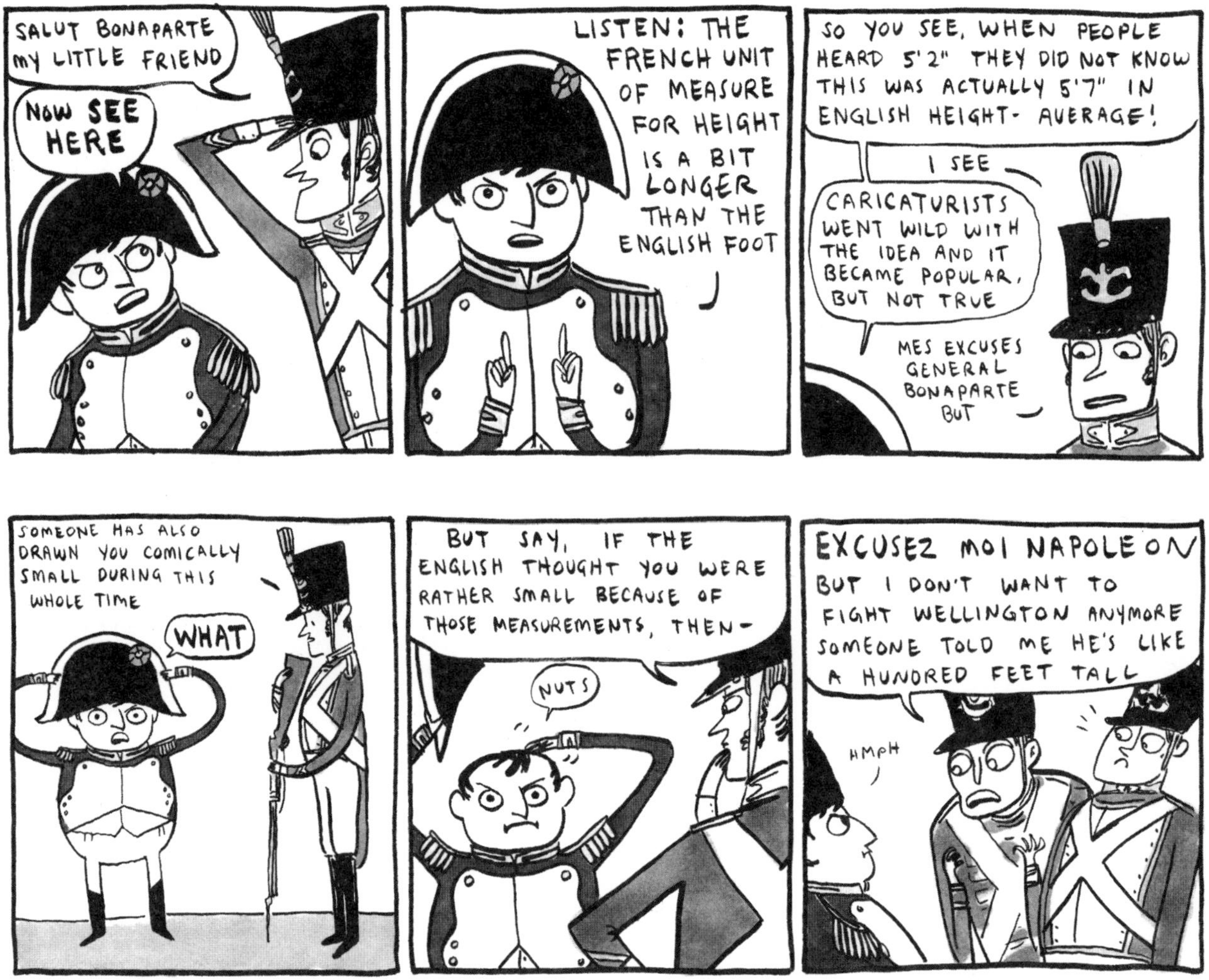

SALUT BONAPARTE my LITTLE FRIEND
NOW SEE HERE
LISTEN: THE FRENCH UNIT OF MEASURE FOR HEIGHT IS A BIT LONGER THAN THE ENGLISH FOOT
SO YOU SEE, WHEN PEOPLE HEARD 5'2" THEY DID NOT KNOW THIS WAS ACTUALLY 5'7" IN ENGLISH HEIGHT- AVERAGE!
I SEE
CARICATURISTS WENT WILD WITH THE IDEA AND IT BECAME POPULAR, BUT NOT TRUE
MES EXCUSES GENERAL BONAPARTE BUT
SOMEONE HAS ALSO DRAWN YOU COMICALLY SMALL DURING THIS WHOLE TIME
WHAT
BUT SAY, IF THE ENGLISH THOUGHT YOU WERE RATHER SMALL BECAUSE OF THOSE MEASUREMENTS, THEN-
NUTS
EXCUSEZ MOI NAPOLEON BUT I DON'T WANT TO FIGHT WELLINGTON ANYMORE SOMEONE TOLD ME HE'S LIKE A HUNDRED FEET TALL
HMPH

Napoleon is something of an unofficial mascot to this comic collection, so sometimes I think I ought to throw him in more. However, as you can see, my round depictions don't really help his, uh, Napoleon complex problem. I blame Gillray.

NEMESIS

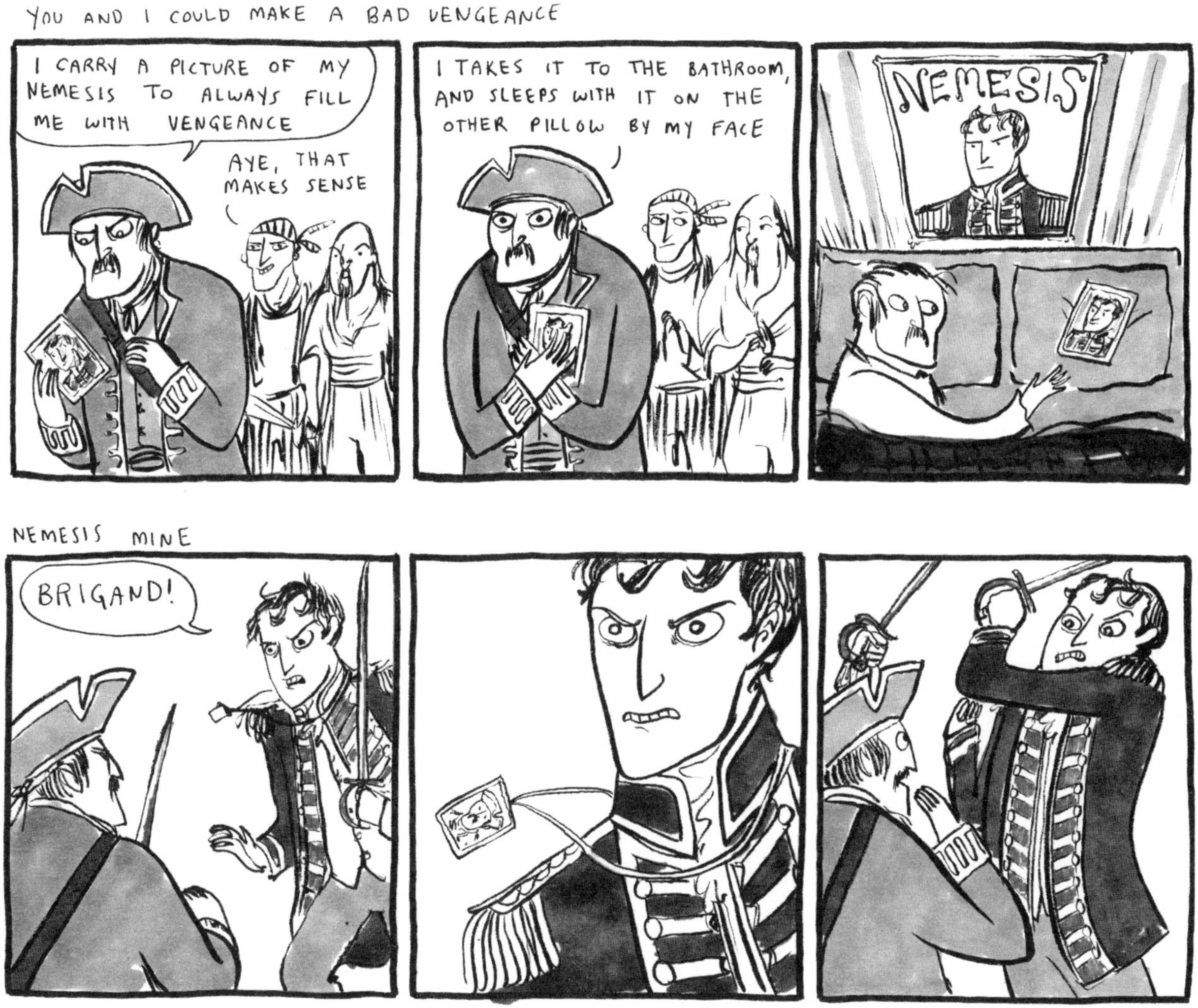

YOU AND I COULD MAKE A BAD VENGEANCE
I CARRY A PICTURE OF MY NEMESIS TO ALWAYS FILL ME WITH VENGEANCE
AYE, THAT MAKES SENSE
I TAKES IT TO THE BATHROOM, AND SLEEPS WITH IT ON THE OTHER PILLOW BY MY FACE
NEMESIS
NEMESIS MINE
BRIGAND!

Sweet antagonism! The joy and the agony. These two popped up in a collection of pirate strips in *Hark! A Vagrant* but you all liked them so much I thought they needed a second, expanded appearance.

LAY DOWN YOUR LOYALTIES

DON'T WORRY CAPTAIN- IF HE GETS TOO CLOSE TO YOU, I CAN TAKE HIM DOWN MYSELF
WOULD YOU NOW
OR I HAVE A SHOT IF HE GETS MORE IN THE CLEAR
POW

DON'T PLAY ME LIKE THIS

HE HAD ORDERS TO BE HERE BY NOW! I KNOW- I INTERCEPTED THEM!
WHY HASN'T HE COME? I'VE BEEN WAITING FOR DAYS
AW HE PROBABLY WOULD HAVE SHOWN UP ON TIME IF HE KNEW YOU INTERCEPTED THEM! HE'S PROBABLY BUSY
UGH JUST LEAVE ME ALONE TO DIE

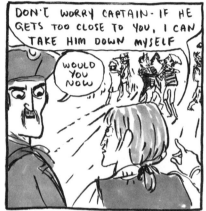

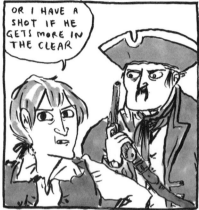

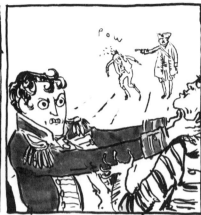

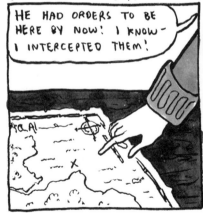

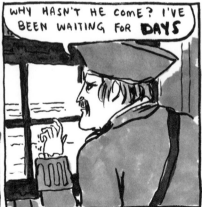

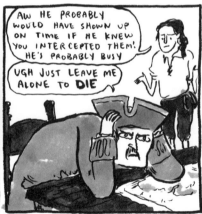

NO ONE ELSE

NO
I DON'T KNOW! HE JUST WON'T GET OUT OF BED
SIR
KNOCK KNOCK

GRAPESHOT MY HEART

SOUND THE CANNONS
ARE WE ATTACKING?
I JUST WANT HIM TO KNOW
I'M HERE
BOOM

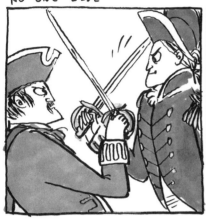

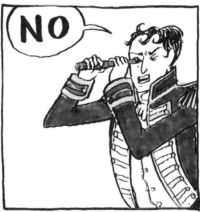

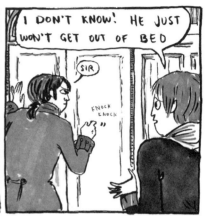

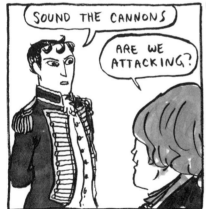

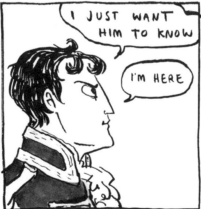

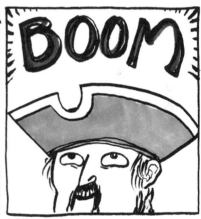

GOREYS

A 619
$1.95
POOR PEOPLE
A LITTLE HERO
Translated, with an Introduction by DAVID MAGARSHACK
FYODOR DOSTOEVSKY
A DOUBLEDAY ANCHOR ORIGINAL
WHO SHALL BE THE CHAMPION OF THE POOR, WHO WILL SAVE US?
I WILL!
PEW PEW
Stendhal: On Love
A Doubleday Anchor Book
EGAD, MY LEGS! REMEMBER WHAT FATHER ALWAYS SAID
MY BOY IF A MAN SPIES THE WOMAN OF HIS DREAMS IT IS NATURAL FOR HIM TO LOSE CONTROL OF HIS BODY, STARTING WITH THE LEGS
WHEW OK
IF YOU LOSE CONTROL OF MORE THAN THAT AND POOP YOUR PANTS THEN MARRY THAT GIRL
SO WISE, FATHER

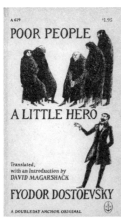

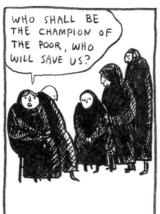

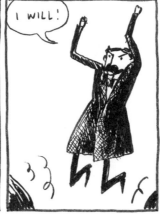

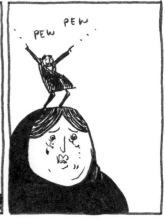

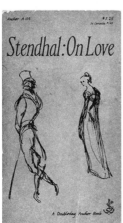

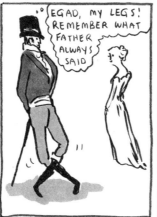

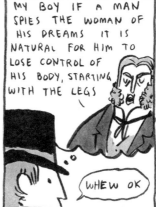

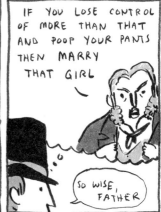

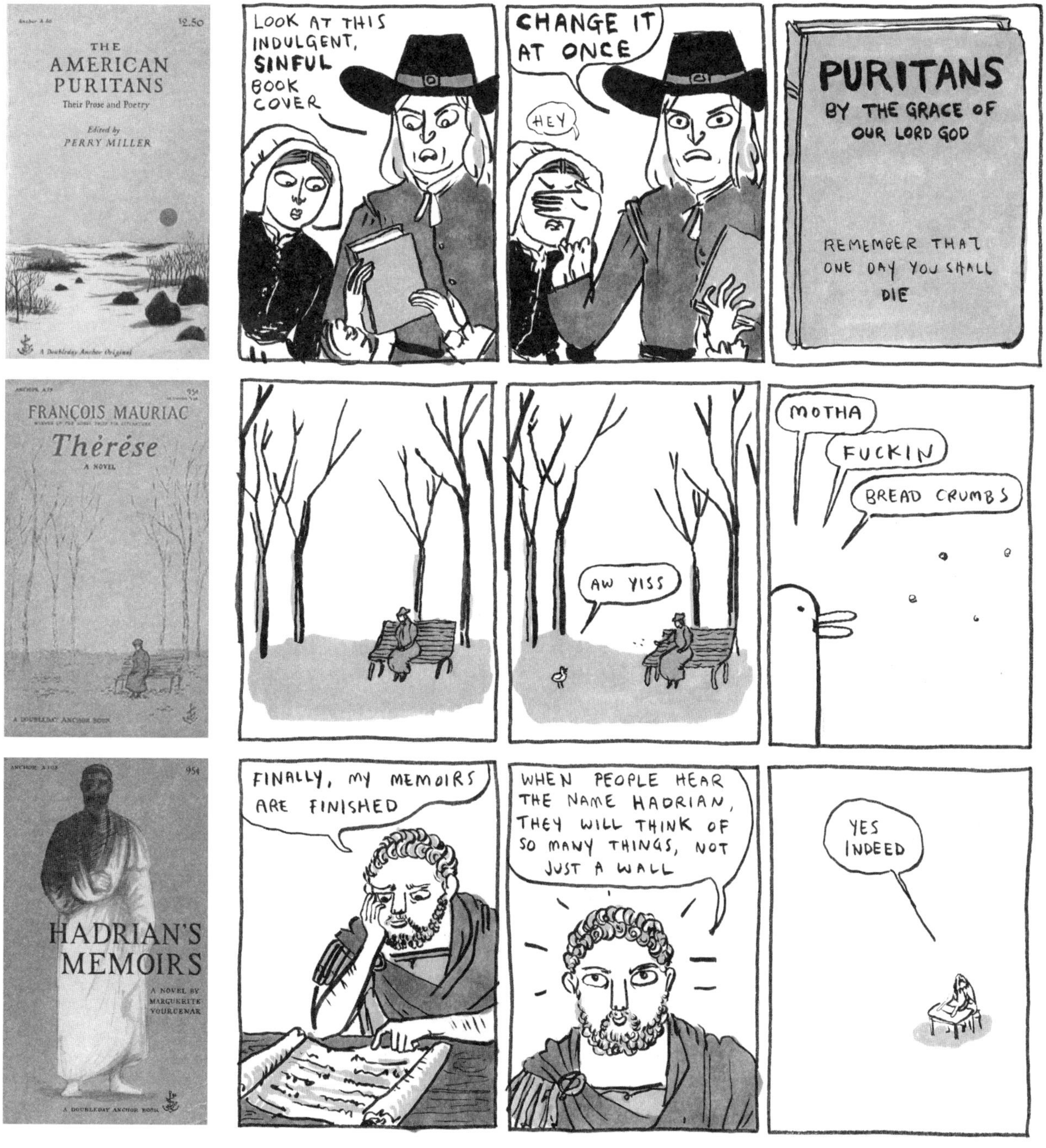
$2.50
THE AMERICAN PURITANS
Their Prose and Poetry
Edited by
PERRY MILLER
A Doubleday Anchor Original
LOOK AT THIS INDULGENT, SINFUL BOOK COVER
CHANGE IT AT ONCE
HEY
PURITANS
BY THE GRACE OF OUR LORD GOD
REMEMBER THAT ONE DAY YOU SHALL DIE
95¢
FRANÇOIS MAURIAC
Thérèse
A NOVEL
A DOUBLEDAY ANCHOR BOOK
AW YISS
MOTHA
FUCKIN
BREAD CRUMBS
95¢
HADRIAN'S MEMOIRS
A NOVEL BY MARGUERITE YOURCENAR
A DOUBLEDAY ANCHOR BOOK
FINALLY, MY MEMOIRS ARE FINISHED
WHEN PEOPLE HEAR THE NAME HADRIAN, THEY WILL THINK OF SO MANY THINGS, NOT JUST A WALL
YES INDEED

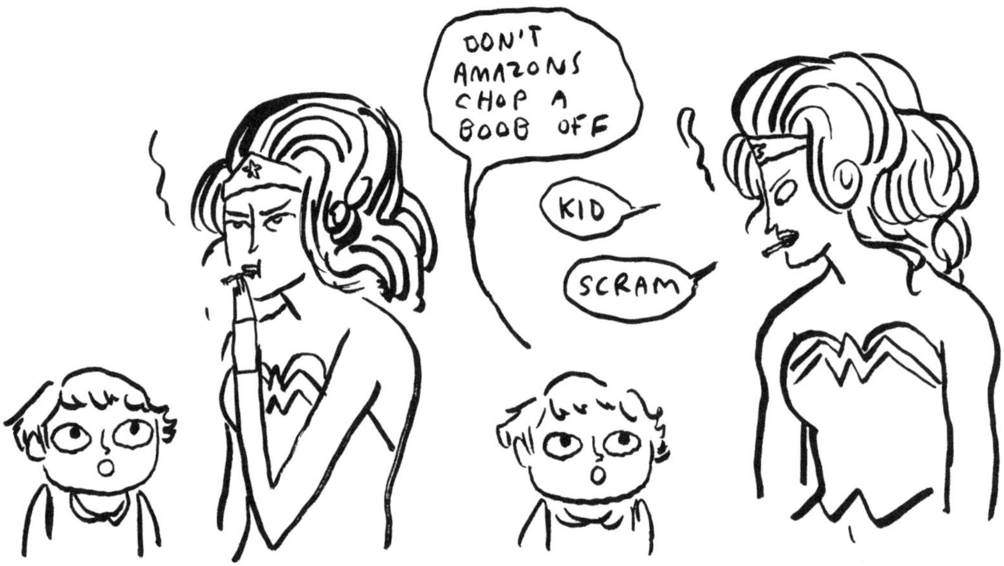
DON'T AMAZONS CHOP A BOOB OFF
KID
SCRAM

WONDER WOMAN

Wonder Woman, we just want her to be great—the first and best of all. What's wrong with that? Maybe she wants to be great too.

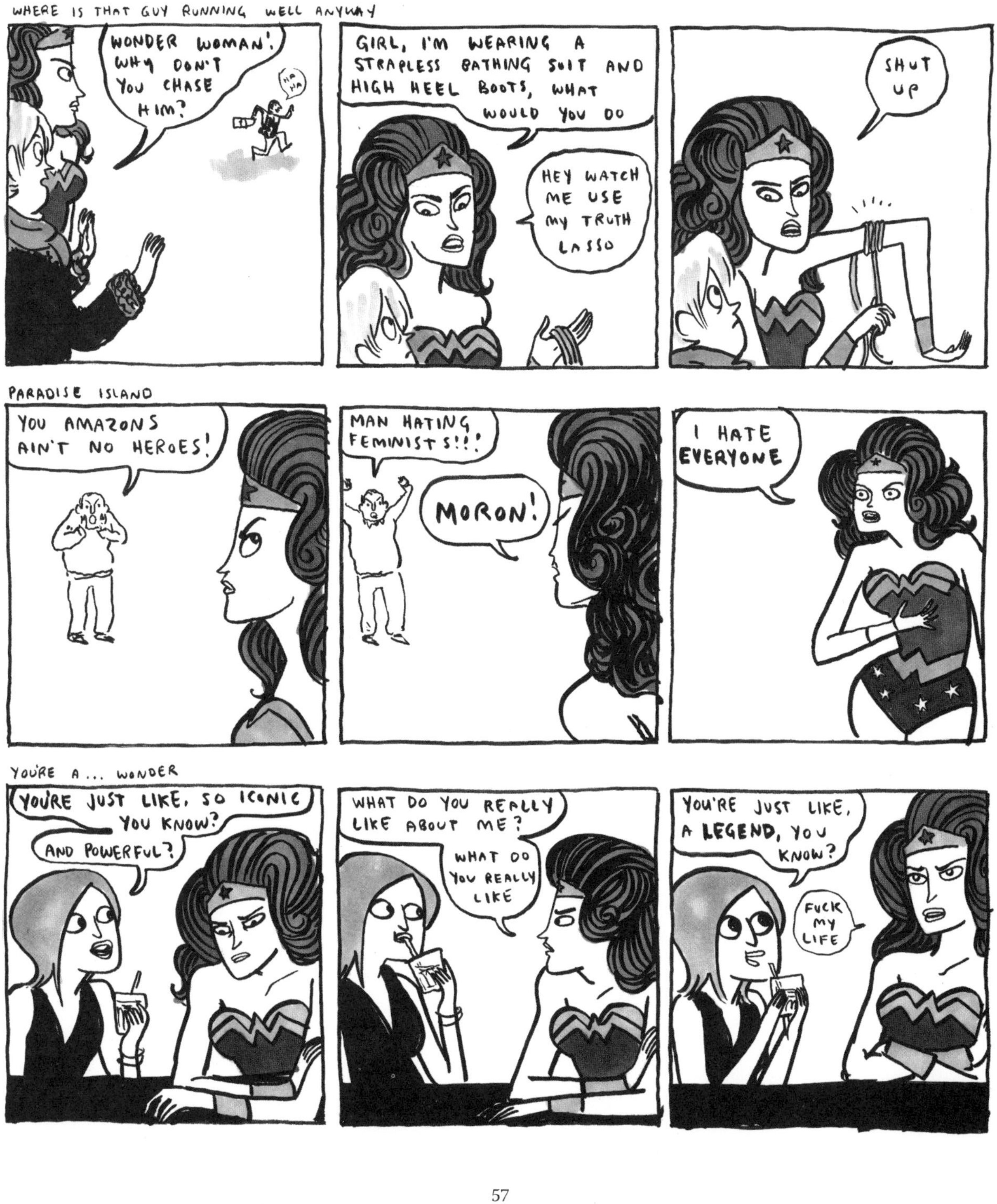

WHERE IS THAT GUY RUNNING WELL ANYWAY
WONDER WOMAN! WHY DON'T YOU CHASE HIM?
HA HA
GIRL, I'M WEARING A STRAPLESS BATHING SUIT AND HIGH HEEL BOOTS, WHAT WOULD YOU DO
HEY WATCH ME USE MY TRUTH LASSO
SHUT UP
PARADISE ISLAND
YOU AMAZONS AIN'T NO HEROES!
MAN HATING FEMINISTS!!!
MORON!
I HATE EVERYONE
YOU'RE A... WONDER
YOU'RE JUST LIKE, SO ICONIC YOU KNOW?
AND POWERFUL?
WHAT DO YOU REALLY LIKE ABOUT ME?
WHAT DO YOU REALLY LIKE
YOU'RE JUST LIKE, A **LEGEND**, YOU KNOW?
FUCK MY LIFE

HEAD OFFICE

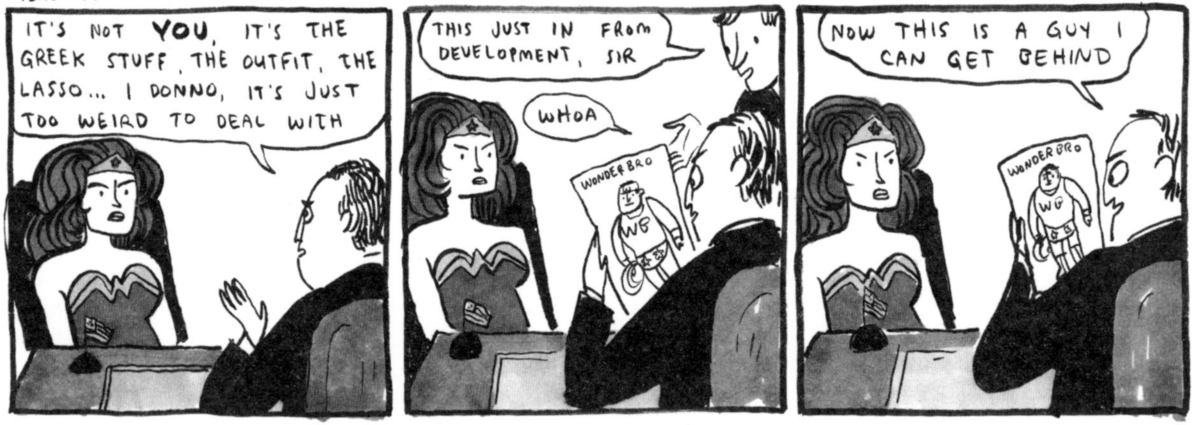
IT'S NOT **YOU**, IT'S THE GREEK STUFF, THE OUTFIT, THE LASSO... I DONNO, IT'S JUST TOO WEIRD TO DEAL WITH
THIS JUST IN FROM DEVELOPMENT, SIR
WHOA
WONDERBRO
WB
NOW THIS IS A GUY I CAN GET BEHIND
WONDERBRO
WB

WEAPONRY

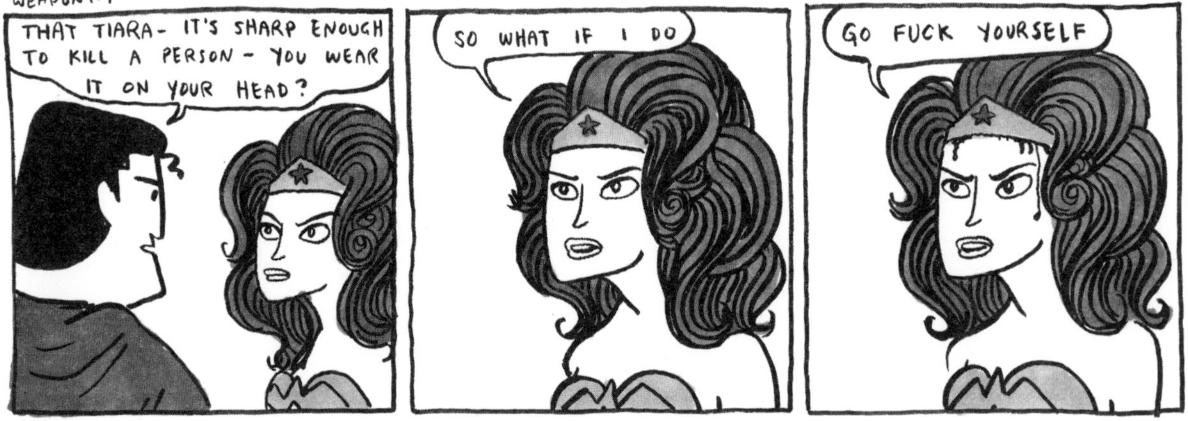
THAT TIARA- IT'S SHARP ENOUGH TO KILL A PERSON - YOU WEAR IT ON YOUR HEAD?
SO WHAT IF I DO
GO FUCK YOURSELF

TRINITY

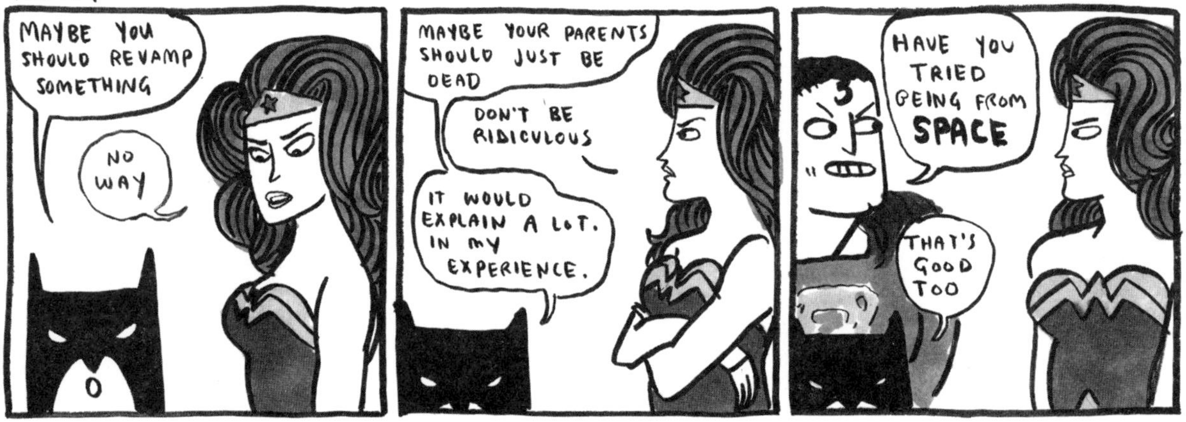
MAYBE YOU SHOULD REVAMP SOMETHING
NO WAY
MAYBE YOUR PARENTS SHOULD JUST BE DEAD
DON'T BE RIDICULOUS
IT WOULD EXPLAIN A LOT. IN MY EXPERIENCE.
HAVE YOU TRIED BEING FROM **SPACE**
THAT'S GOOD TOO

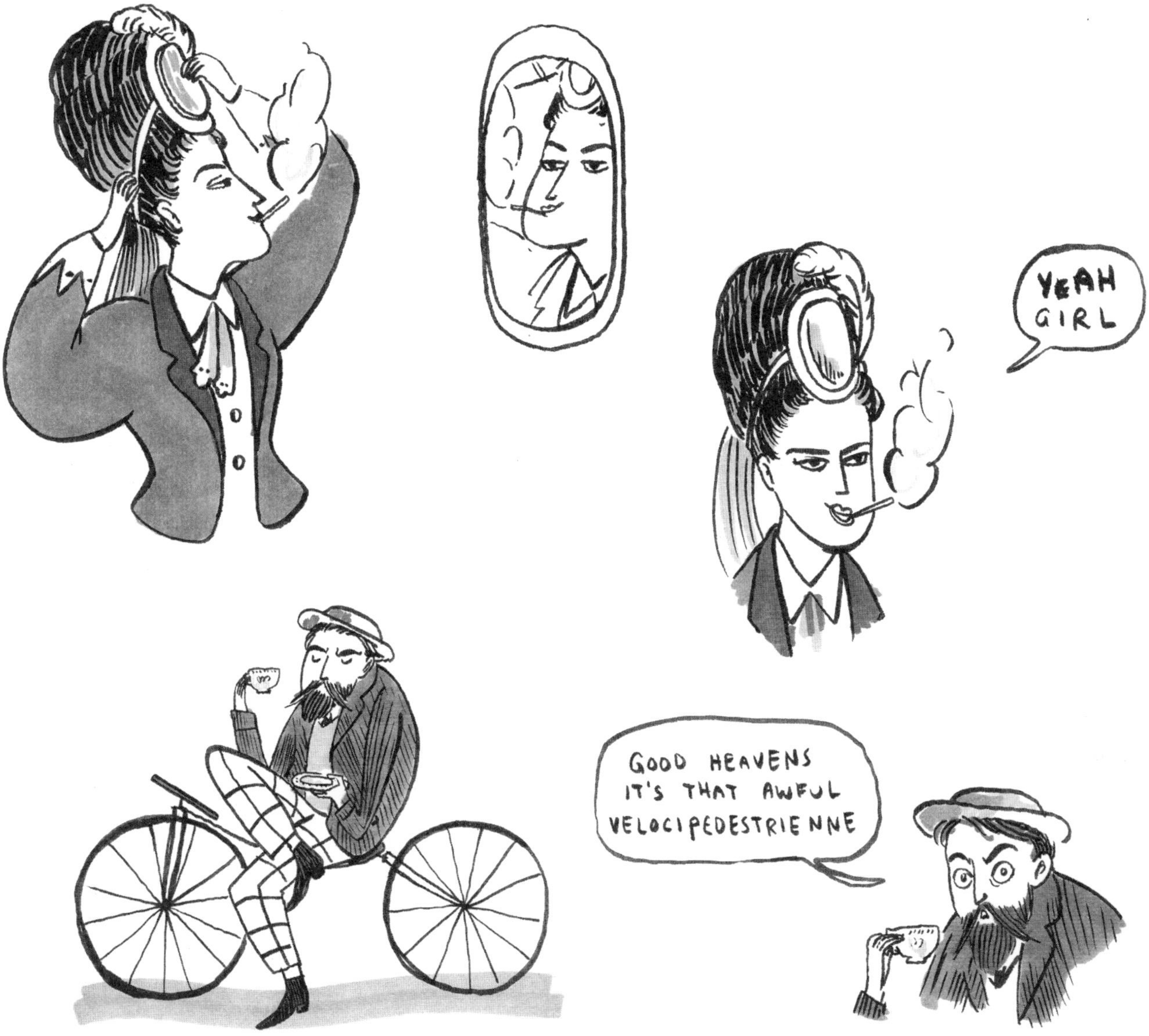
YEAH GIRL
GOOD HEAVENS IT'S THAT AWFUL VELOCIPEDESTRIENNE

When bicycles were invented and women started to ride them, a whole bunch of satirical cartoons came out depicting the women as shocking and inappropriate, not knowing that in our time, we would look at those cartoons and think those women look AWESOME. It was folly, but the good kind, poor fools.

THE AWFUL EFFECTS OF VELOCIPEDING.

PUBLIC NUISANCE!

60

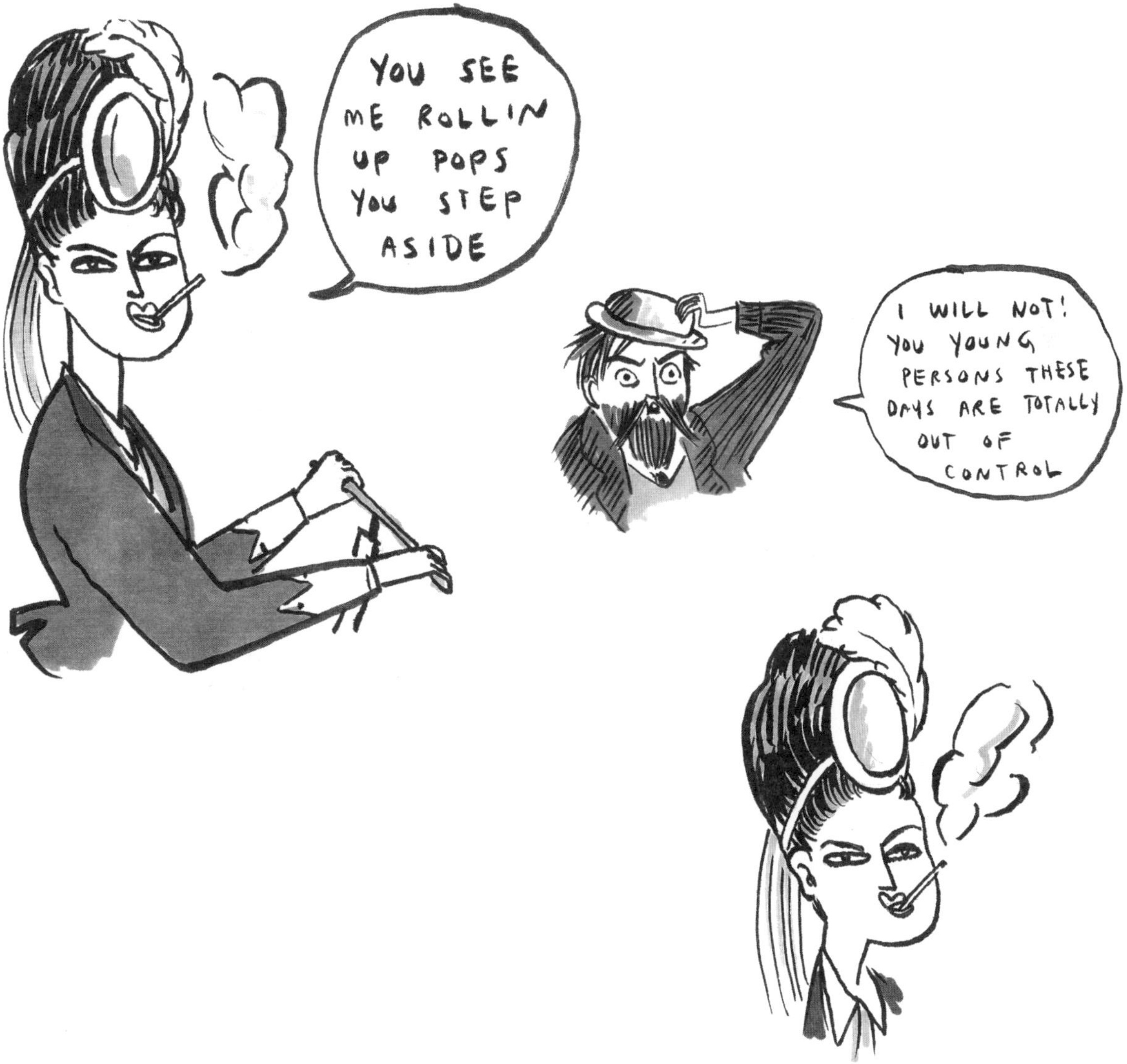
YOU SEE ME ROLLIN UP POPS YOU STEP ASIDE
I WILL NOT! YOU YOUNG PERSONS THESE DAYS ARE TOTALLY OUT OF CONTROL

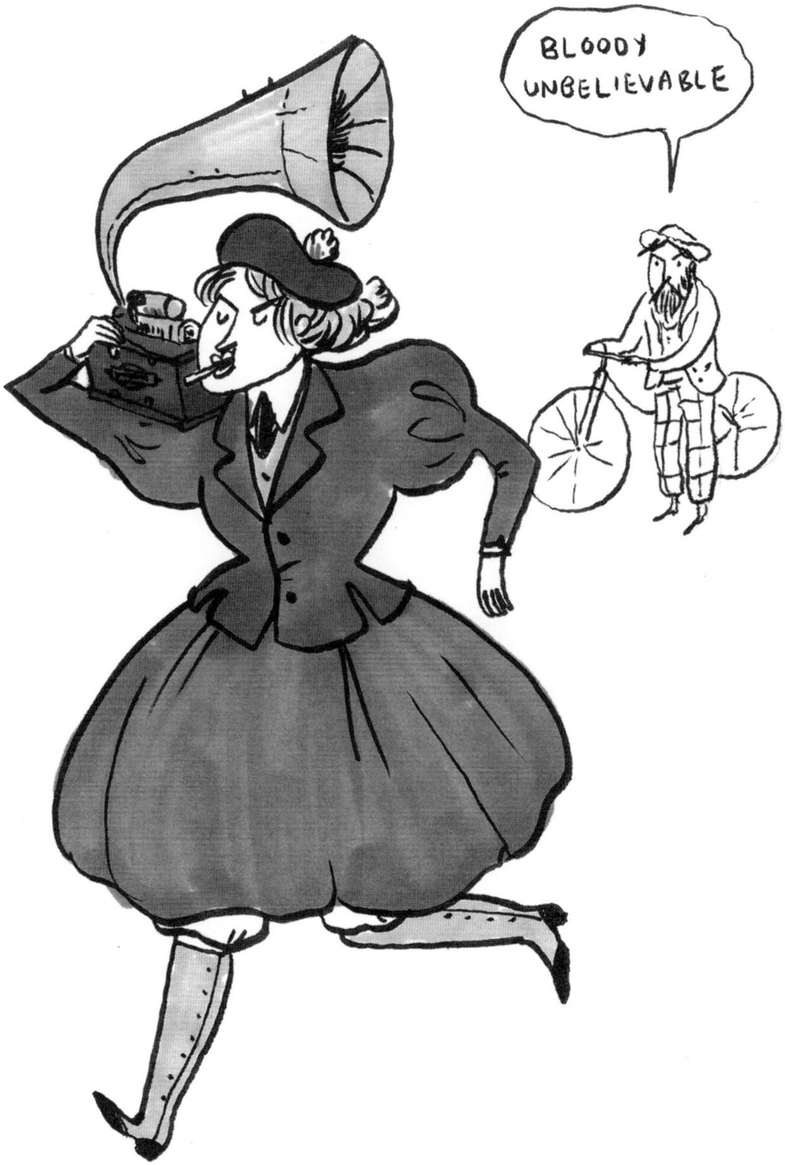
BLOODY UNBELIEVABLE

PEASANT COMICS

THESPIAN

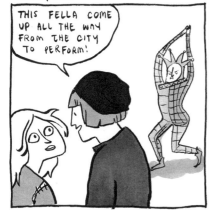

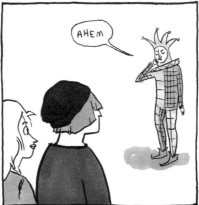

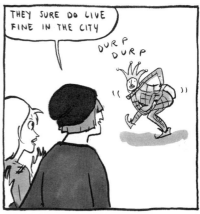

THIS FELLA COME UP ALL THE WAY FROM THE CITY TO PERFORM!
AHEM
THEY SURE DO LIVE FINE IN THE CITY
DURP DURP

ALLER-WHAT?

A BABY!!? YOU DIDN'T TELL ME!
OH NO - IT'S THAT OTHER THING FROM THE SHELLFISH AGAIN
I TOLD THE EVIL-EYE LADY TO STOP PUTTING SPELLS ON THE SHELLFISH

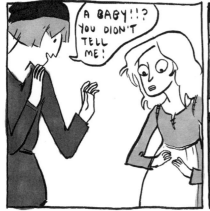

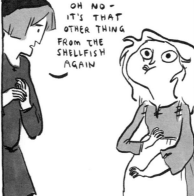

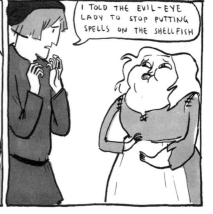

So fond of these little guys. They're going to make it! Unless plague or war or famine or etc.

ARE YOU NOT ENTERTAINED

AW I SAW THIS ONE ALREADY, HE KNOCKS THE OTHER FELLOW UP THE ARSE WITH A MALLET AND THEN IT'S ALL OVER

BIT SILLY REALLY

TOXIC

AW NO- YOU GOT MESSED UP ON WATER AGAIN! THERE'S TOO MUCH INSANE CRAP IN THERE!

YOU KNOW THAT YOU'RE ONLY SUPPOSED TO DRINK BEER! I HOPE THE TEMPERANCE SOCIETY DOESN'T SEE THIS

WATER IS the devil's DRINK

WHATEVER WORKS

WHAT ARE YOU MAKING!!
IS IT APPLE JUICE

REVOLT

PEASANTS ARE DOING AN UPRISING BABY GET YOUR CLOAK ON
PAFF

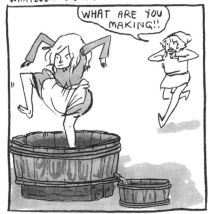

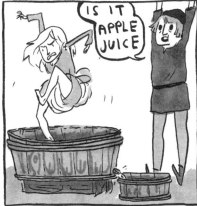

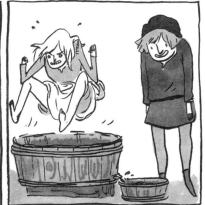

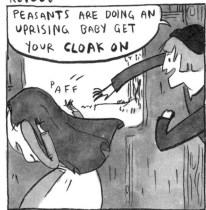

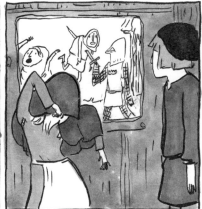

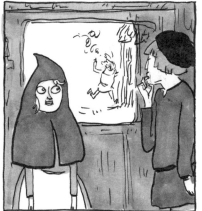

DR. SARA JOSEPHINE BAKER SAVES THE BABIES AND DOES OTHER THINGS

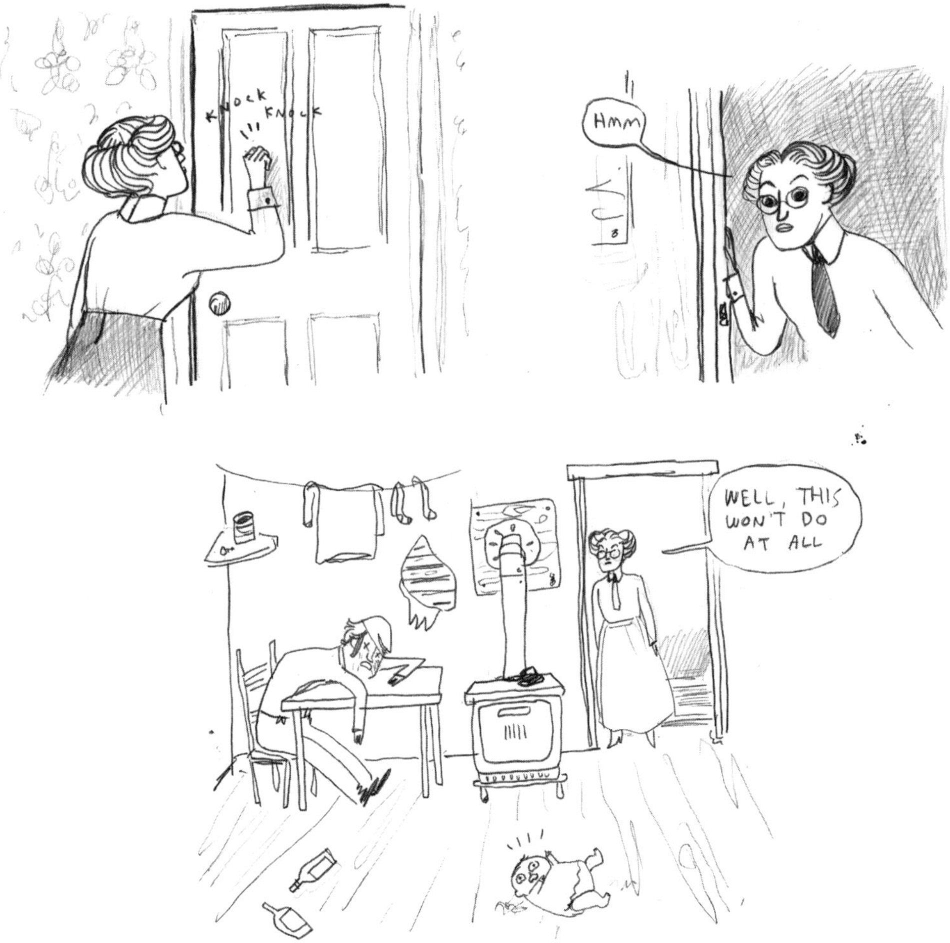
KNOCK KNOCK
Hmm
WELL, THIS WON'T DO AT ALL

Sara Baker was all about preventative care before its time. She's an LGBT icon too. She was so good at saving babies that the city of New York created a Bureau of Child Hygiene and just said "ok, you're in charge." She was known (adorably) as Dr. Jo by the people who loved her best—the countless mothers whose children were healthy and alive because of her.

TEACHING THE BASICS

MY BABY SICK
YOUR BABY IS UPSIDE-DOWN
MY BABY SICK!
WE MUSN'T CARRY BABIES LIKE THAT

EDUCATION

IS THAT BOY GOING TO SCHOOL?
IN THAT CONDITION?
AW HE AIN'T CONTAGIOUS
HUAGHH
PROBABLY

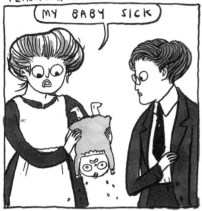

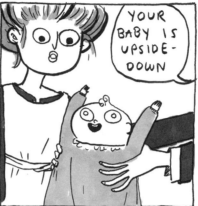

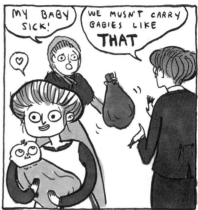

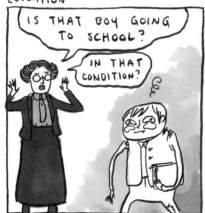

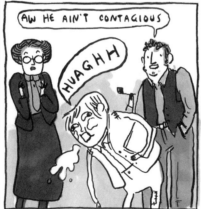

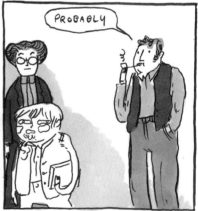

NEW IDEAS

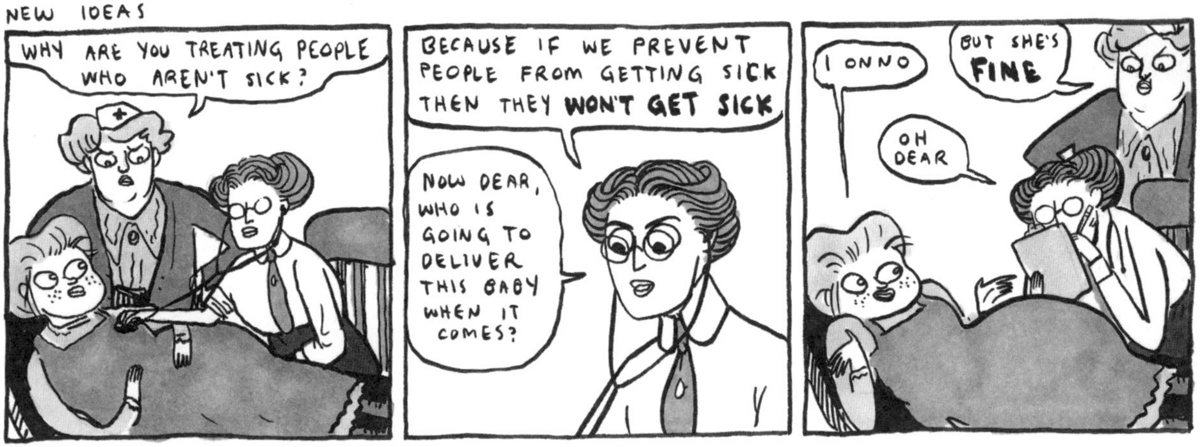
WHY ARE YOU TREATING PEOPLE WHO AREN'T SICK?
BECAUSE IF WE PREVENT PEOPLE FROM GETTING SICK THEN THEY **WON'T GET SICK**
NOW DEAR, WHO IS GOING TO DELIVER THIS BABY WHEN IT COMES?
I ONNO
BUT SHE'S **FINE**
OH DEAR

FOR THE PUBLIC GOOD

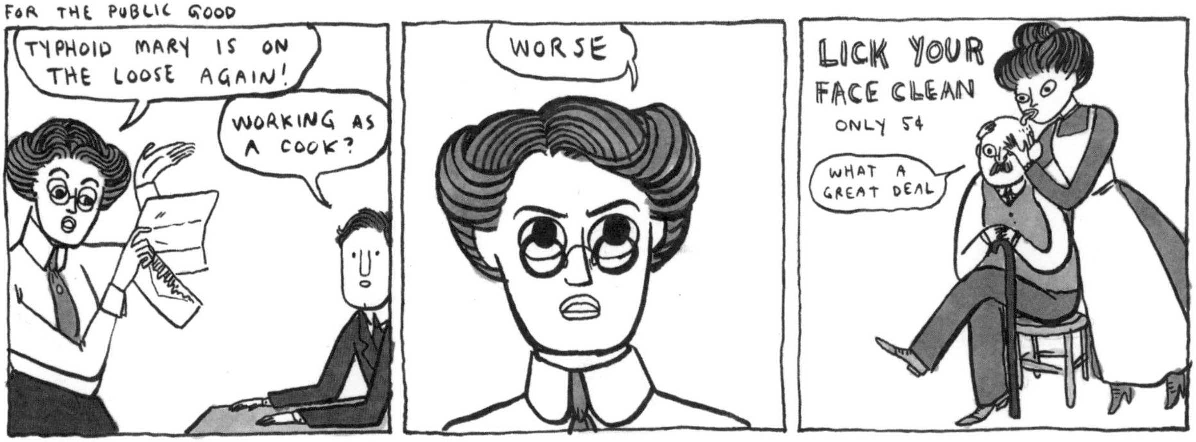
TYPHOID MARY IS ON THE LOOSE AGAIN!
WORKING AS A COOK?
WORSE
LICK YOUR FACE CLEAN
ONLY 5¢
WHAT A GREAT DEAL

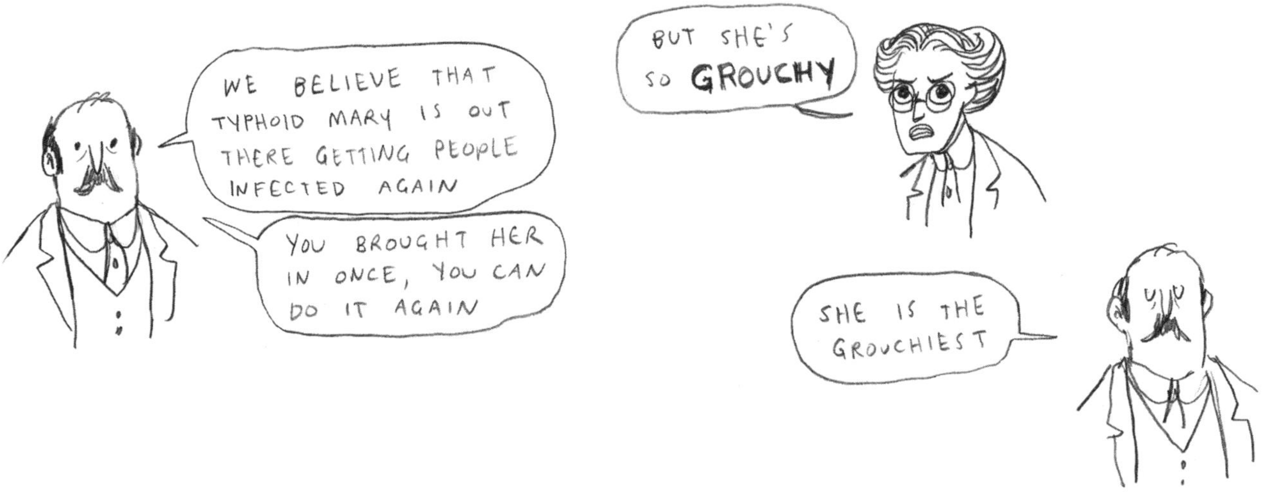
WE BELIEVE THAT TYPHOID MARY IS OUT THERE GETTING PEOPLE INFECTED AGAIN
YOU BROUGHT HER IN ONCE, YOU CAN DO IT AGAIN
BUT SHE'S SO **GROUCHY**
SHE IS THE GROUCHIEST

IDLER

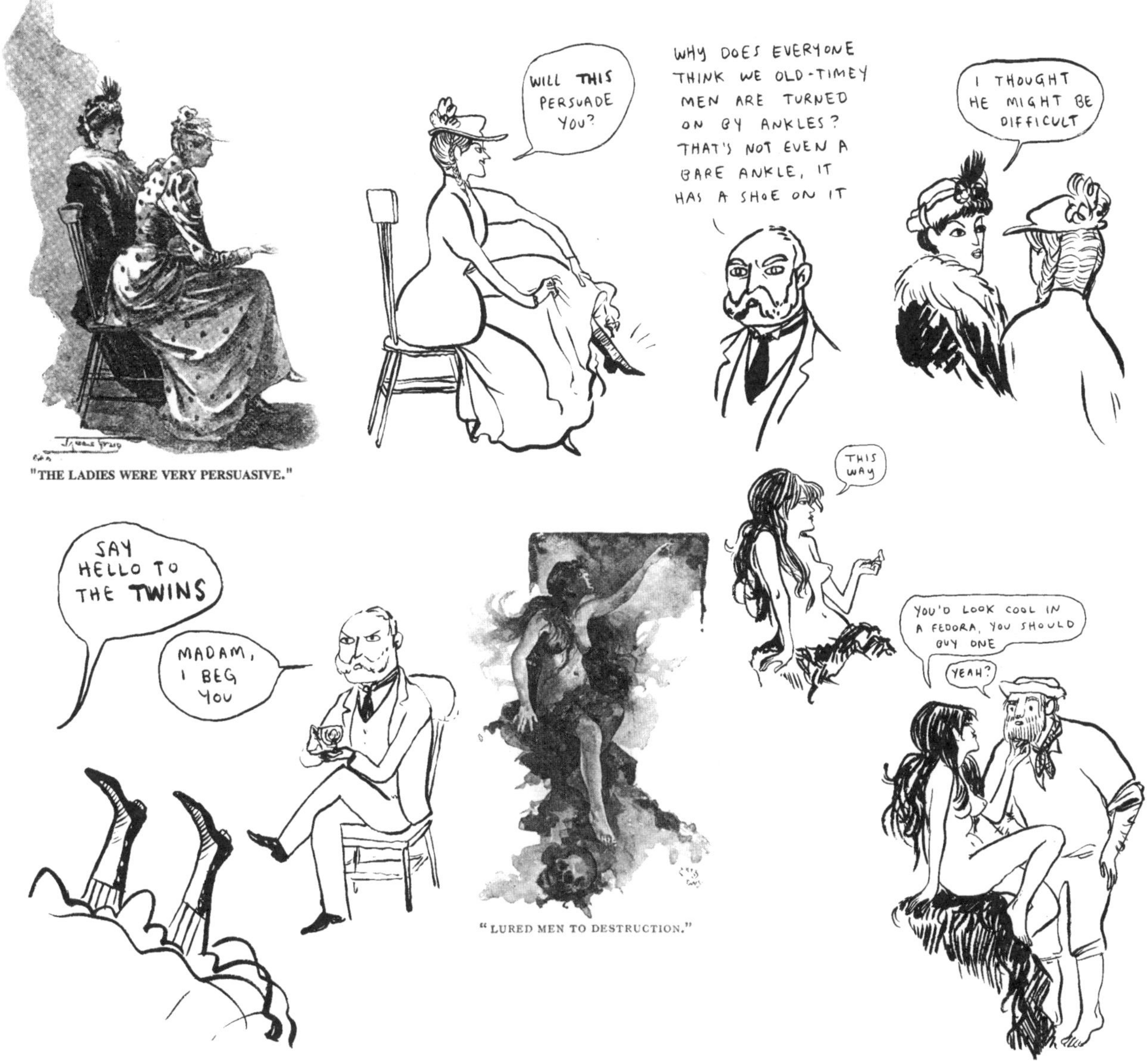
"THE LADIES WERE VERY PERSUASIVE."
WILL THIS PERSUADE YOU?
WHY DOES EVERYONE THINK WE OLD-TIMEY MEN ARE TURNED ON BY ANKLES? THAT'S NOT EVEN A BARE ANKLE, IT HAS A SHOE ON IT
I THOUGHT HE MIGHT BE DIFFICULT
SAY HELLO TO THE TWINS
MADAM, I BEG YOU
"LURED MEN TO DESTRUCTION."
THIS WAY
YOU'D LOOK COOL IN A FEDORA, YOU SHOULD BUY ONE
YEAH?

Just going through some old magazines. One-hundred-year-old magazines. All these images came from *Idler* and were found at gutenberg.org! Go forth! It's an endless supply of interesting things.

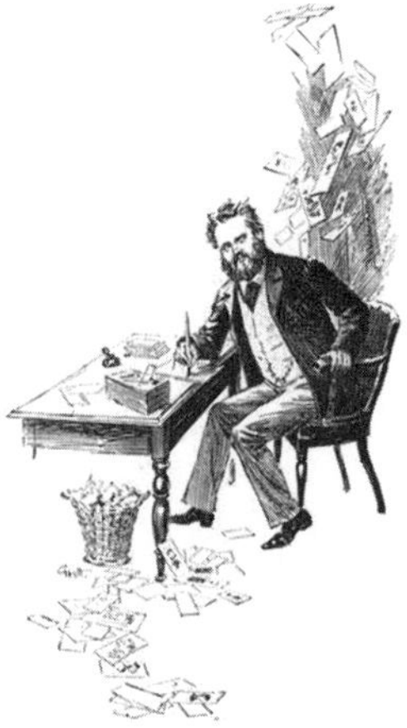

"I WORK VERY QUICKLY."

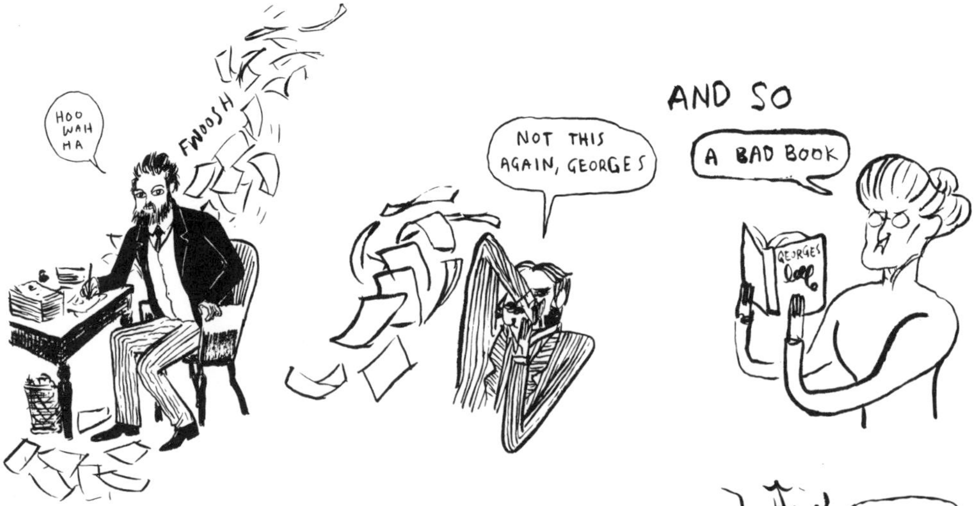
HOO WAH HA
FWOOSH
NOT THIS AGAIN, GEORGES
AND SO
A BAD BOOK
GEORGES

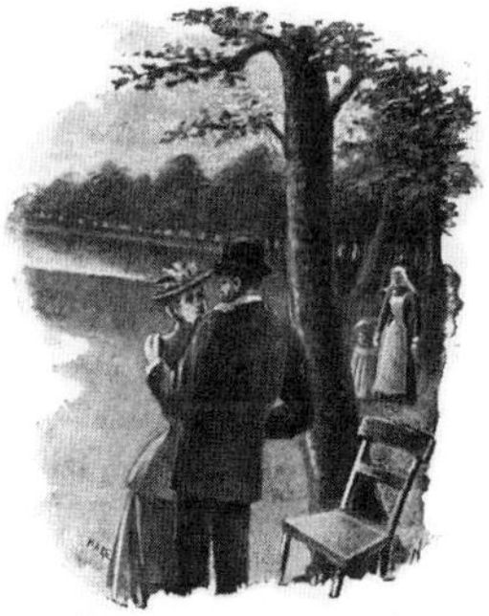

"FORGIVE ME—MY HUSBAND"

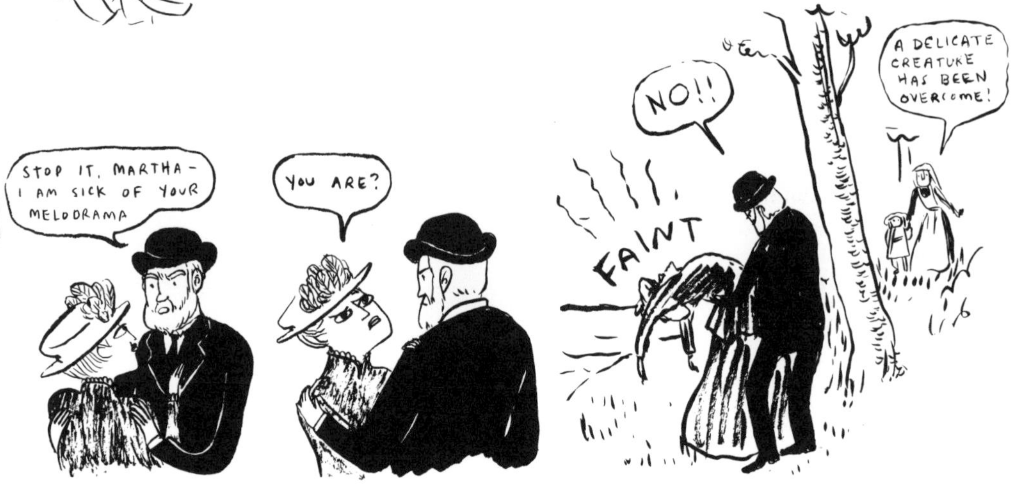
STOP IT, MARTHA - I AM SICK OF YOUR MELODRAMA
YOU ARE?
FAINT
NO!!
A DELICATE CREATURE HAS BEEN OVERCOME!

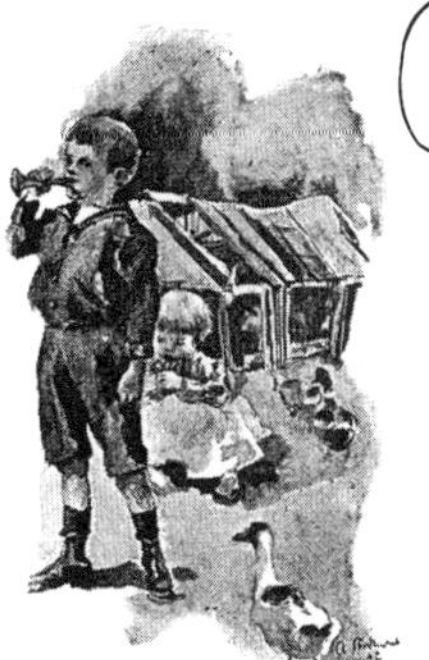

' TOM'S CHILDREN "

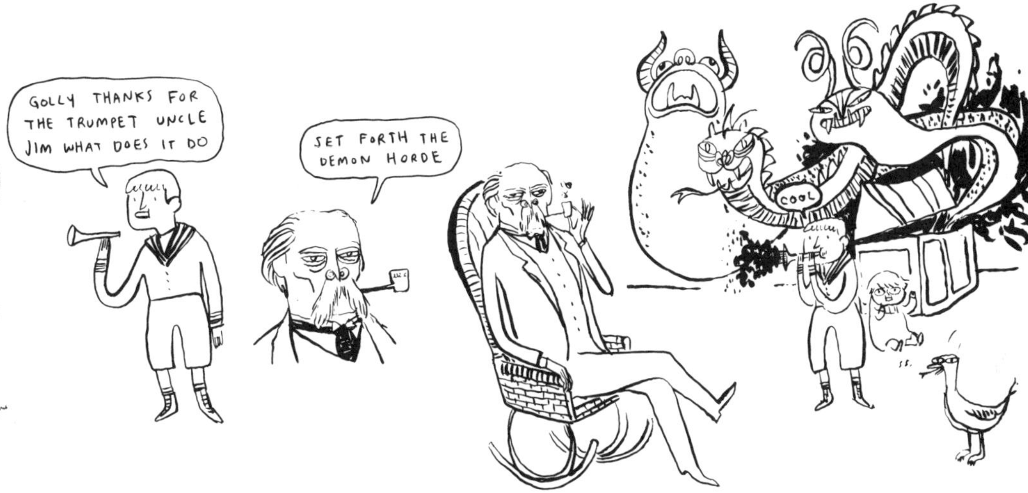
GOLLY THANKS FOR THE TRUMPET UNCLE JIM WHAT DOES IT DO
SET FORTH THE DEMON HORDE
COOL

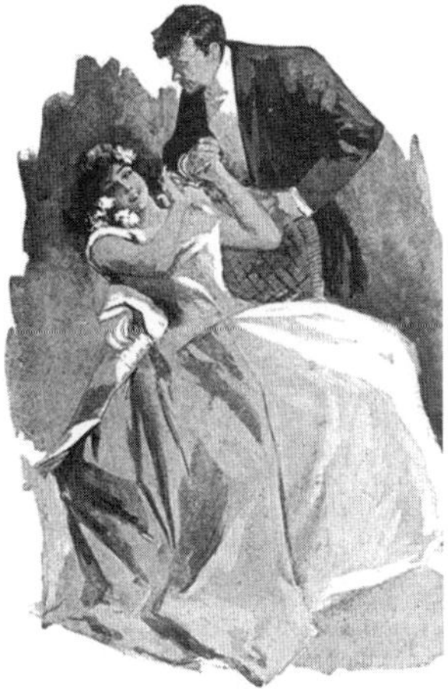

"SHE LAUGHED AT THEM."

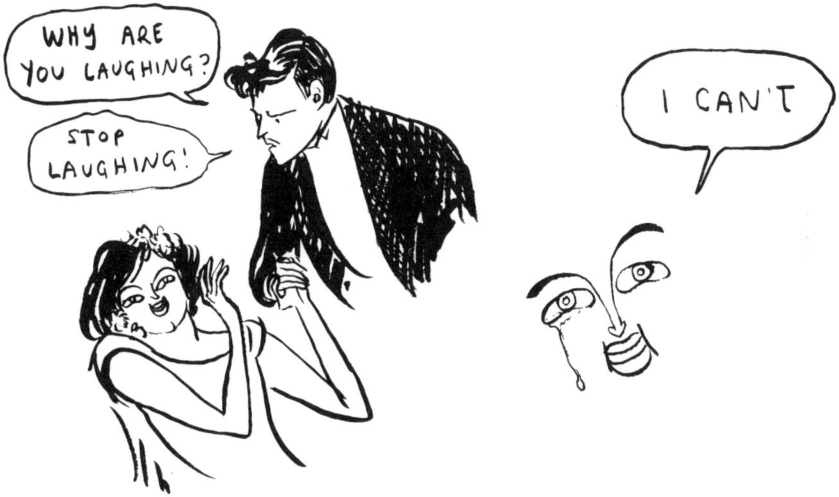
WHY ARE YOU LAUGHING?
STOP LAUGHING!
I CAN'T

THE SECRET GARDEN

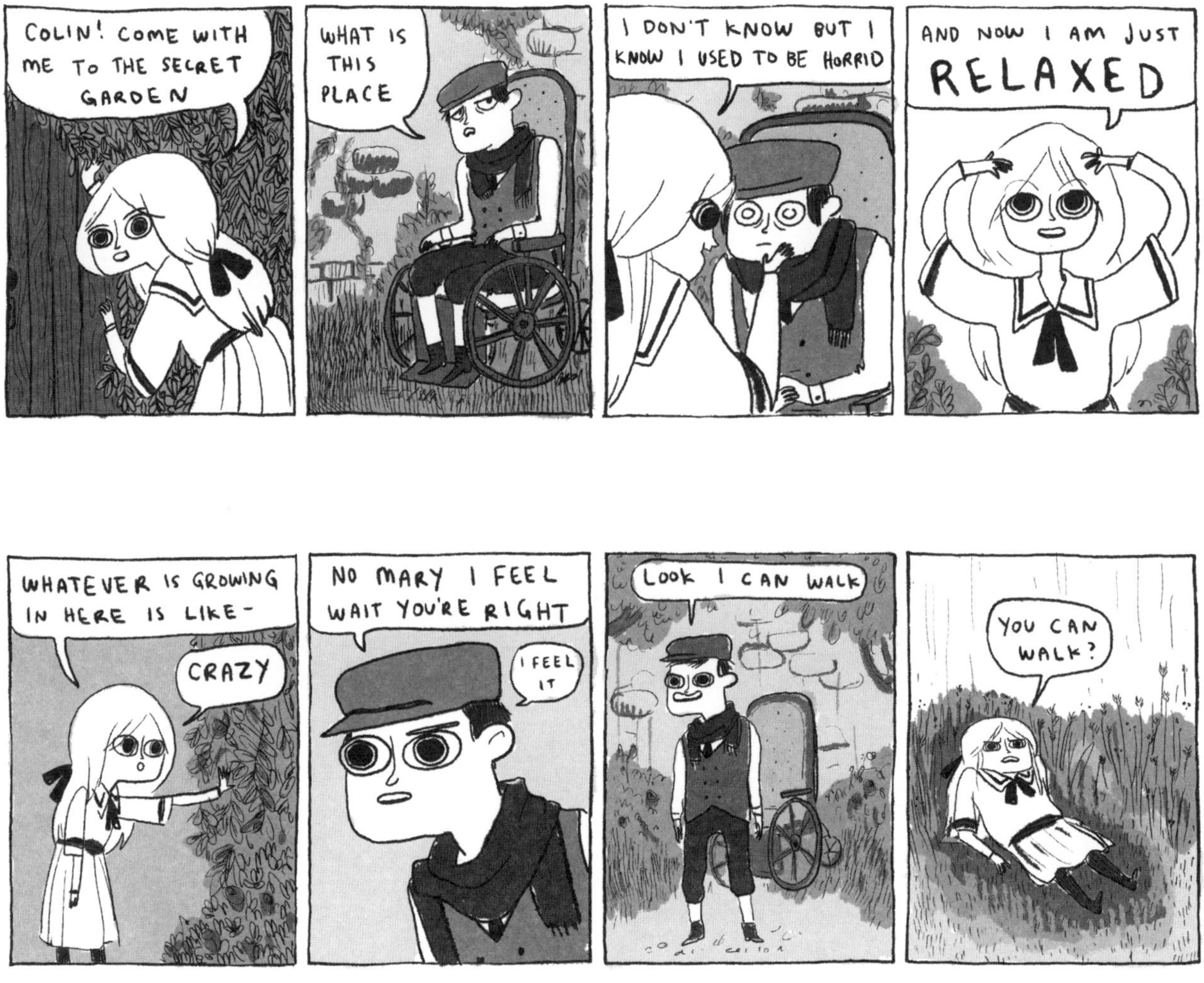
COLIN! COME WITH ME TO THE SECRET GARDEN
WHAT IS THIS PLACE
I DON'T KNOW BUT I KNOW I USED TO BE HORRID
AND NOW I AM JUST RELAXED
WHATEVER IS GROWING IN HERE IS LIKE-
CRAZY
NO MARY I FEEL WAIT YOU'RE RIGHT
I FEEL IT
LOOK I CAN WALK
YOU CAN WALK?

Well, it *was* a life changing garden.

COLIN YOU'RE LIKE FREAKING ME OUT
I'M FREAKING OUT RIGHT NOW

SIR- THE CHILDREN HAVE FOUND THE GARDEN
MY LATE WIFE'S
I USED TO FIND HER IN THERE, DAYS AFTER SHE'D DISAPPEAR, ROLLING ON THE GROUND
TALKING TO NO ONE, BISCUITS STREWN EVERYWHERE
SHE LOVED THAT GARDEN

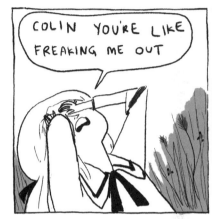

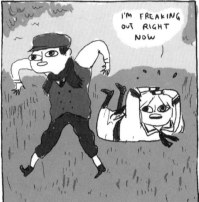

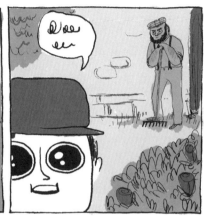

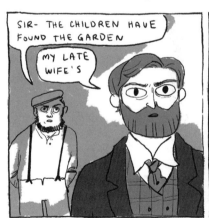

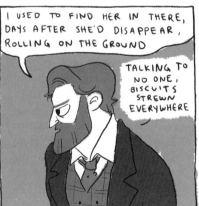

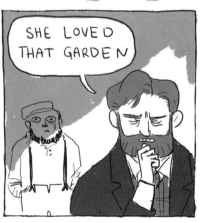

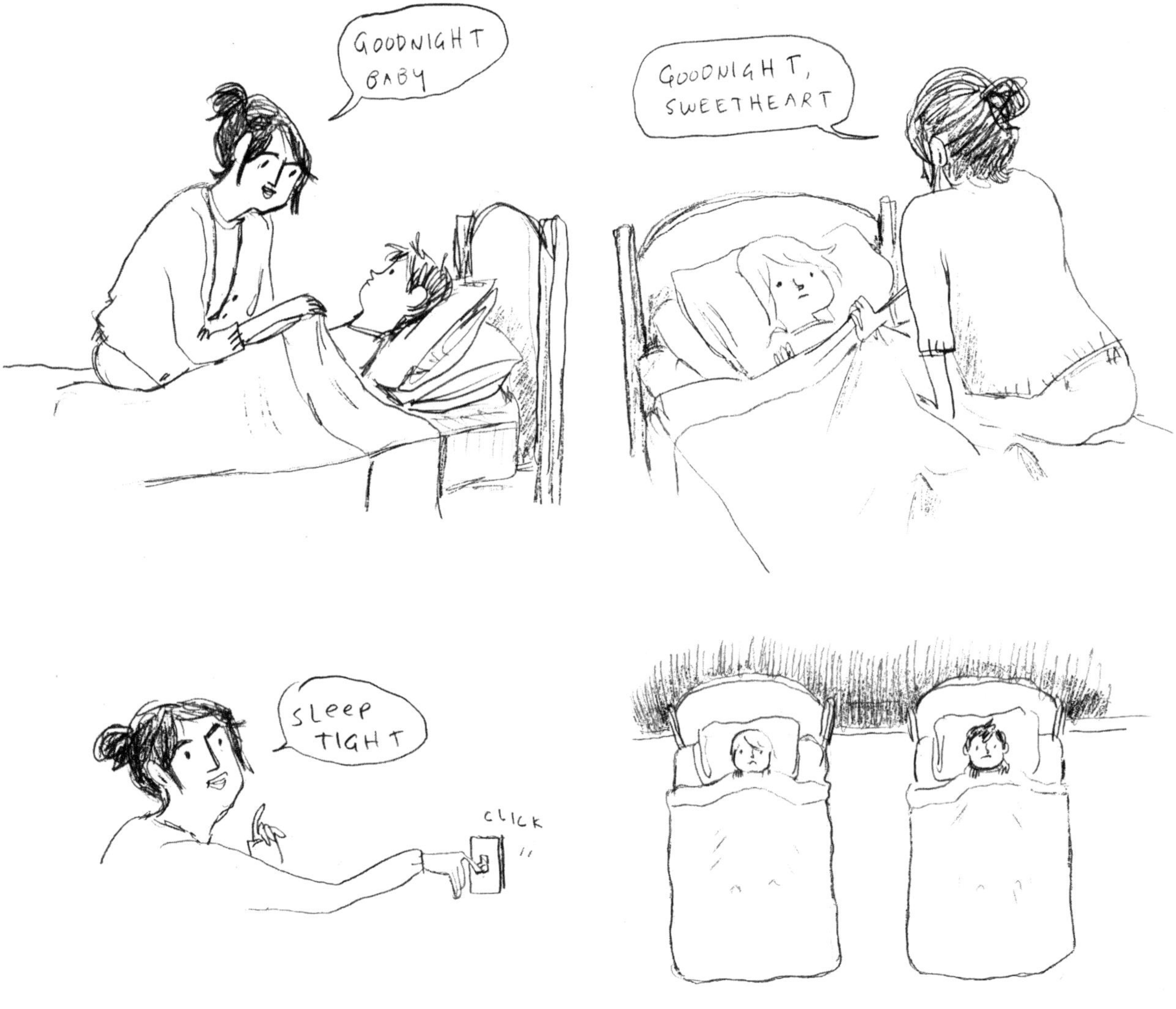
GOODNIGHT BABY
GOODNIGHT, SWEETHEART
SLEEP TIGHT
CLICK

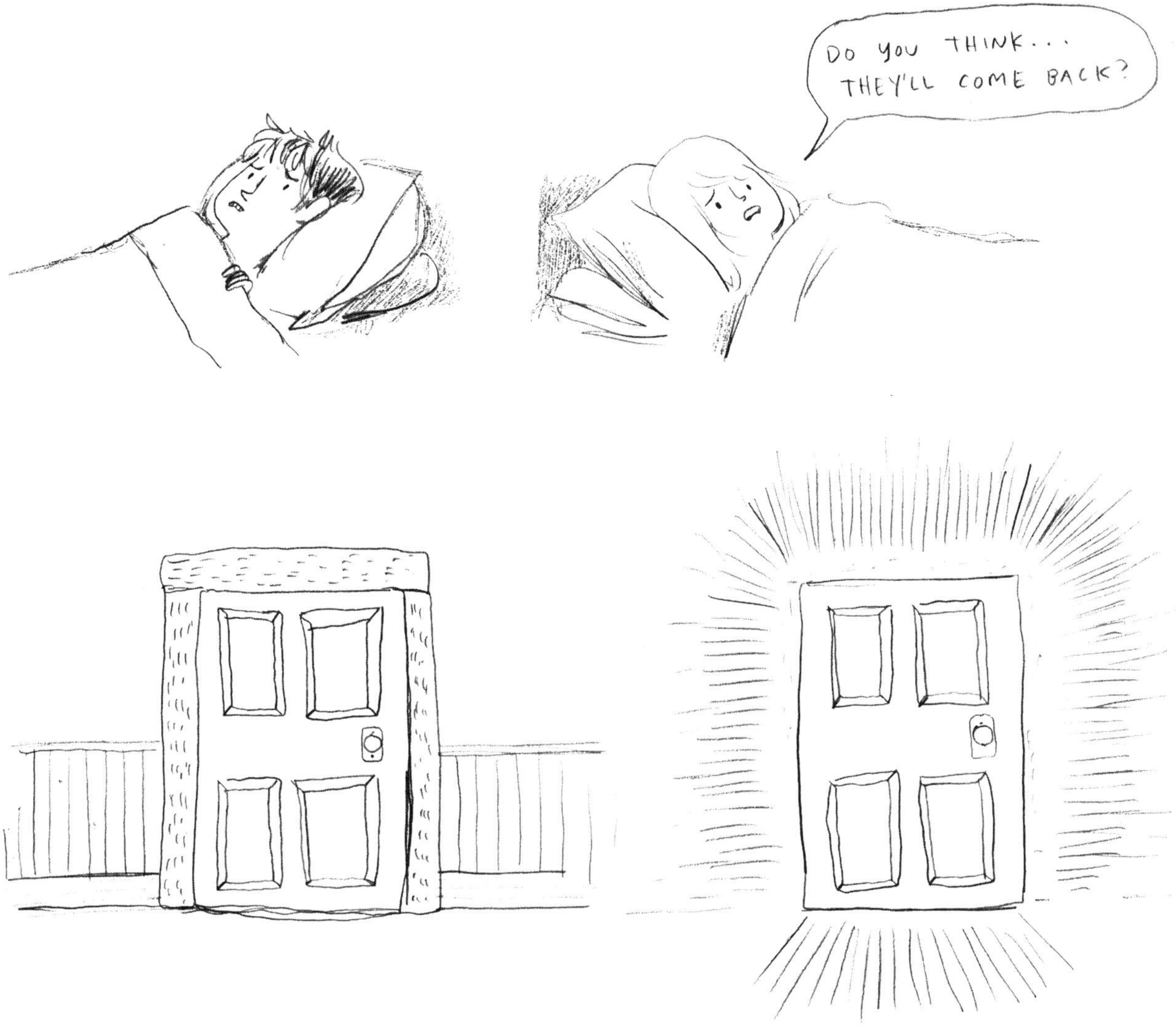
DO YOU THINK...
THEY'LL COME BACK?

STRAW FEMINISTS IN THE CLOSET

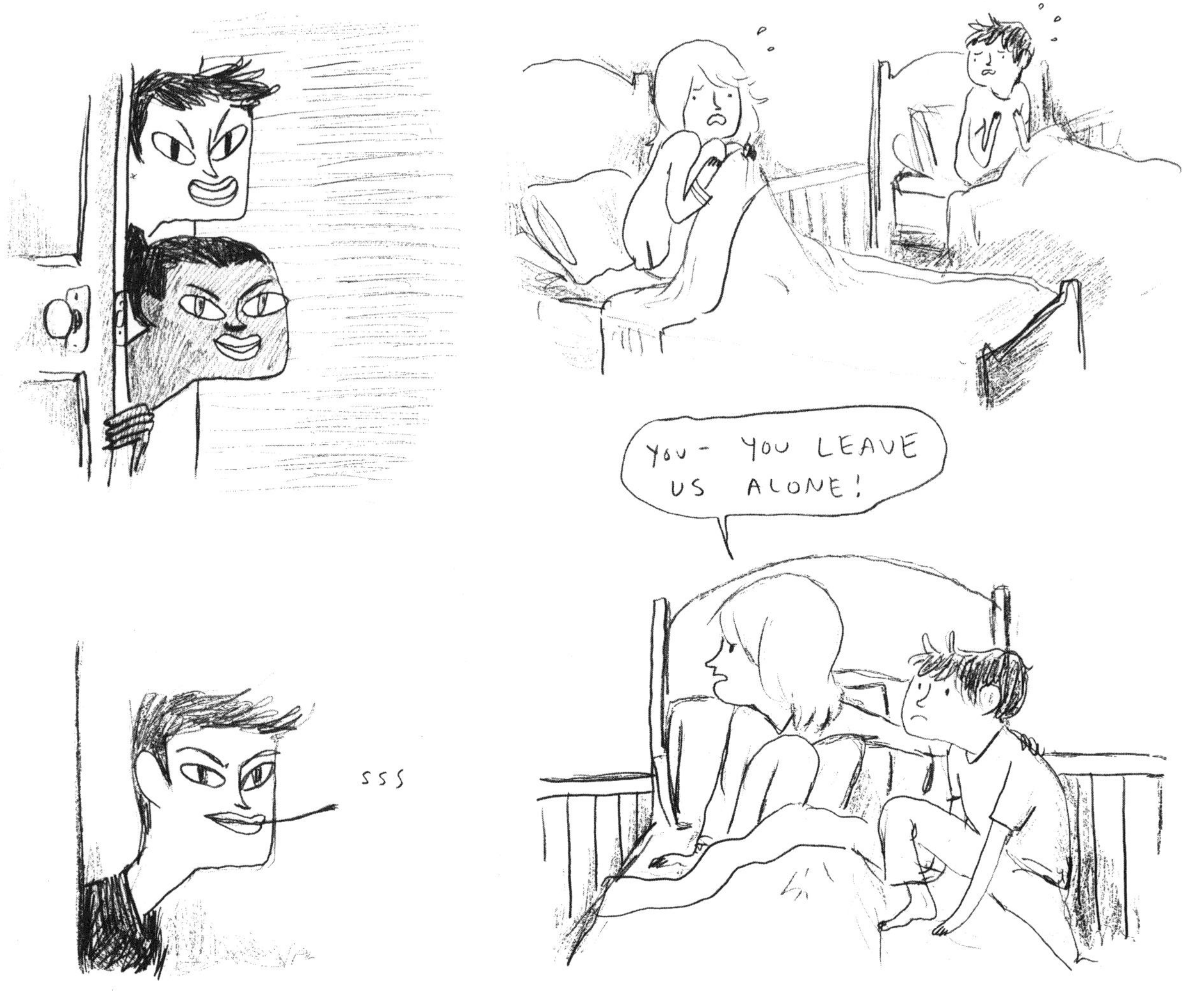
sss
YOU- YOU LEAVE US ALONE!

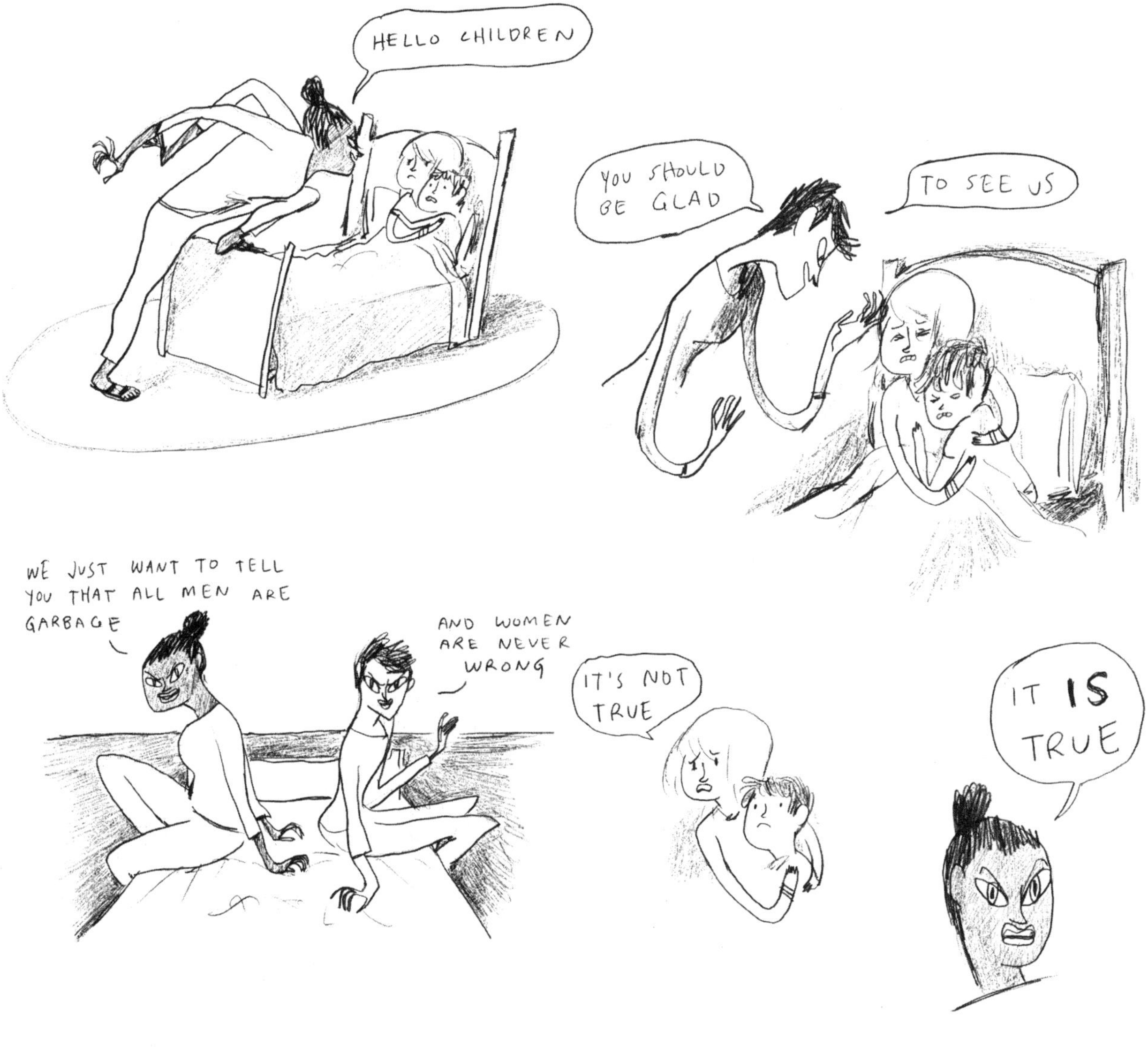
HELLO CHILDREN
YOU SHOULD BE GLAD
TO SEE US
WE JUST WANT TO TELL YOU THAT ALL MEN ARE GARBAGE
AND WOMEN ARE NEVER WRONG
IT'S NOT TRUE
IT IS TRUE

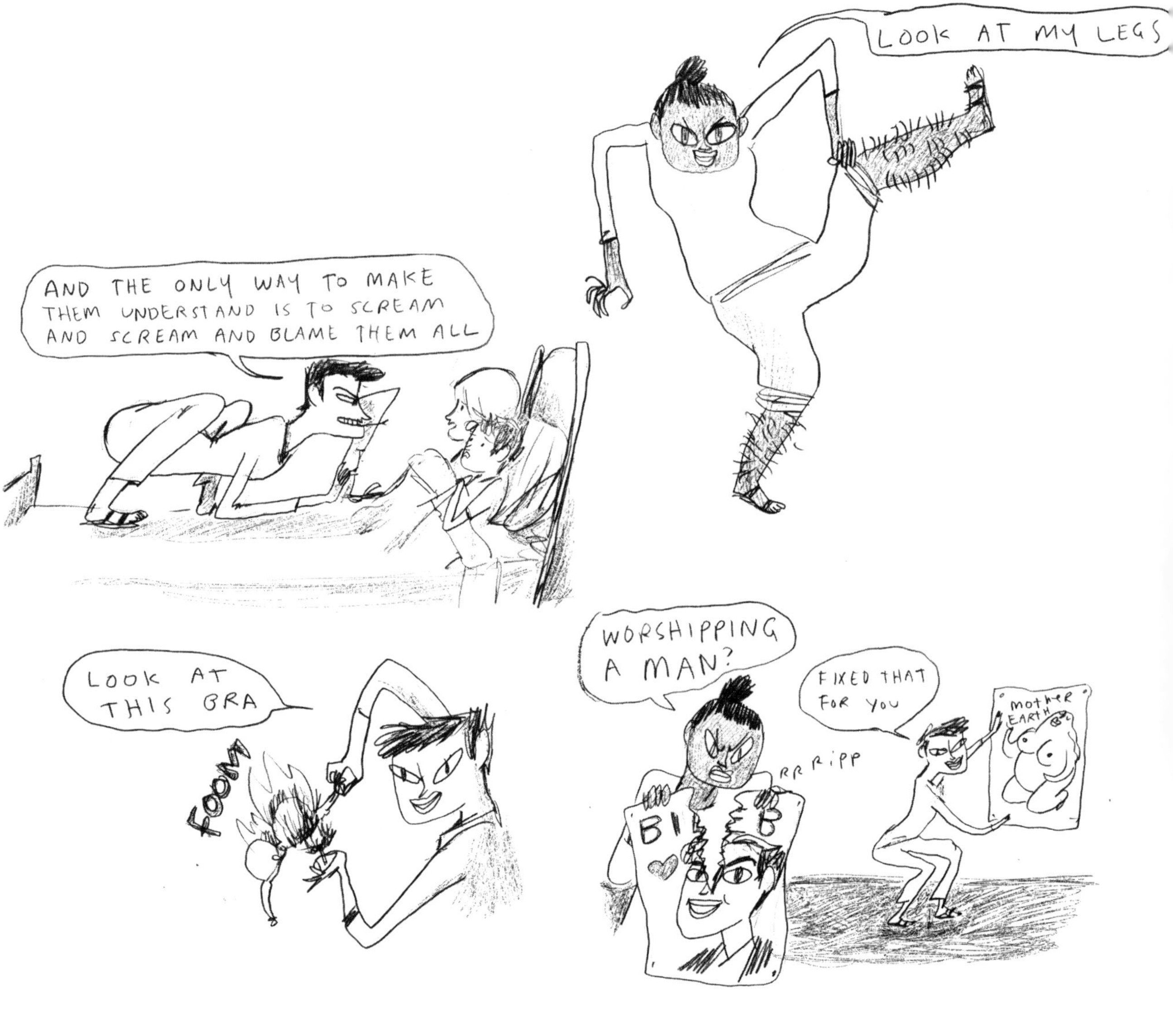
LOOK AT MY LEGS
AND THE ONLY WAY TO MAKE THEM UNDERSTAND IS TO SCREAM AND SCREAM AND BLAME THEM ALL
LOOK AT THIS BRA
FOOM
WORSHIPPING A MAN?
RRRIPP
FIXED THAT FOR YOU
mother EARTH

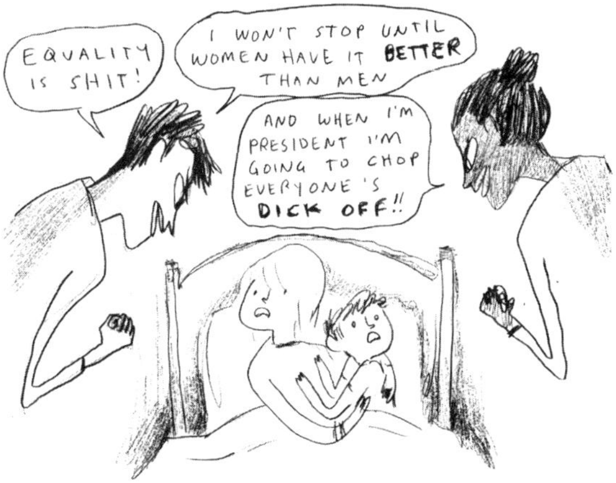
EQUALITY IS SHIT!
I WON'T STOP UNTIL WOMEN HAVE IT BETTER THAN MEN
AND WHEN I'M PRESIDENT I'M GOING TO CHOP EVERYONE'S DICK OFF!!

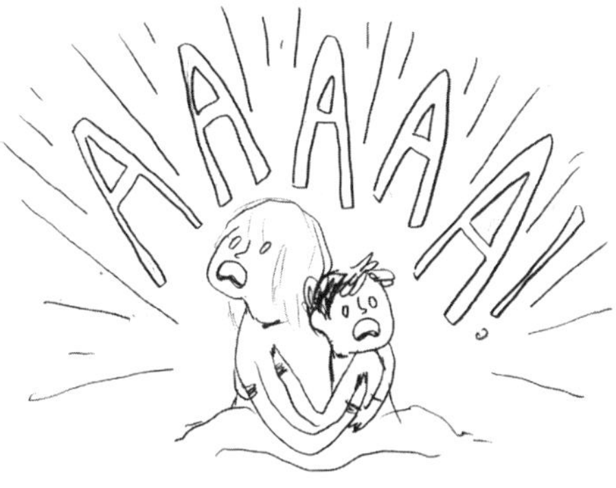
AAAAA!

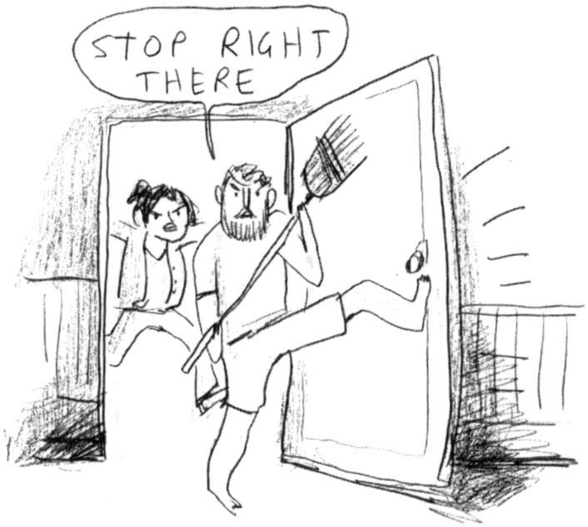
STOP RIGHT THERE

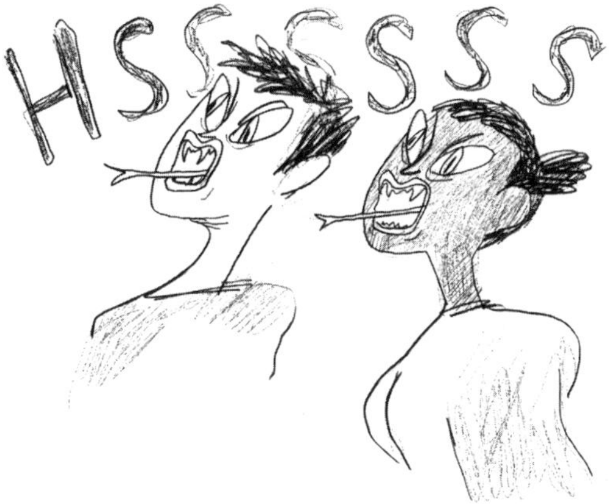
HSSSSSS

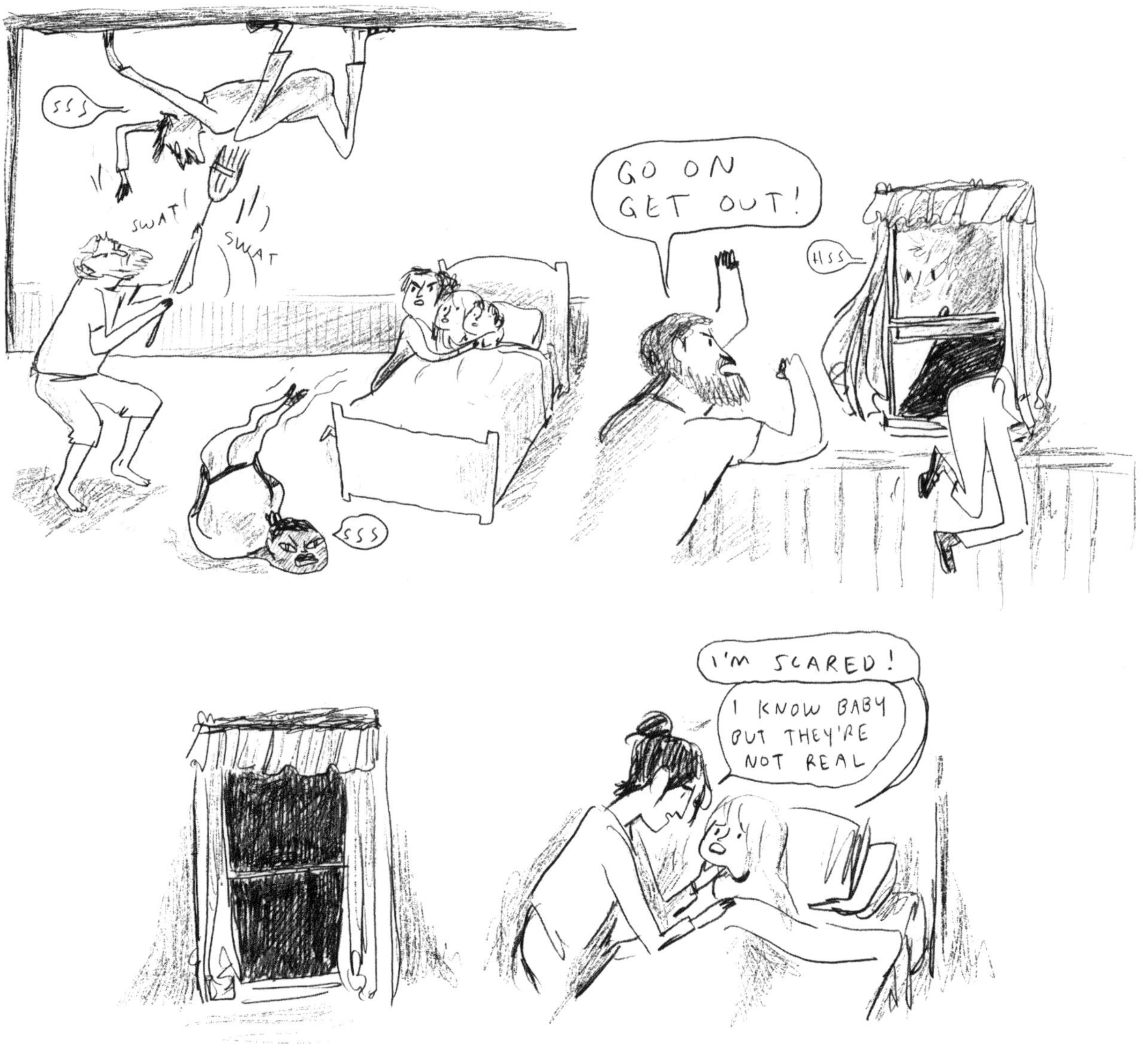
SSS
SWAT!
SWAT
SSS
GO ON GET OUT!
HSS
I'M SCARED!
I KNOW BABY BUT THEY'RE NOT REAL

THEY FELT REAL!
AH LITTLE BUDDY THAT'S THE PROBLEM A LOT OF PEOPLE HAVE WITH THEM
THEY DON'T JUST HAUNT CHILDREN, THEY HAUNT A LOT OF THINGS
BUT THEY'RE GONE FOR NOW. TRY TO SLEEP
POOR KIDS...
TOO SOON, TOO SOON FOR ALL THAT

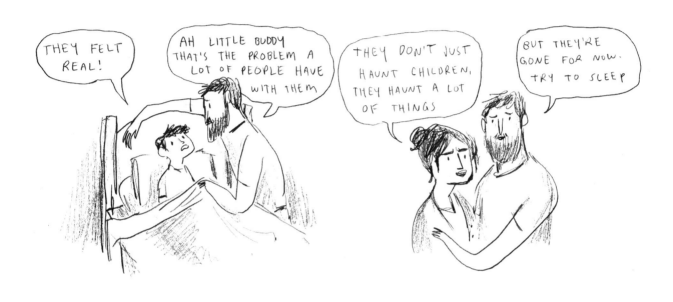

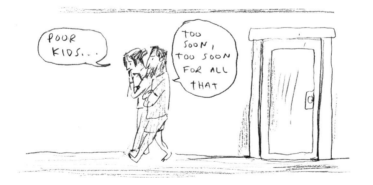

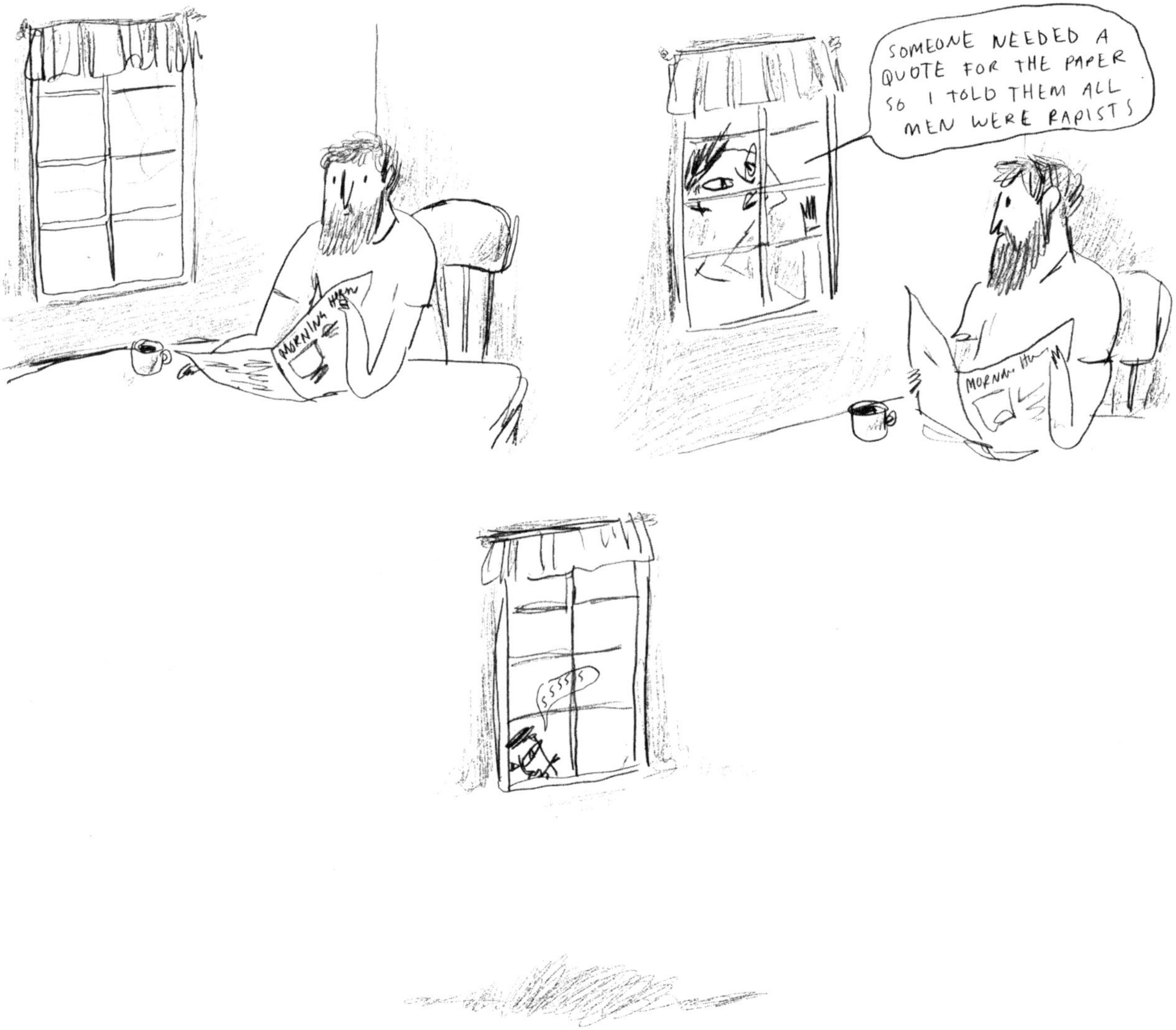
SOMEONE NEEDED A QUOTE FOR THE PAPER SO I TOLD THEM ALL MEN WERE RAPISTS
SSSSS

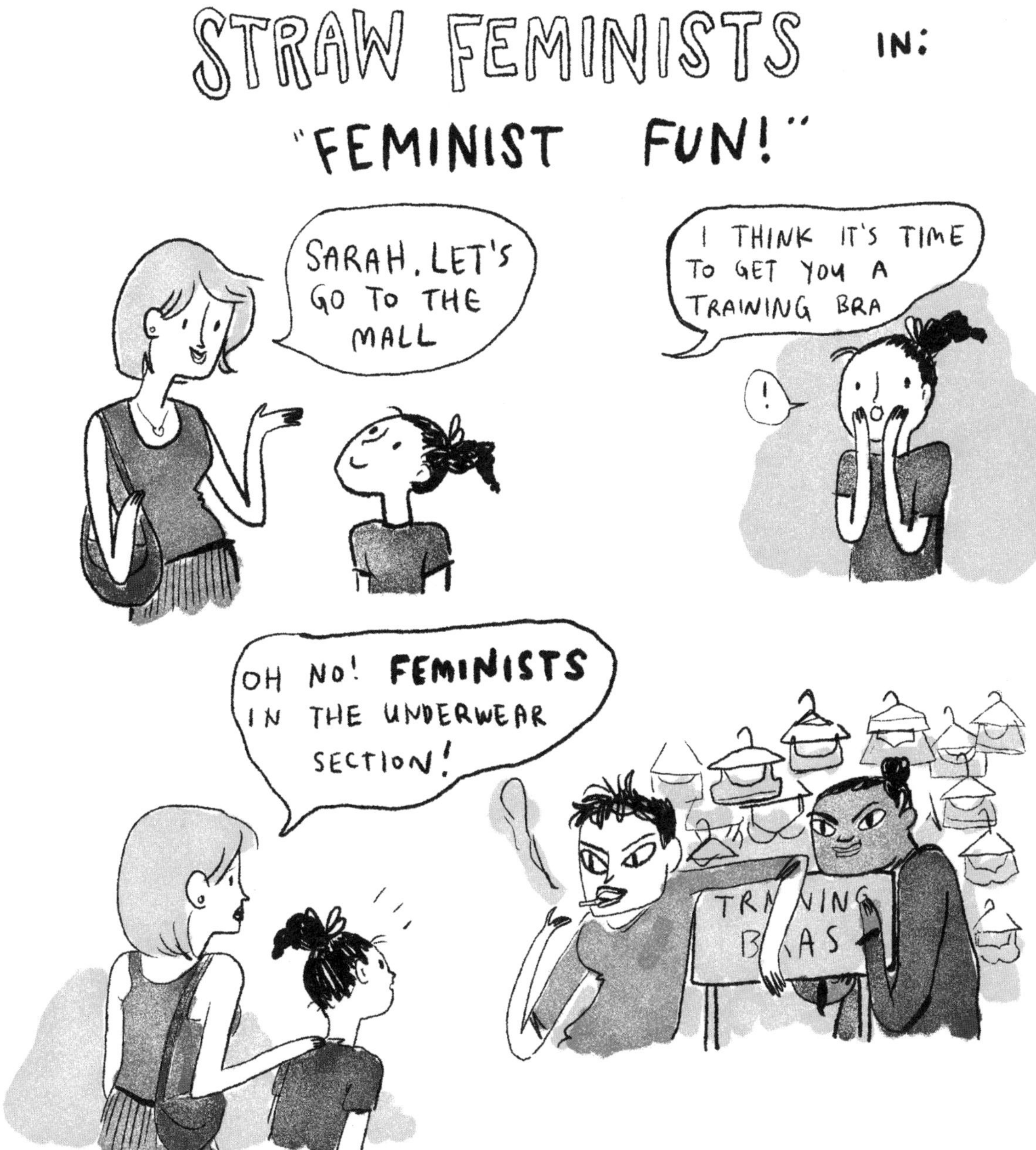
STRAW FEMINISTS IN:
"FEMINIST FUN!"
SARAH, LET'S GO TO THE MALL
I THINK IT'S TIME TO GET YOU A TRAINING BRA
!
OH NO! FEMINISTS IN THE UNDERWEAR SECTION!
TRAINING BRAS

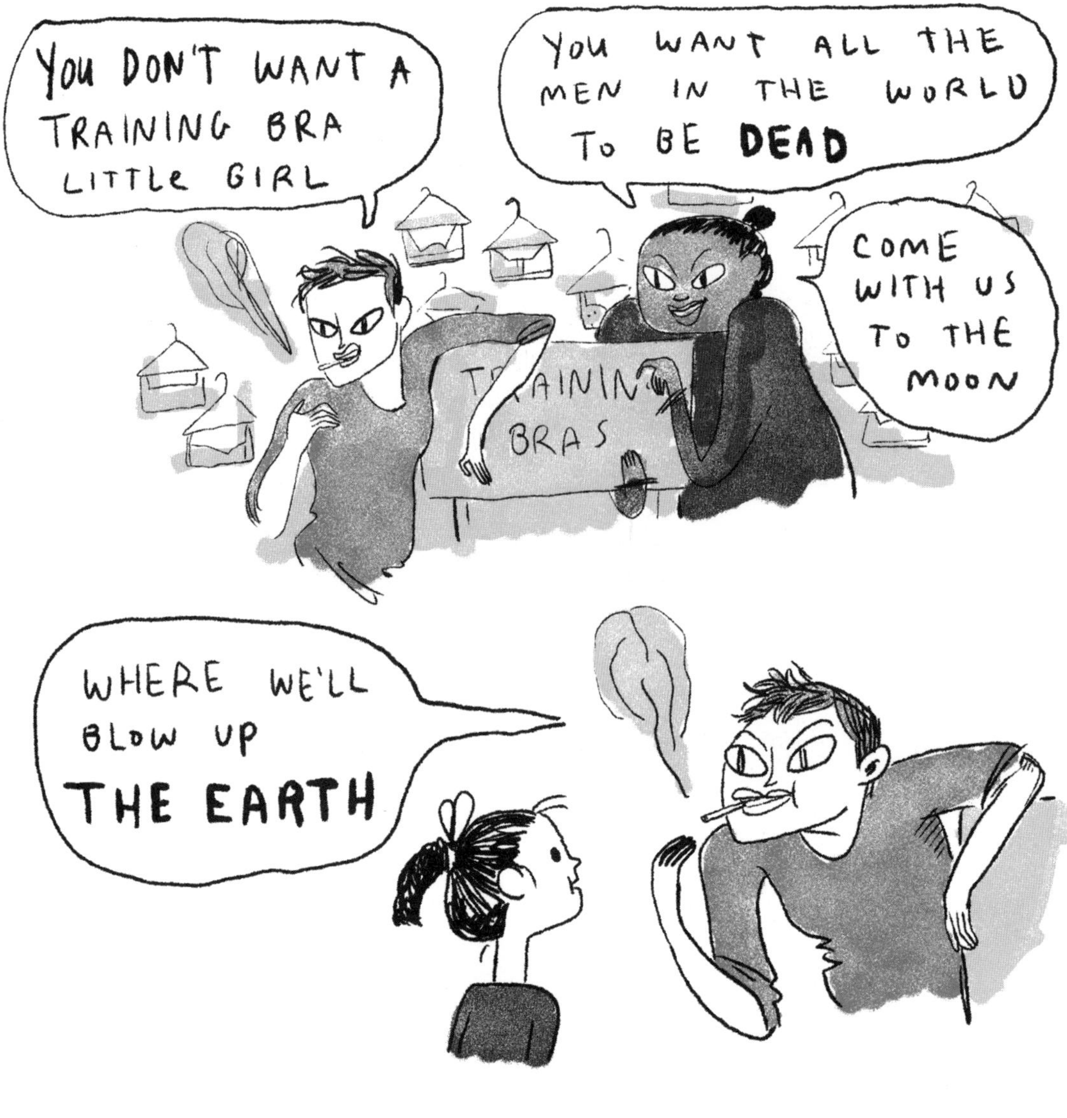
YOU DON'T WANT A TRAINING BRA LITTLE GIRL
YOU WANT ALL THE MEN IN THE WORLD TO BE DEAD
COME WITH US TO THE MOON
TRAINING BRAS
WHERE WE'LL BLOW UP THE EARTH

A MEDIEVAL FILM

PLACES, EVERYONE!

VICTORY OF THE PEOPLE

OK: YOU'RE A PEASANT. KING JOHN IS GOING TO SIGN THE MAGNA CARTA. THIS IS LIKE, THE BEST DAY OF YOUR **LIFE**. IT'S BASICALLY YOUR DECLARATION OF INDEPENDENCE

OK, COOL

ACTION!

KING JOHN HAS SIGNED TO THE BARONS' DEMANDS. WE ARE VICTORIOUS!

YAYY

PEASANTS! LIE DOWN SO I MAY USE YOUR BODIES AS A VICTORY CARPET

INVASION

A LOAD OF VIKINGS! HEADED THIS WAY!!

GOOD HEAVENS!

ᚦᚨᛗᚢᚱ?

NOT THOSE GUYS! **THESE** GUYS!

OH

YAR HAR

No one would ever try to shoot a movie in Chaucer-y English like in the fourth comic, and if they did, they probably wouldn't know their way around the actual grammar if Chaucer himself were on hand to explain it. That business is hard!

85

WHAT TO WEAR

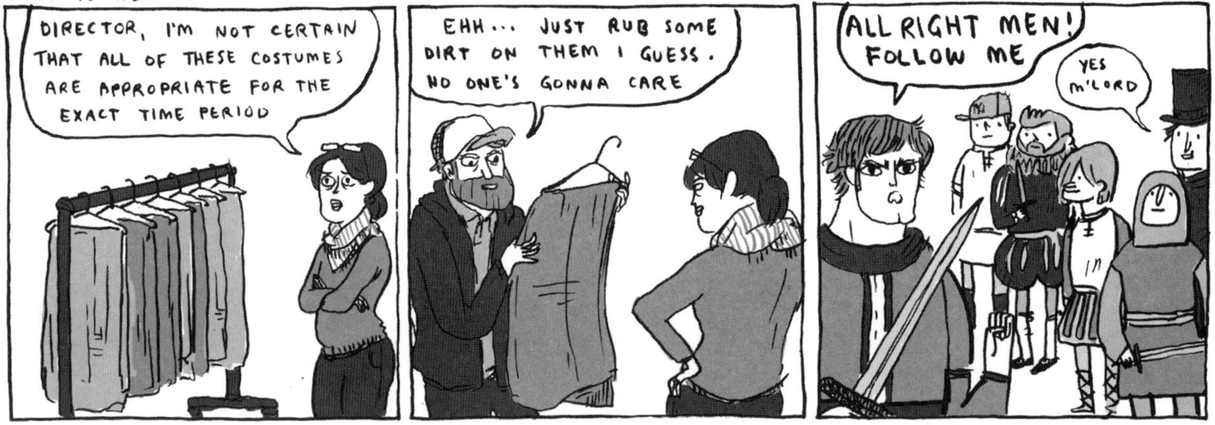
DIRECTOR, I'M NOT CERTAIN THAT ALL OF THESE COSTUMES ARE APPROPRIATE FOR THE EXACT TIME PERIOD
EHH... JUST RUB SOME DIRT ON THEM I GUESS. NO ONE'S GONNA CARE
ALL RIGHT MEN! FOLLOW ME
YES M'LORD

OF OLD ENGLISH AND NOBLES

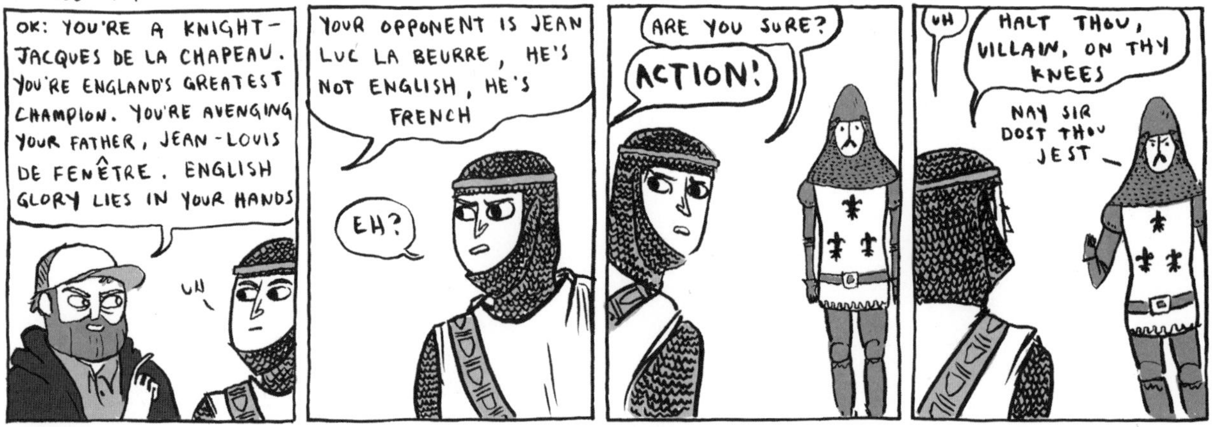
OK: YOU'RE A KNIGHT- JACQUES DE LA CHAPEAU. YOU'RE ENGLAND'S GREATEST CHAMPION. YOU'RE AVENGING YOUR FATHER, JEAN-LOUIS DE FENÊTRE. ENGLISH GLORY LIES IN YOUR HANDS
UH
YOUR OPPONENT IS JEAN LUC LA BEURRE, HE'S NOT ENGLISH, HE'S FRENCH
EH?
ARE YOU SURE?
ACTION!
UH
HALT THOU, VILLAIN, ON THY KNEES
NAY SIR DOST THOU JEST

THE WAY IT IS

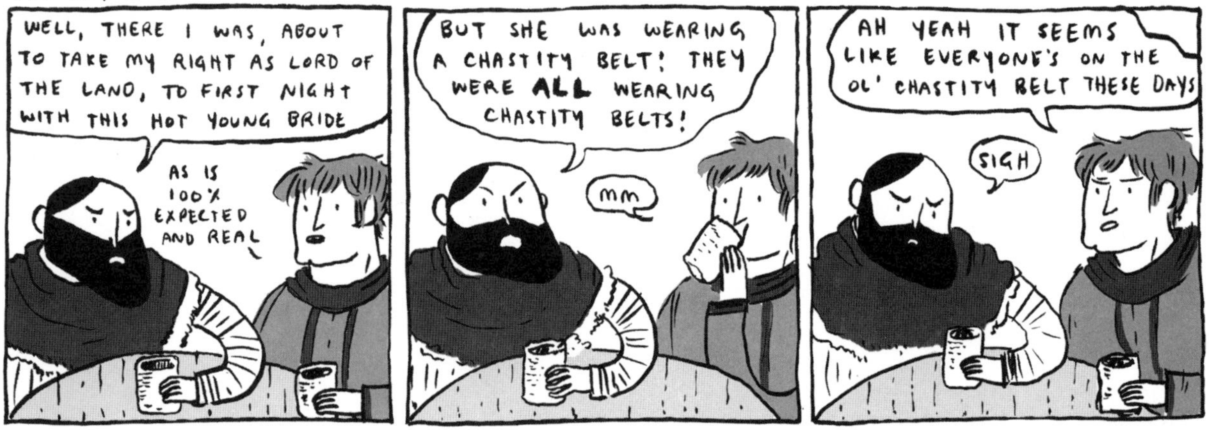
WELL, THERE I WAS, ABOUT TO TAKE MY RIGHT AS LORD OF THE LAND, TO FIRST NIGHT WITH THIS HOT YOUNG BRIDE
AS IS 100% EXPECTED AND REAL
BUT SHE WAS WEARING A CHASTITY BELT! THEY WERE ALL WEARING CHASTITY BELTS!
MM
AH YEAH IT SEEMS LIKE EVERYONE'S ON THE OL' CHASTITY BELT THESE DAYS
SIGH

CINDERELLA

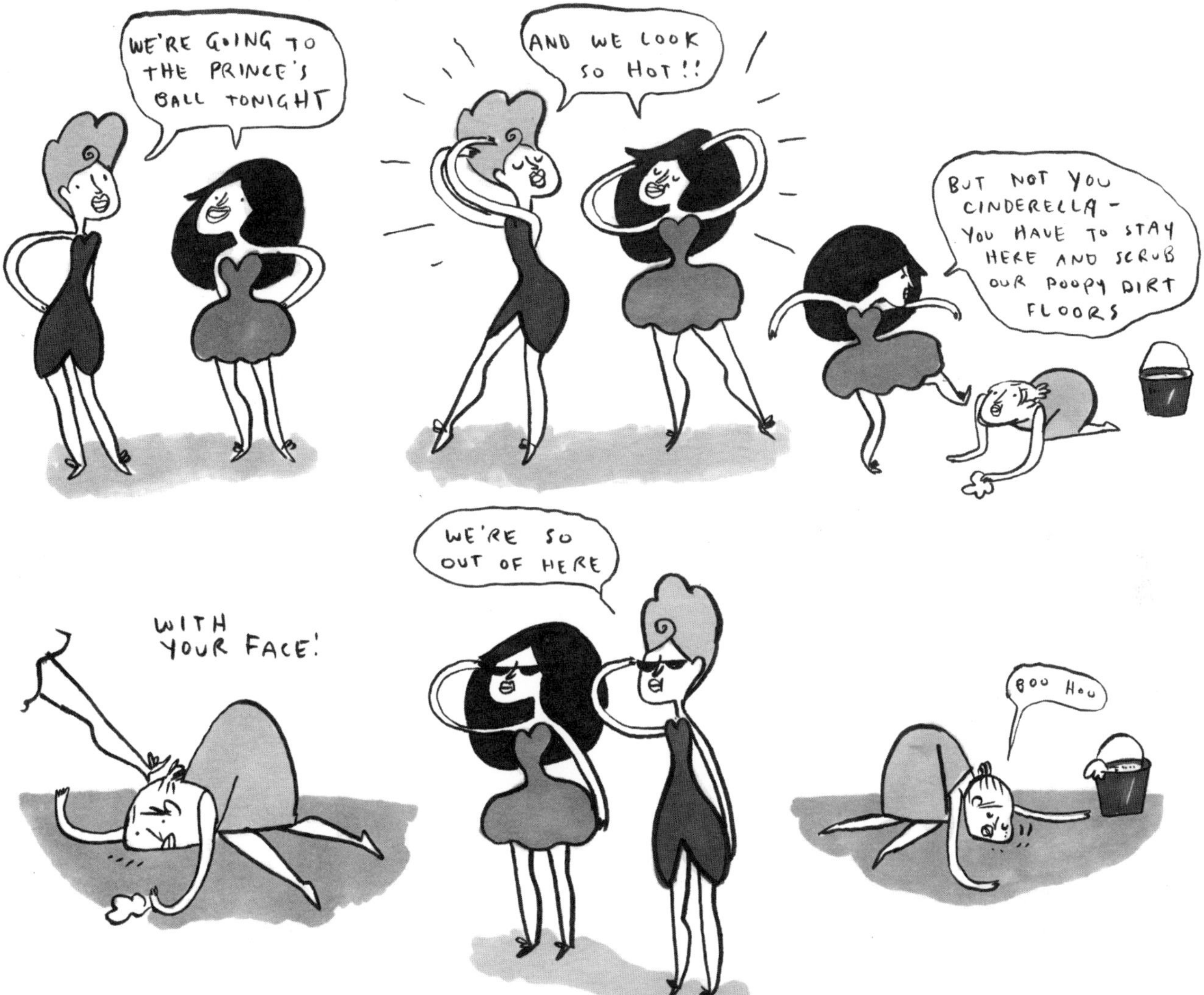
WE'RE GOING TO THE PRINCE'S BALL TONIGHT
AND WE LOOK SO HOT!!
BUT NOT YOU CINDERELLA - YOU HAVE TO STAY HERE AND SCRUB OUR POOPY DIRT FLOORS
WITH YOUR FACE!
WE'RE SO OUT OF HERE
BOO HOO

I like to work out, don't you?

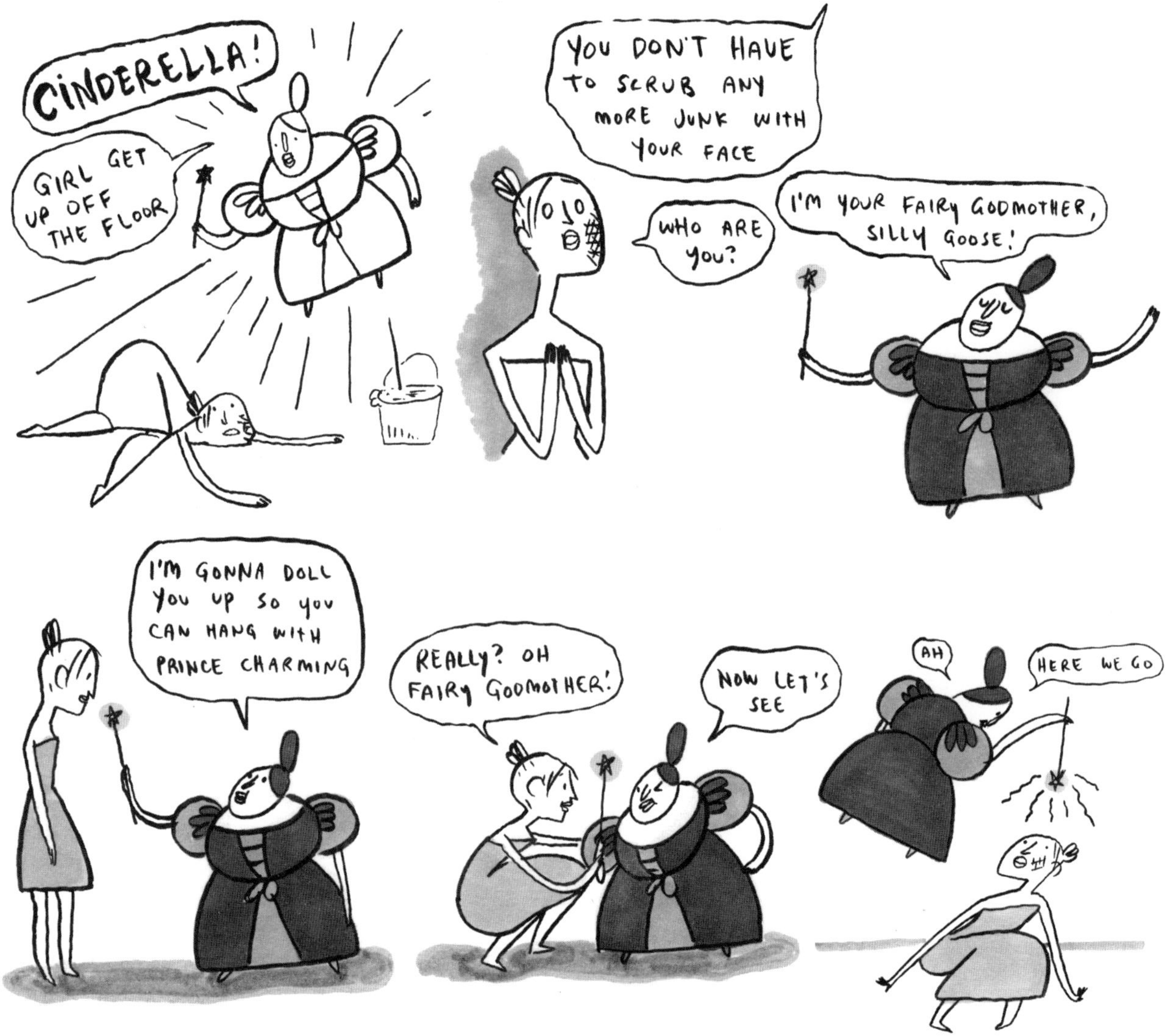
CINDERELLA!
GIRL GET UP OFF THE FLOOR
YOU DON'T HAVE TO SCRUB ANY MORE JUNK WITH YOUR FACE
WHO ARE YOU?
I'M YOUR FAIRY GODMOTHER, SILLY GOOSE!
I'M GONNA DOLL YOU UP SO YOU CAN HANG WITH PRINCE CHARMING
REALLY? OH FAIRY GODMOTHER!
NOW LET'S SEE
AH
HERE WE GO

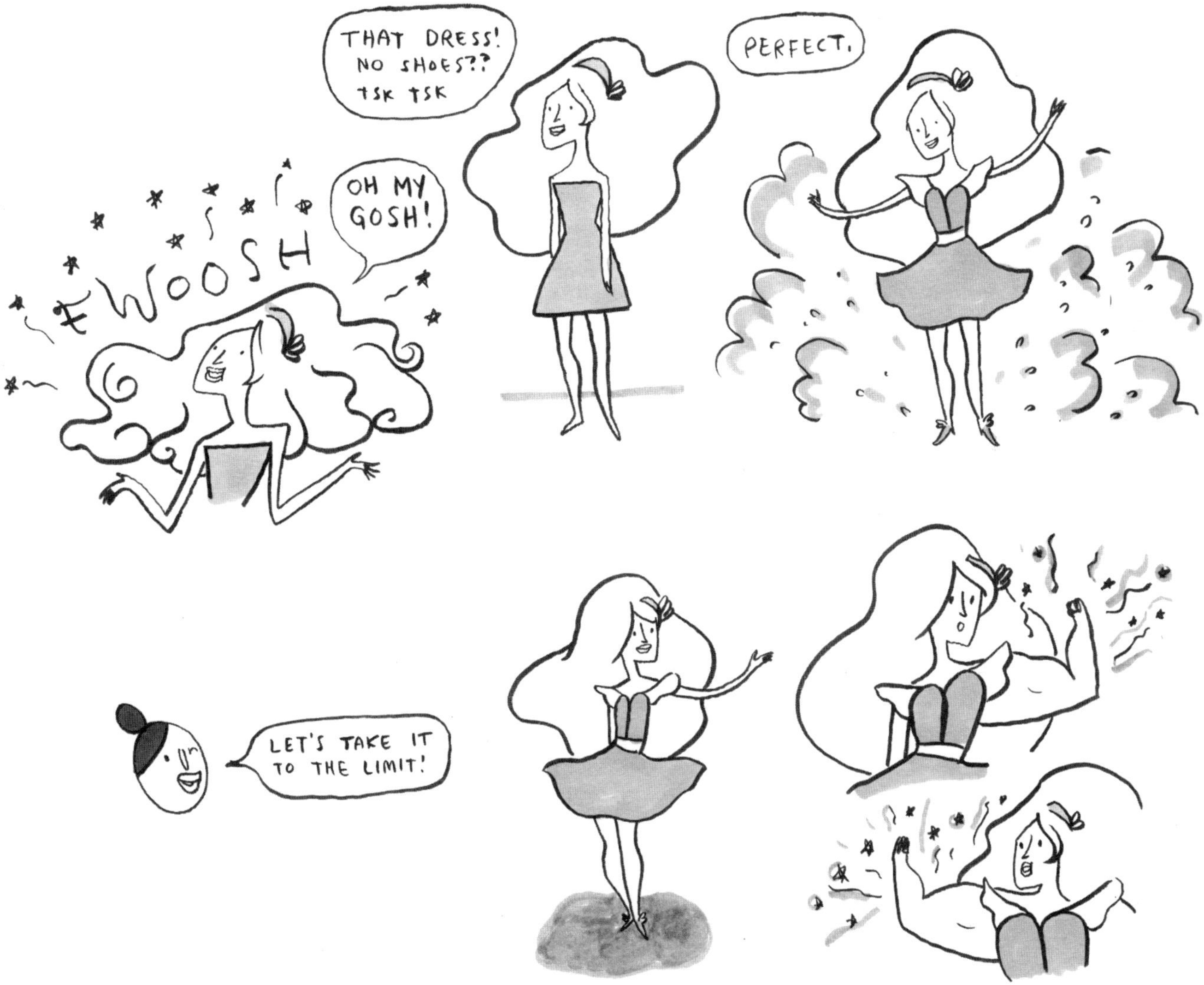

WOOSH
OH MY GOSH!
THAT DRESS! NO SHOES?? TSK TSK
PERFECT.
LET'S TAKE IT TO THE LIMIT!

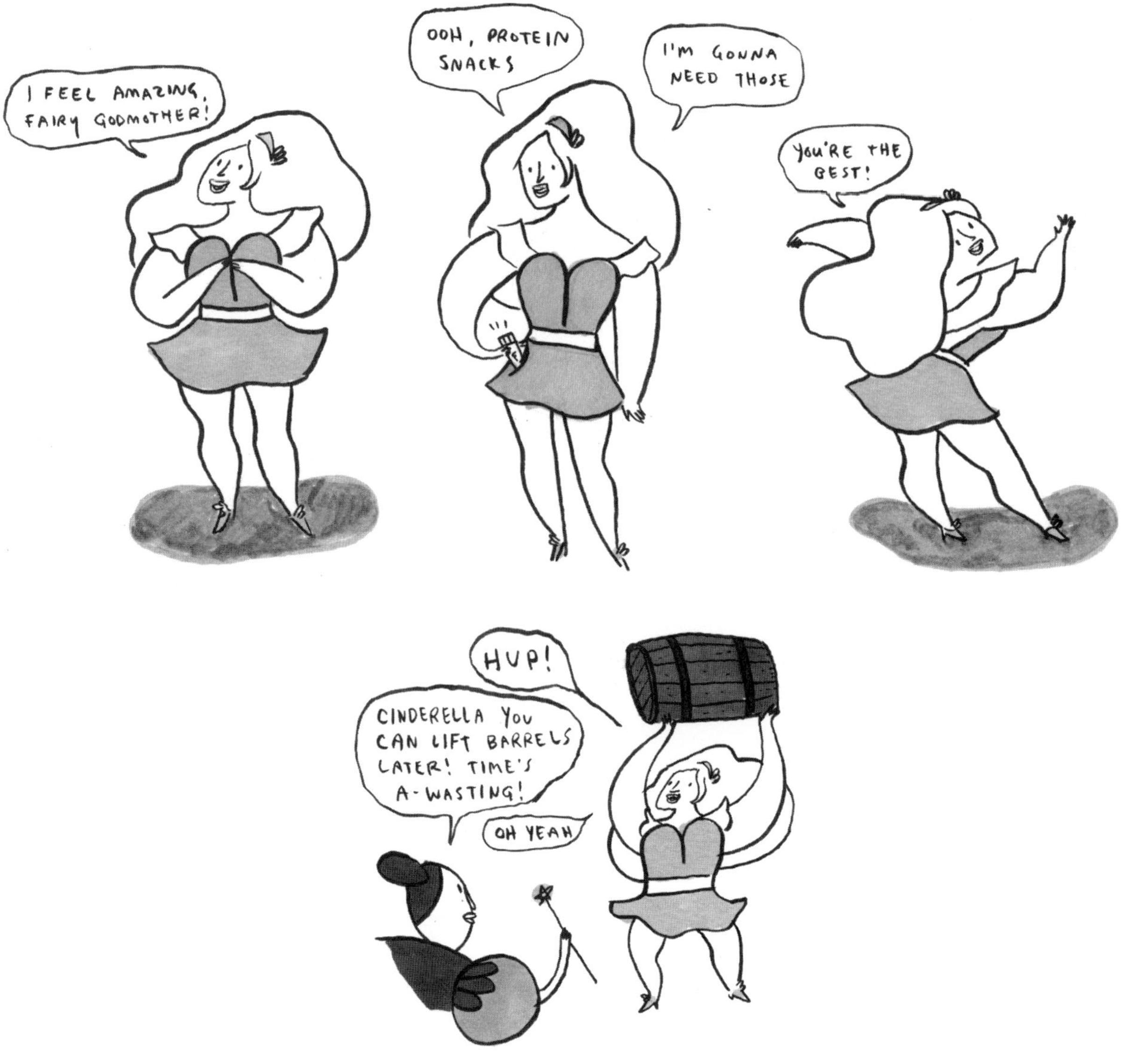
I FEEL AMAZING, FAIRY GODMOTHER!
OOH, PROTEIN SNACKS
I'M GONNA NEED THOSE
YOU'RE THE BEST!
HUP!
CINDERELLA YOU CAN LIFT BARRELS LATER! TIME'S A-WASTING!
OH YEAH

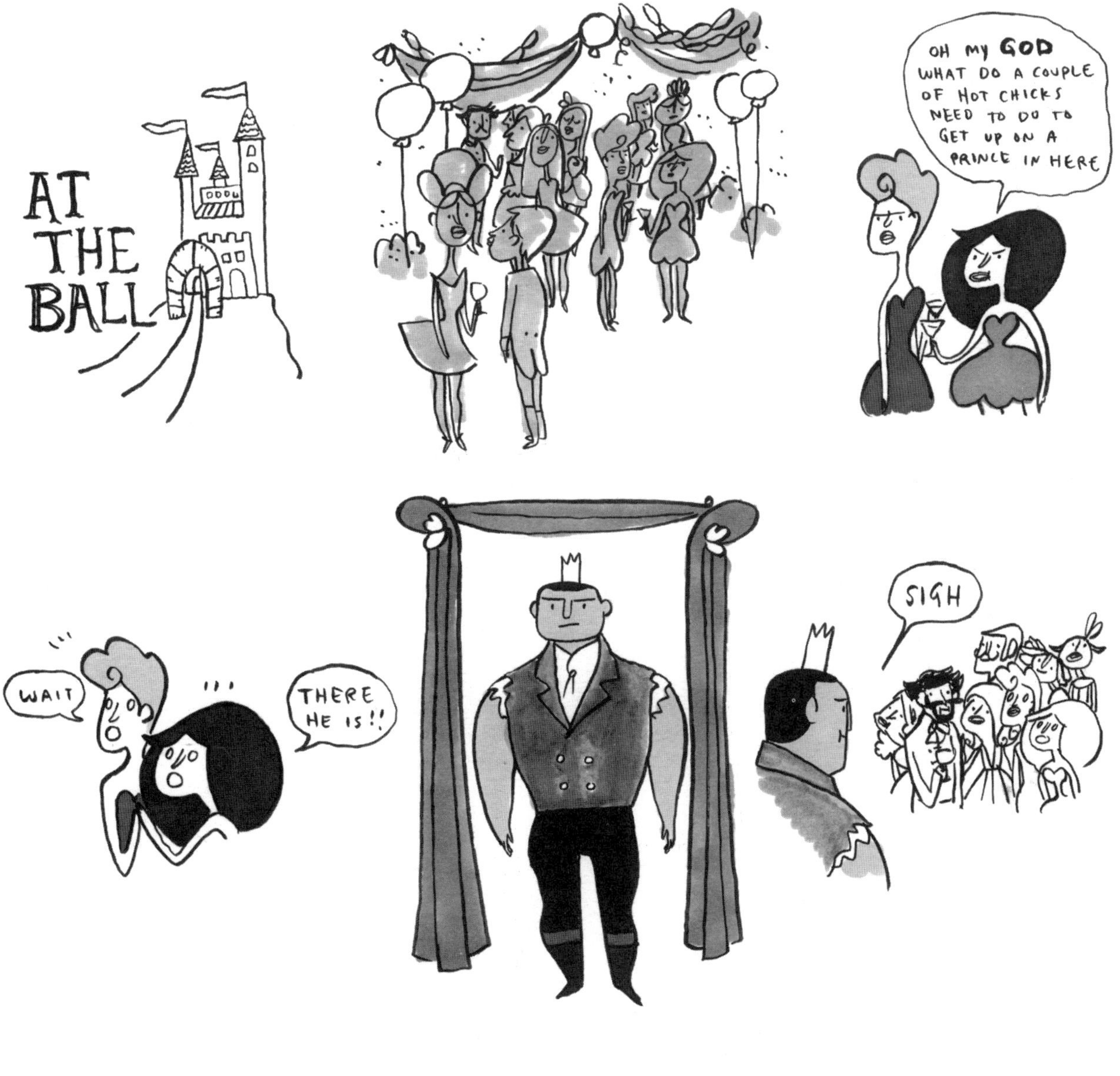
AT THE BALL
OH MY GOD WHAT DO A COUPLE OF HOT CHICKS NEED TO DO TO GET UP ON A PRINCE IN HERE
WAIT
THERE HE IS!!
SIGH

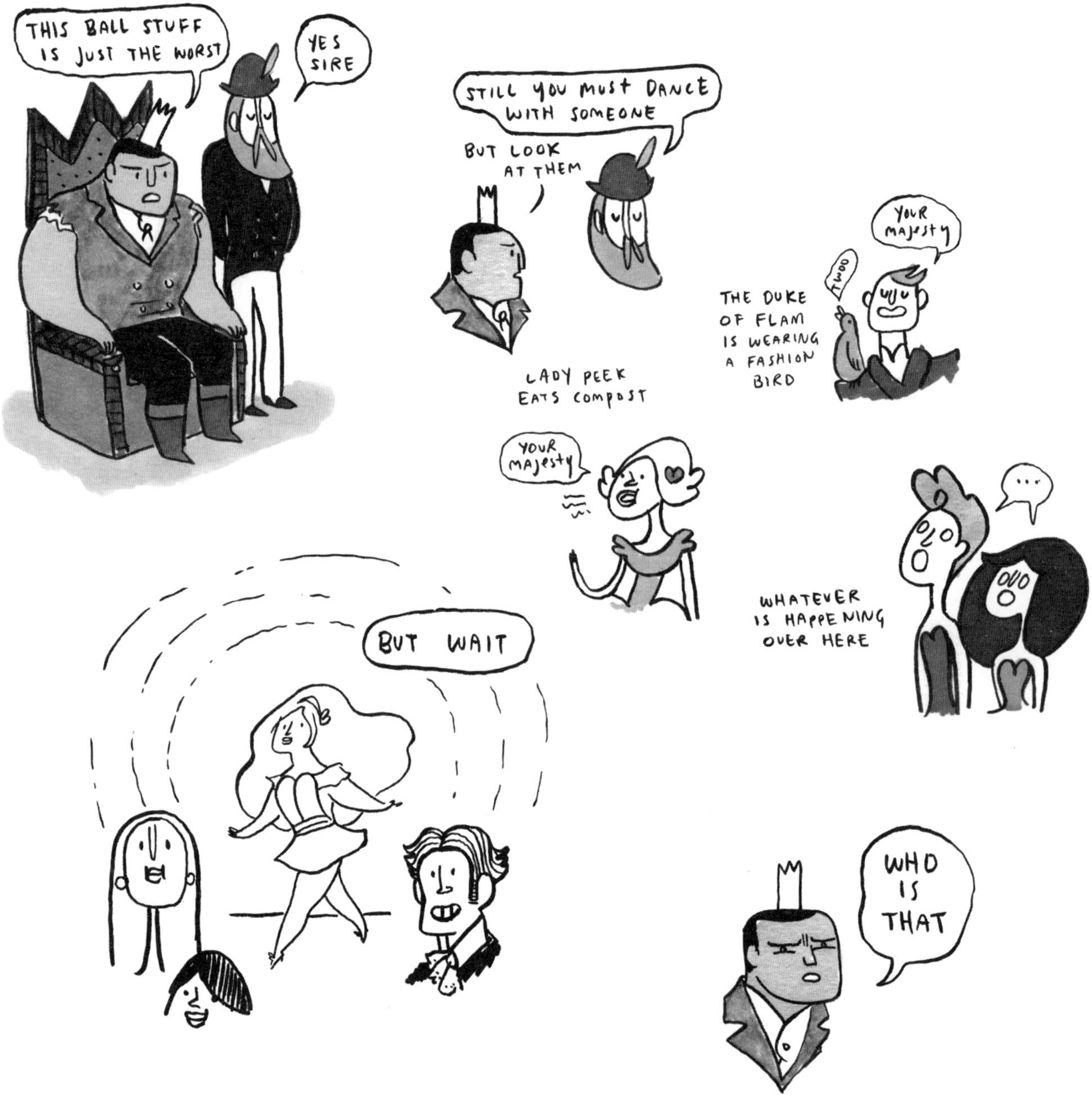
THIS BALL STUFF IS JUST THE WORST
YES SIRE
STILL YOU MUST DANCE WITH SOMEONE
BUT LOOK AT THEM
YOUR majesty
TWOO
THE DUKE OF FLAM IS WEARING A FASHION BIRD
LADY PEEK EATS COMPOST
YOUR majesty
...
WHATEVER IS HAPPENING OVER HERE
BUT WAIT
WHO IS THAT

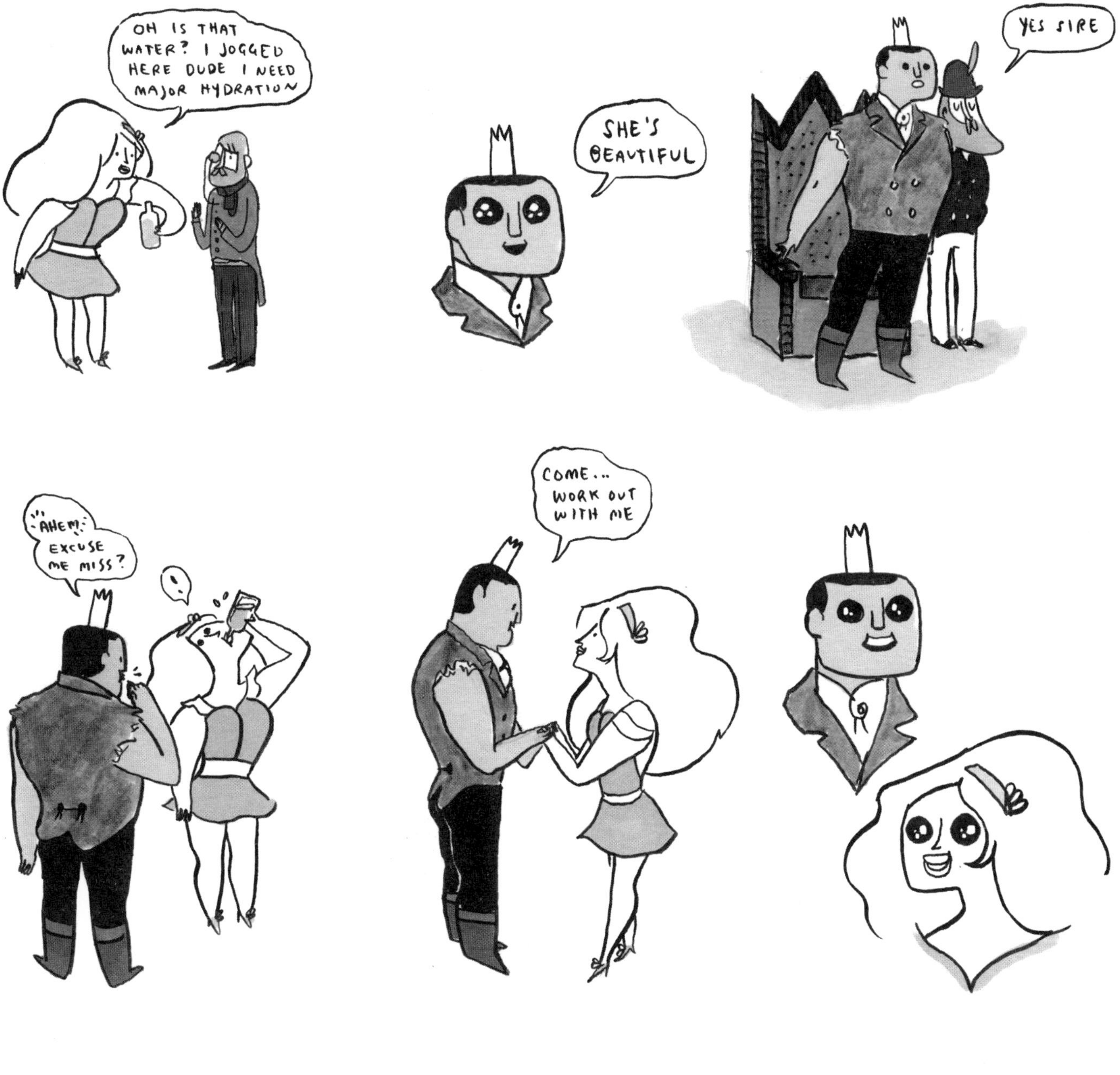
OH IS THAT WATER? I JOGGED HERE DUDE I NEED MAJOR HYDRATION
SHE'S BEAUTIFUL
YES SIRE
AHEM EXCUSE ME MISS?
!
COME... WORK OUT WITH ME

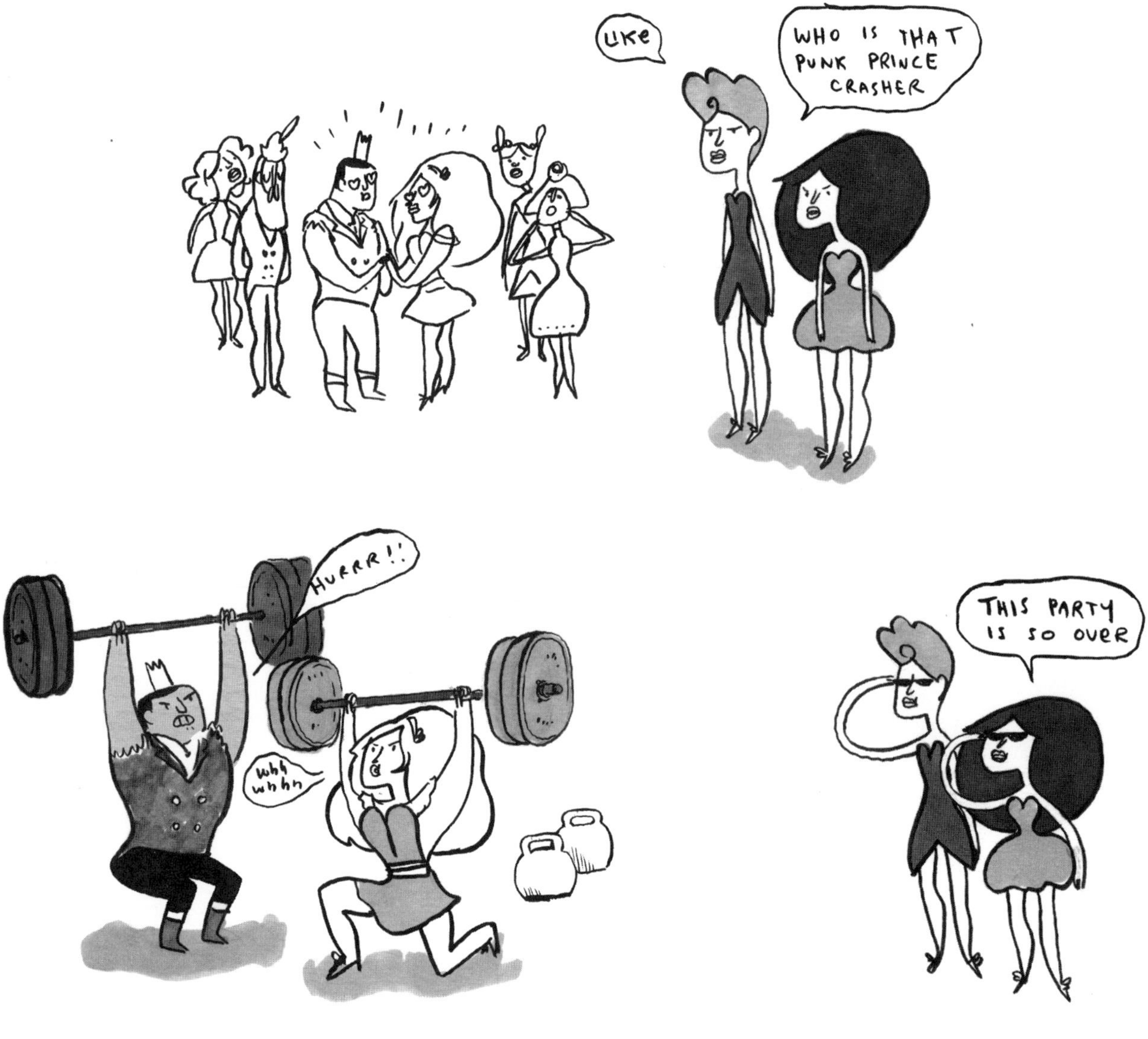
LIKE
WHO IS THAT PUNK PRINCE CRASHER
HURRR!!
THIS PARTY IS SO OVER

NASTY

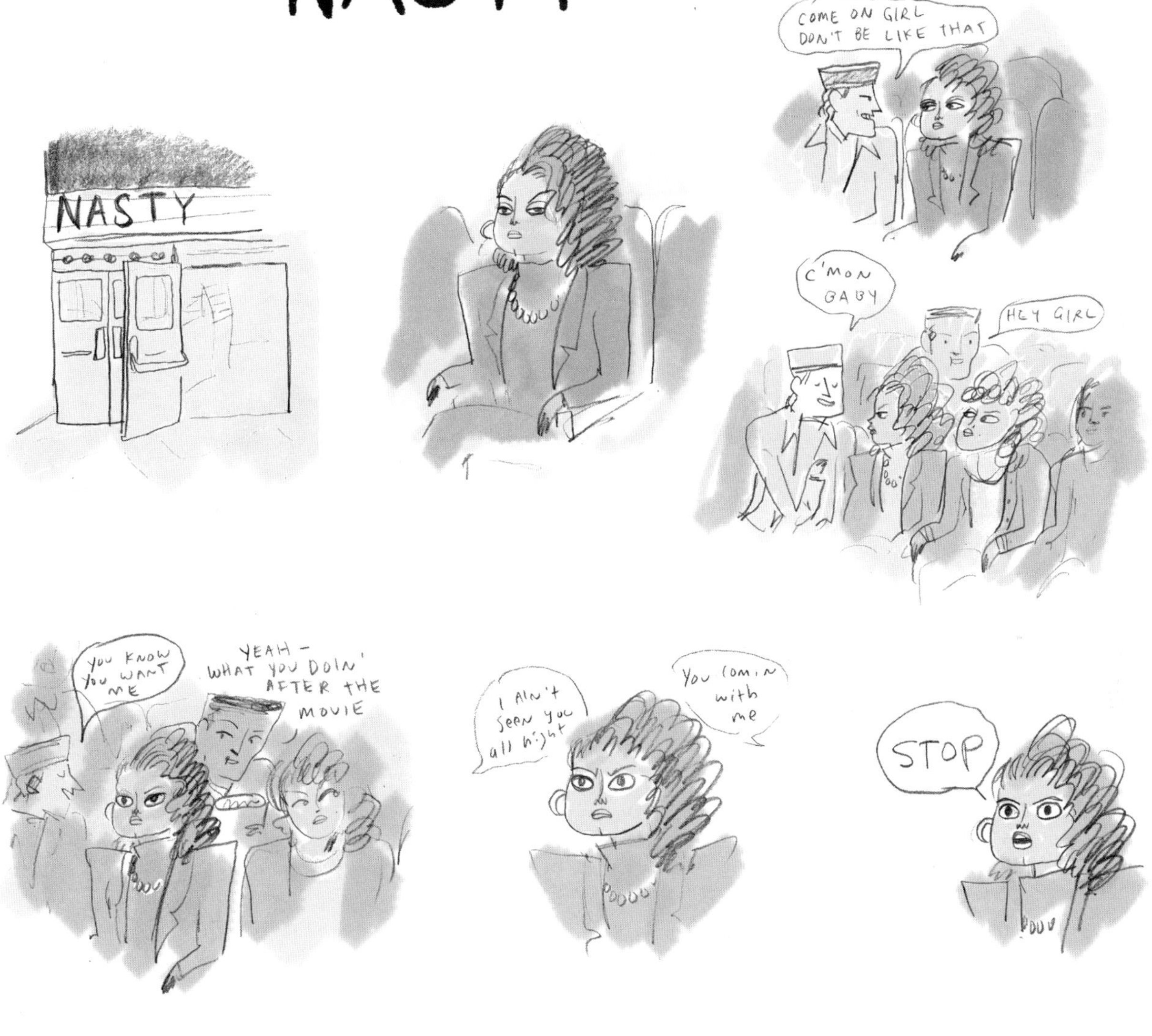
NASTY
COME ON GIRL DON'T BE LIKE THAT
C'MON BABY
HEY GIRL
YOU KNOW YOU WANT ME
YEAH - WHAT YOU DOIN' AFTER THE MOVIE
I AIN'T SEEN YOU ALL NIGHT
YOU COMIN WITH ME
STOP

"Why do you make such esoteric history jokes?" they ask. "Why don't you make comics about things people know about, like the man who was in the first three seconds of a decades-old Janet Jackson music video? That's what the people want."

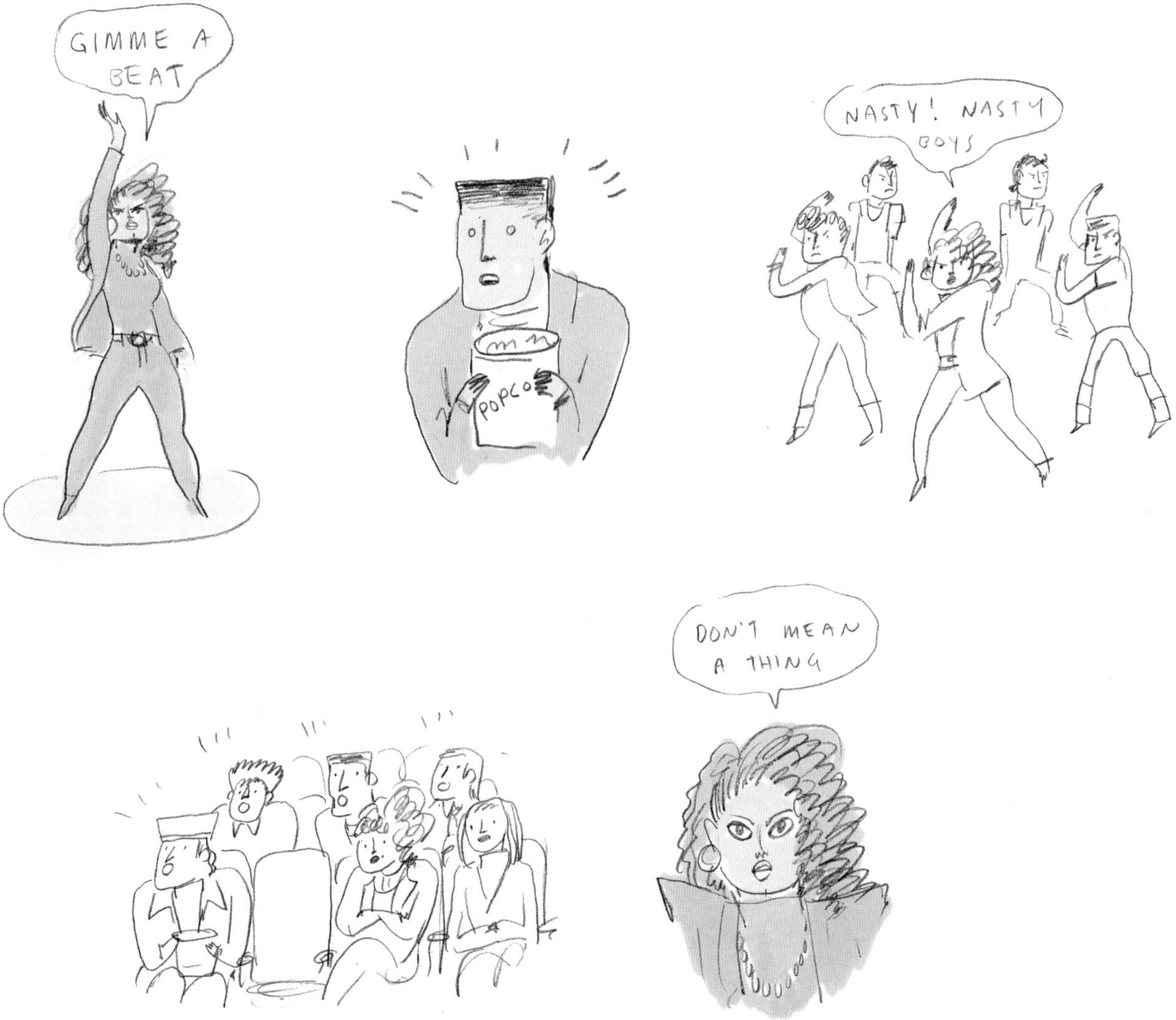
GIMME A BEAT
POPCO
NASTY! NASTY BOYS
DON'T MEAN A THING

OH YOU NASTY BOYS

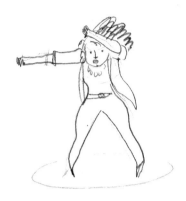

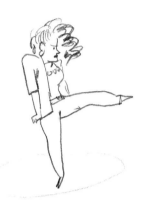

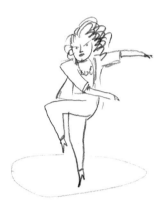

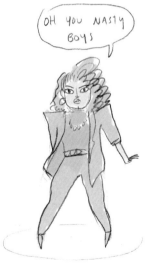

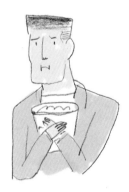

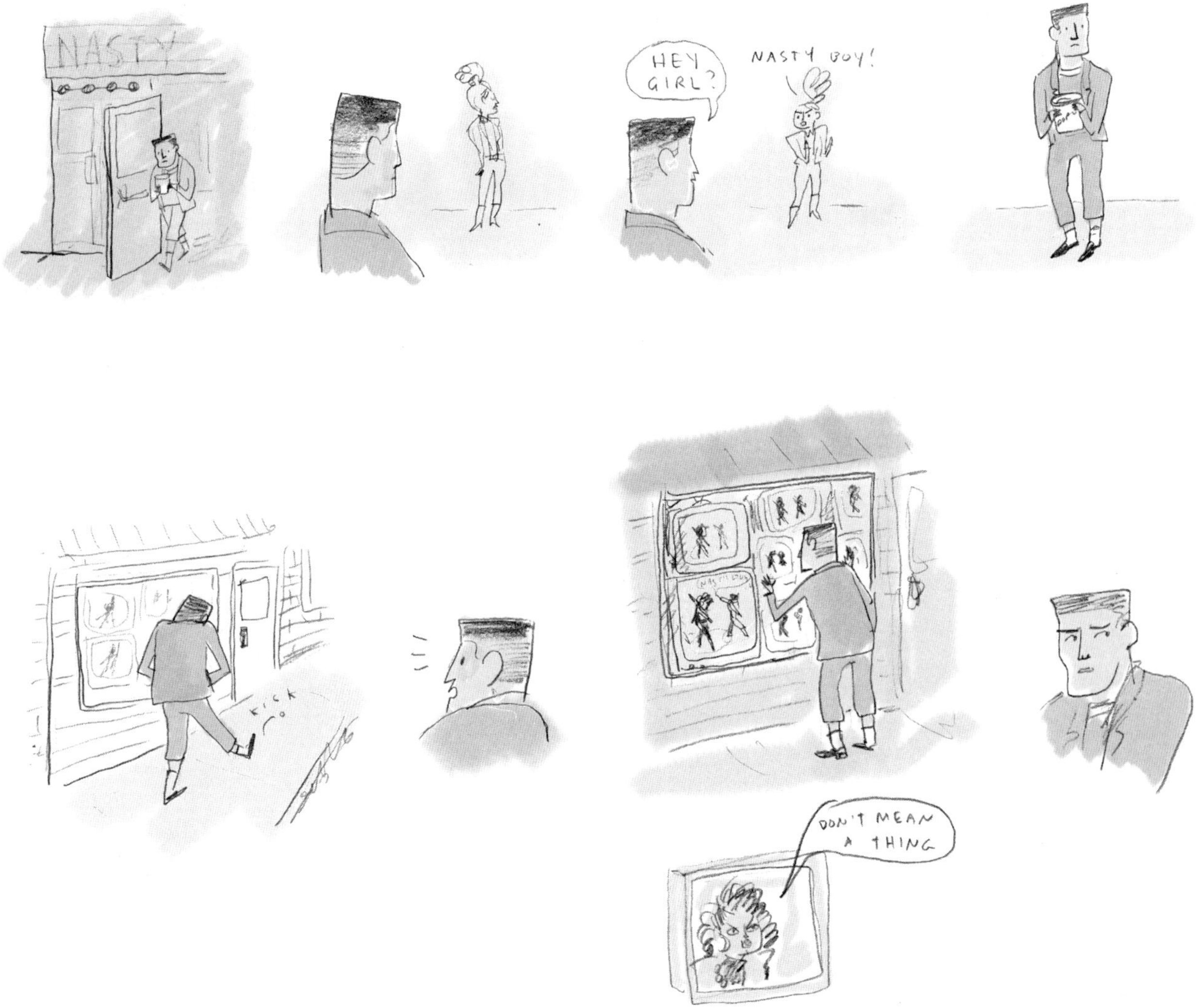
NASTY
HEY GIRL?
NASTY BOY!
KICK
DON'T MEAN A THING

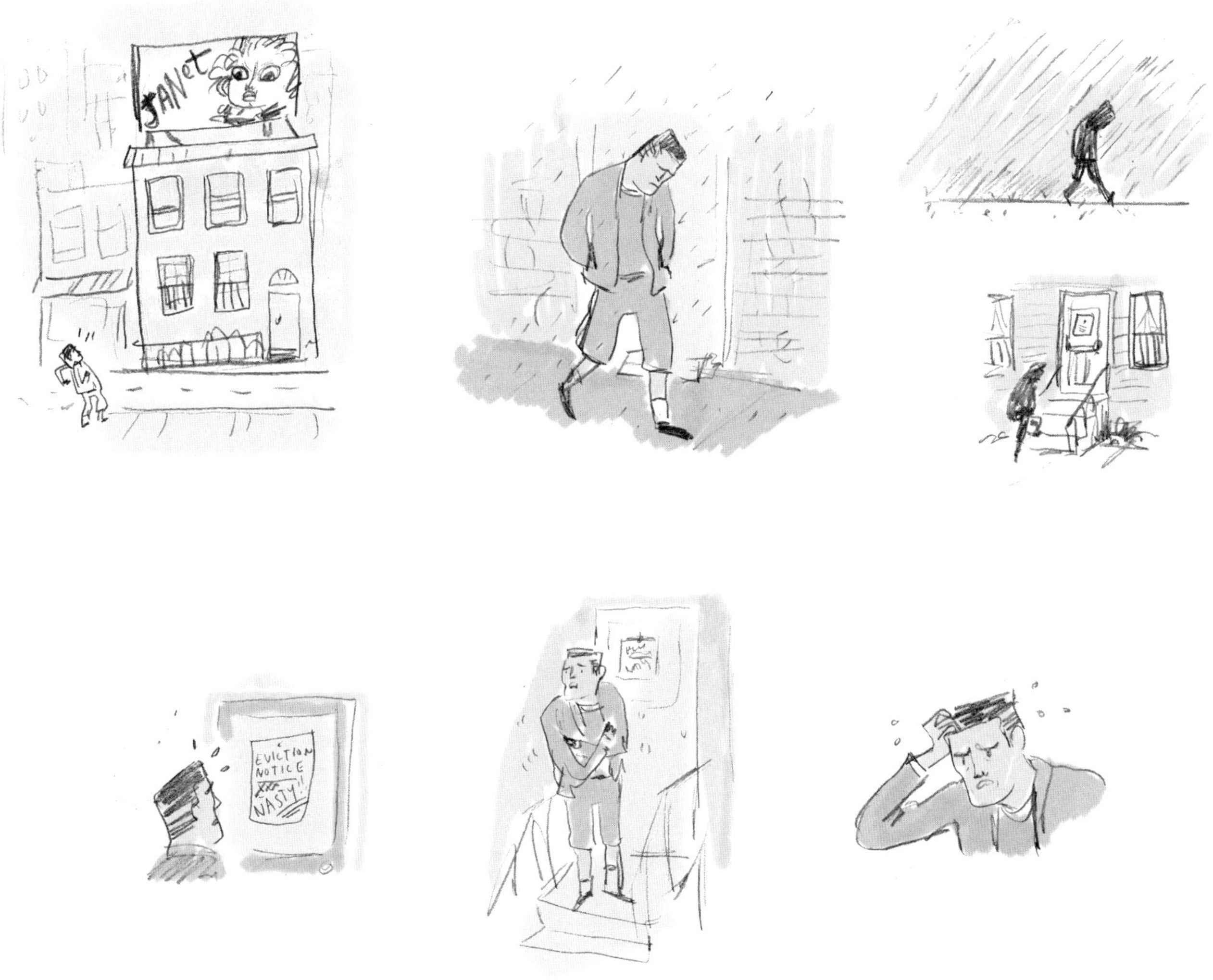
JANet
EVICTION NOTICE
NASTY!!

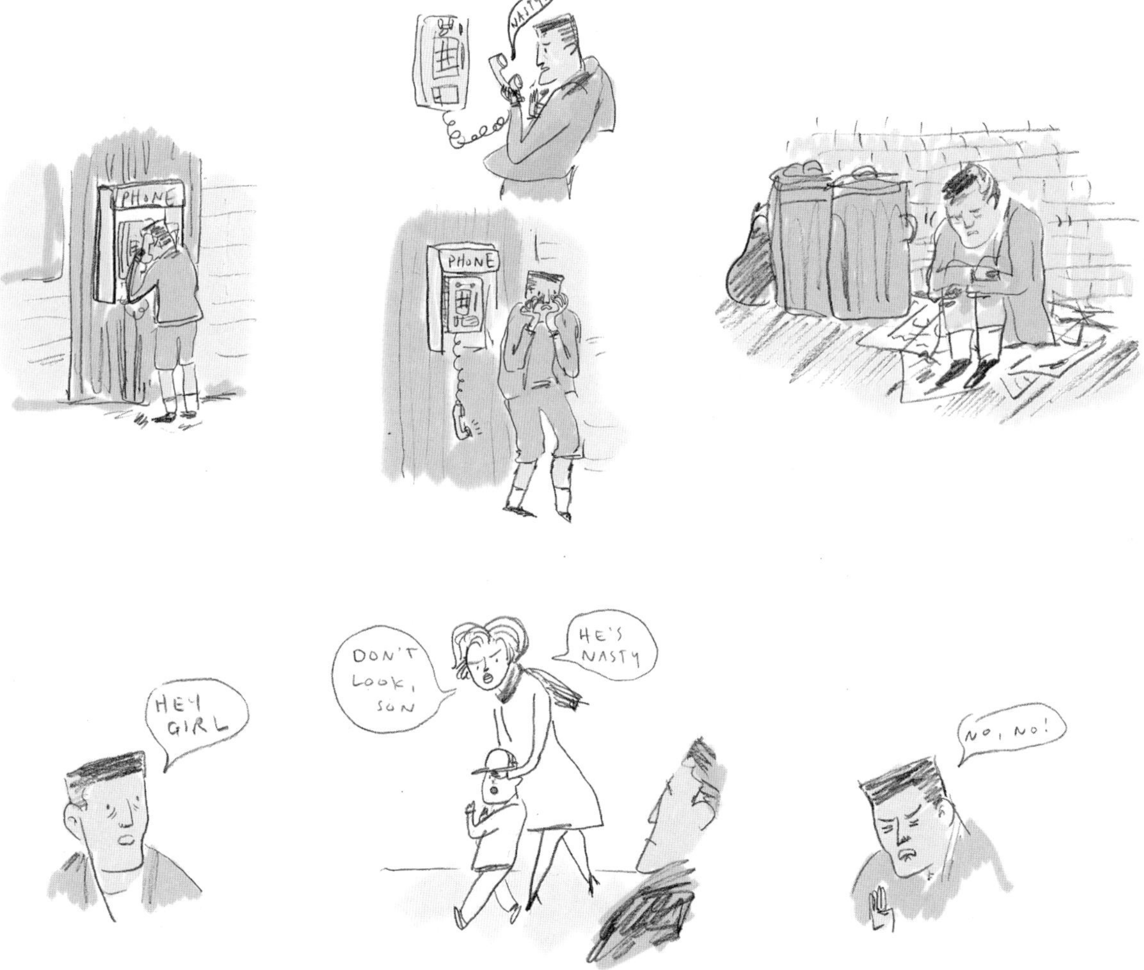
NASTY!
HEY GIRL
DON'T LOOK, SON
HE'S NASTY
NO, NO!

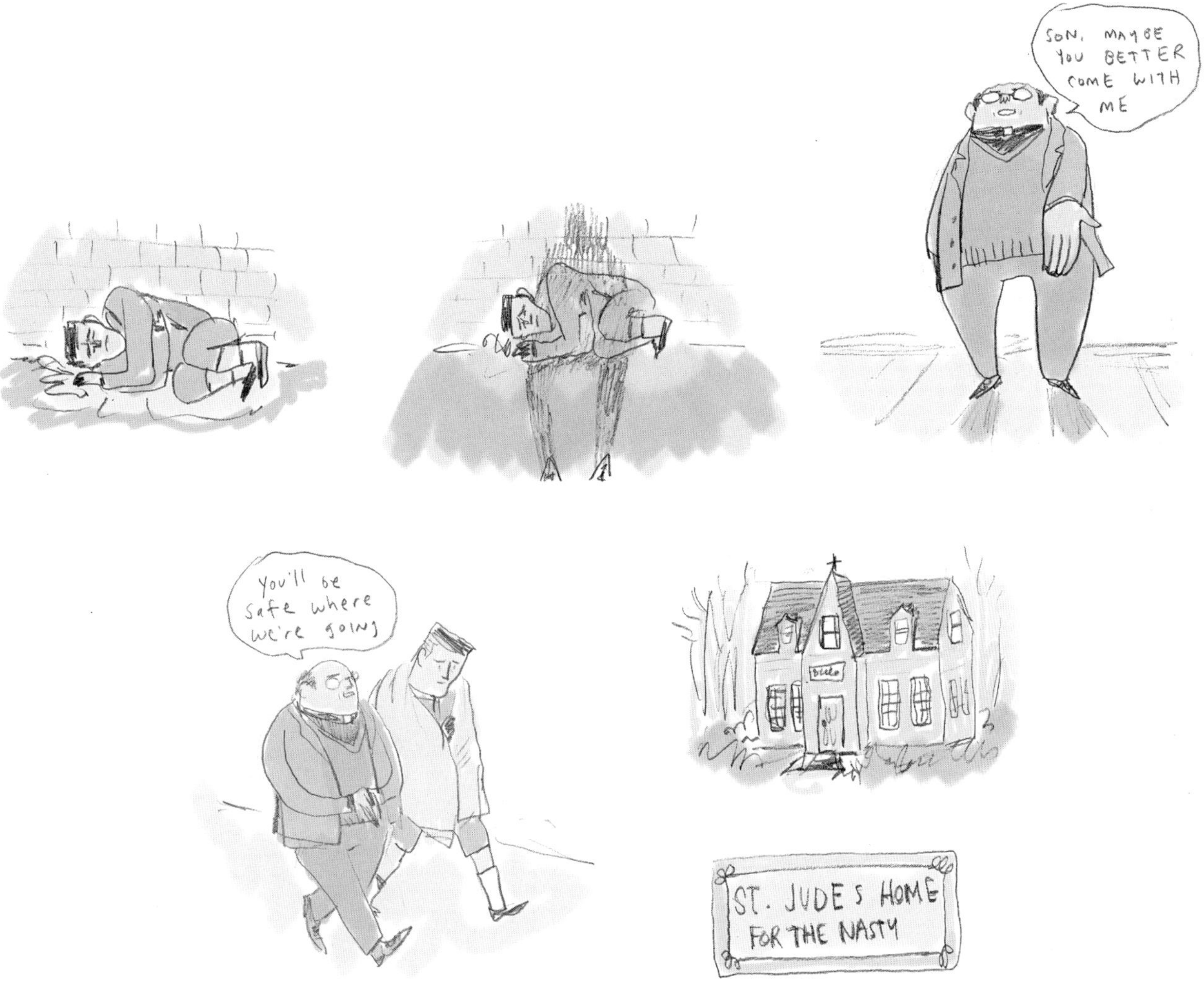
SON, MAYBE YOU BETTER COME WITH ME
you'll be safe where we're going
ST. JUDE S HOME FOR THE NASTY

Hey
How YOU DOIN'
AND SO
YOU'RE DOING SO WELL!
THANKS BABY YEAH
SO MUCH MORE CONFIDENCE, I HARDLY RECOGNIZE THE MAN I FOUND ON THE STREET
NEVER BE ASHAMED OF WHO YOU ARE
A HEH

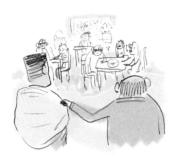

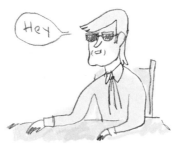

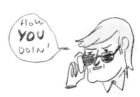

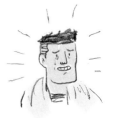

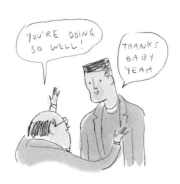

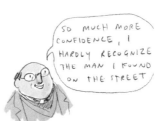

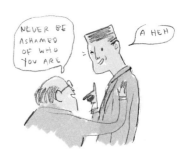

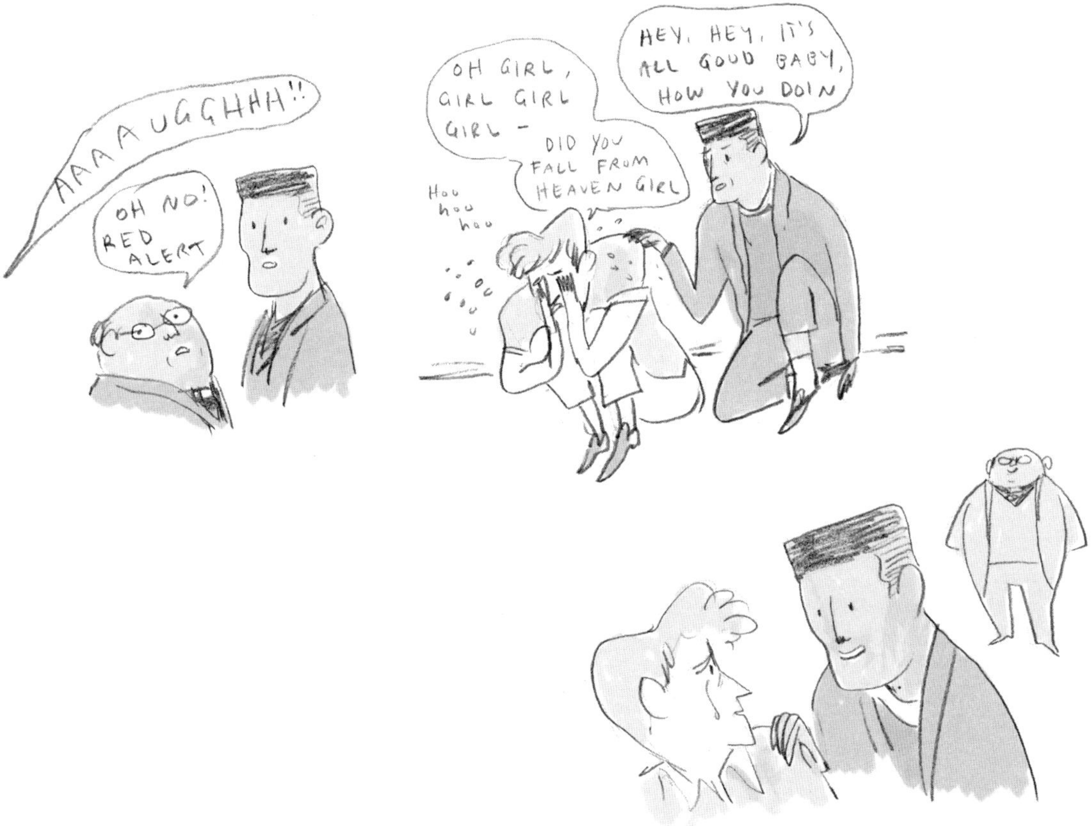
AAAAUGGHHH!!
OH NO! RED ALERT
HEY, HEY, IT'S ALL GOOD BABY, HOW YOU DOIN
OH GIRL, GIRL GIRL GIRL -
DID YOU FALL FROM HEAVEN GIRL
Hoo hoo hoo

DING DONG
OH DEAR
HOW UNFORTUNATE
HE WAS BORN NASTY — I'M SORRY PLEASE TAKE CARE OF HIM
I WILL RAISE HIM AS MY OWN

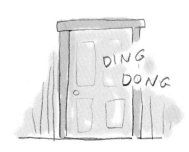

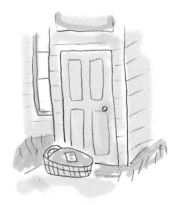

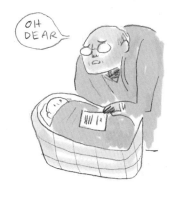

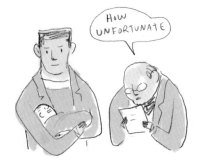

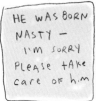

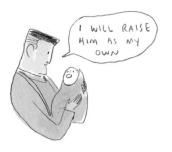

40 YEARS LATER

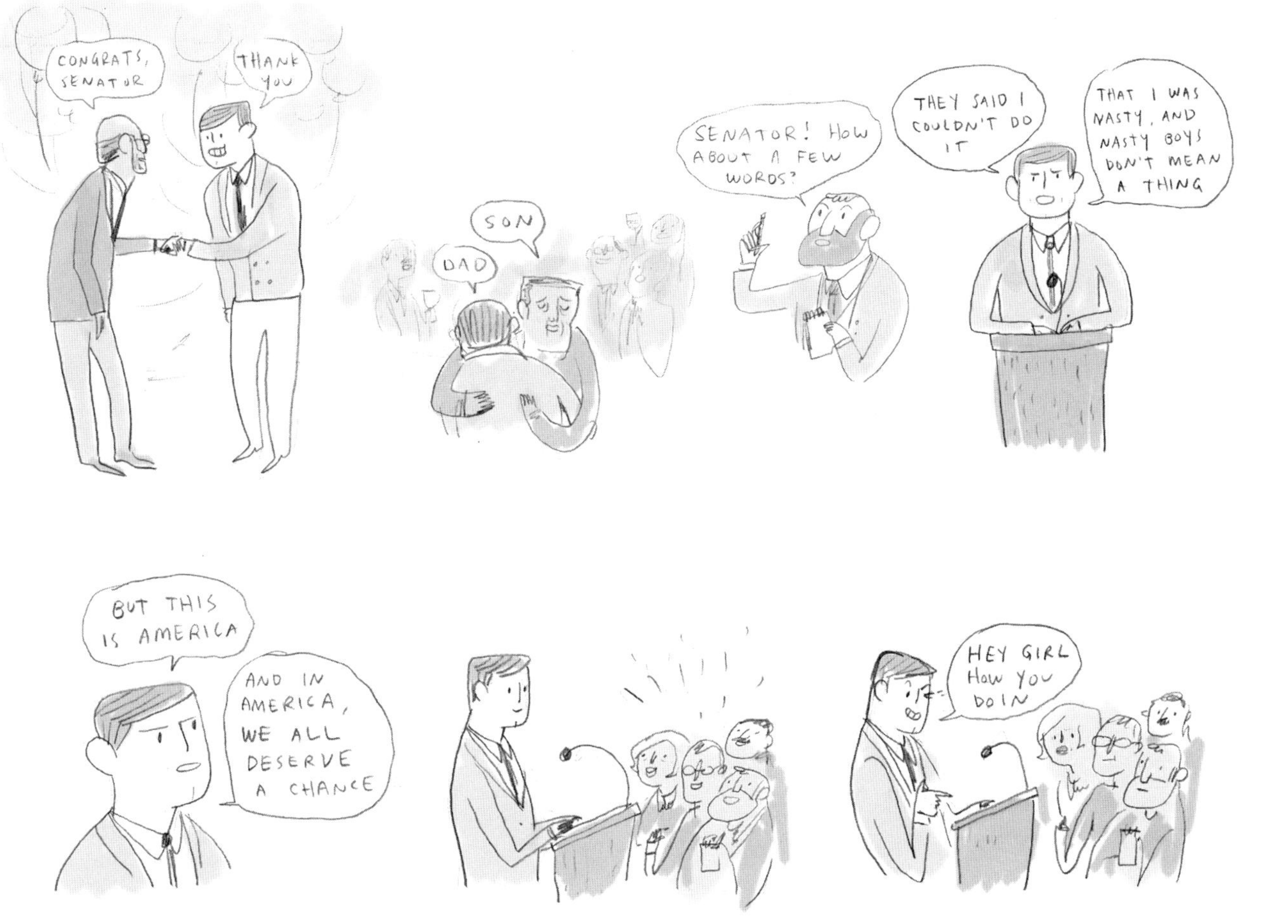
CONGRATS, SENATOR
THANK YOU
SON
DAD
SENATOR! HOW ABOUT A FEW WORDS?
THEY SAID I COULDN'T DO IT
THAT I WAS NASTY, AND NASTY BOYS DON'T MEAN A THING
BUT THIS IS AMERICA
AND IN AMERICA, WE ALL DESERVE A CHANCE
HEY GIRL HOW YOU DOIN

Famous Alexanders

Alexander Pushkin at a Cat Show

This one is the winner
SERGEI
lil' PUSHKINS
JUDGE
You DARE
SMACK
PISTOLS At –
You HAve Like three other duels at dawn

Alexander the Great Plays Monopoly

YES, PARK PLACE AND BOARDWALK ARE MINE! THE SHOE OF SILVER IS AGAIN VICTORIOUS
PARK PLACE
LUXURY TAX
BOARDWALK
UM, I HAVE A HOTEL ON PARK PLACE AND HOUSES ON BOARD-WALK, THEY'RE MY PROPERTIES
NO – I GET IT, BUT THAT'S STILL NOT HOW YOU PLAY THE GAME
RIGHT

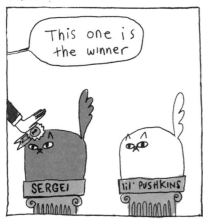

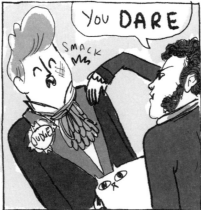

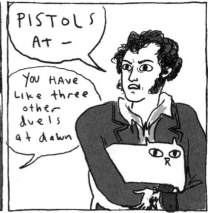

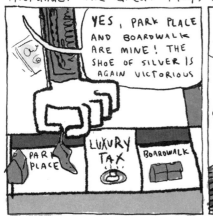

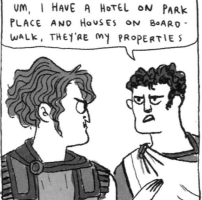

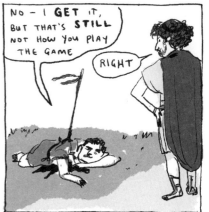

Alexander Pope is misquoted at a party

DON'T WORRY ABOUT IT BRO—
TO ERROR IS HUMAN, RIGHT

YEAH, I GUESS SO

"TO ERR IS HUMAN"

ugh

IT'S LIKE, THAT KIND OF PEDANTIC NERD IS THE WORST

NO I KNOW WHAT YOU MEAN

Alexander Graham Bell sends a pic

watson come here

DID YOU REALLY PUT YOUR BUTT ON MY LUNCH

AYE

Black Canary

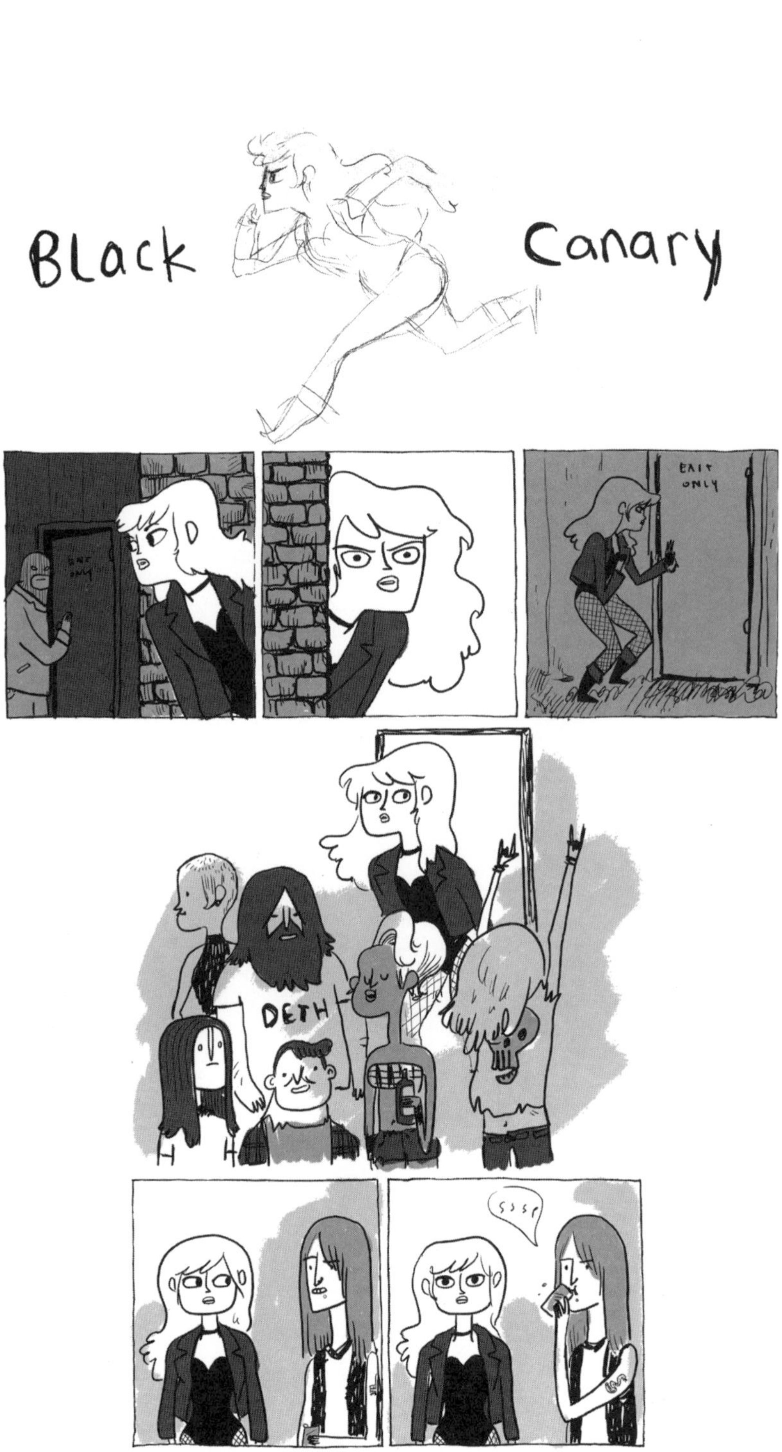
EXIT ONLY
EXIT ONLY
DETH

NICE TIGHTS.
...
NOD
NOD
SCREAM

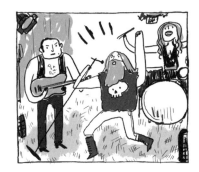

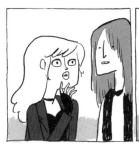

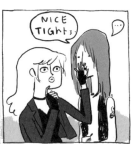

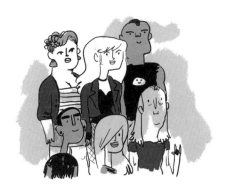

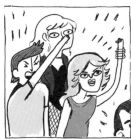

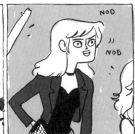

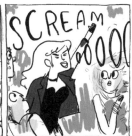

the end

SPOOKY POSTCARDS

Passing shadows Halloween
THE WITCHES ARE COMING TO PICK THE FLESH FROM YOUR BONES
JOHN STOP
AND BURY YOU WHERE NO ONE WILL EVER FIND YOU
JOHN PLEASE
HEH HEH
I DON'T LIKE THIS

ON HALLOWE'EN LOOK IN THE GLASS,
YOUR FUTURE HUSBAND'S FACE WILL PASS.
WHY HELLO THERE!
DING
OOH DICK PICS
scroll scroll

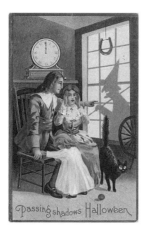

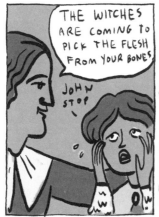

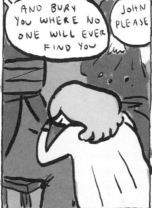

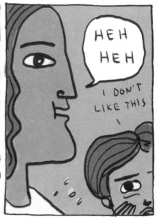

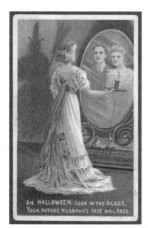

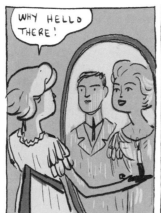

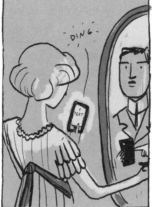

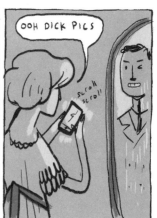

Spooky, right? I wonder where that tradition stopped—where you look in the mirror on Halloween and see your future husband's face? Judging by this card collections, it was pretty popular!

With Best Wishes for Hallowe'en.
GET OFF THAT COUCH
QUIET OPRAH I'M IN LOVE
THAT JOKE IS TOO OLD
YOU KNOW WHAT — NEVERMIND
WHATEVER. YOU JEALOUS

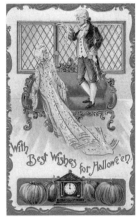

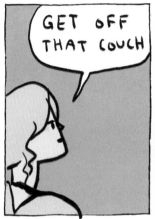

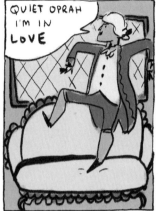

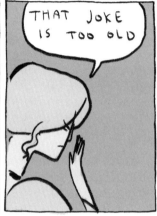

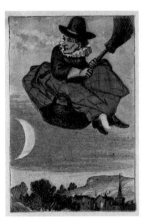

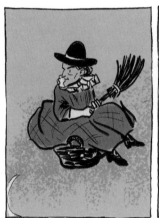

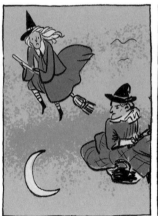

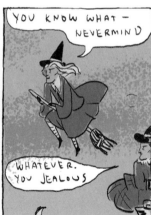

Bewitching Halloween
Don't dive for apples or grab for fruits beyond your reach – you've something here and she's a peach
HEY BOYS
OH JESUS
UGH
FUCKING HELL

BEST WISHES FOR HALLOWE'EN
PUT YOUR HAND IN THE BOWL AND GUESS WHAT'S IN IT
IS IT DICK PICS?
UM, NO?
WHY WOULD IT BE
WHAT KIND OF A PARTY IS THIS

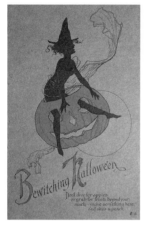

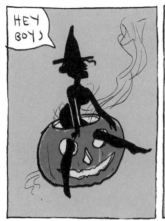

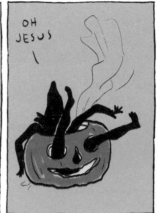

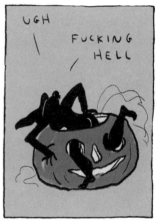

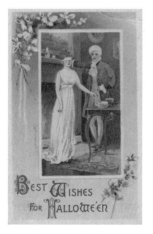

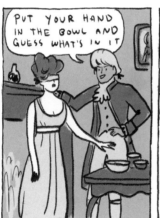

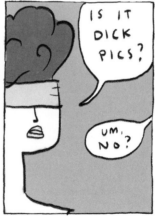

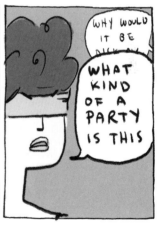

THE BLACK PRINCE

TEEN GLORY

HOW ARE YOU FEELING ABOUT BEING A HERO OF THE BATTLE OF CRÉCY?

BRO I AM STOKED

THIS IS QUITE A MOMENTOUS EVENT SO FAR IN THE WAR...

THOSE FRENCH GUYS WERE LIKE, WHOAAAA

I KEEP FORGETTING YOU ARE SIXTEEN

AND MY ARMY WAS LIKE EAT IT

KA CHOW!!

A TRUE KNIGHT

I SLEW THAT GUY SO HARD TODAY

THEN I HELD HIM IN MY ARMS UNTIL HIS SWEET SOUL DEPARTED FROM THAT NOBLE BODY

WICKED CHIVALROUS

GAP

Who says you can't be the "Flower of English Chivalry" on one hand and a brutal warlord on the other? History has shown us that it is possible to have your cake and murder it too.

DUTY

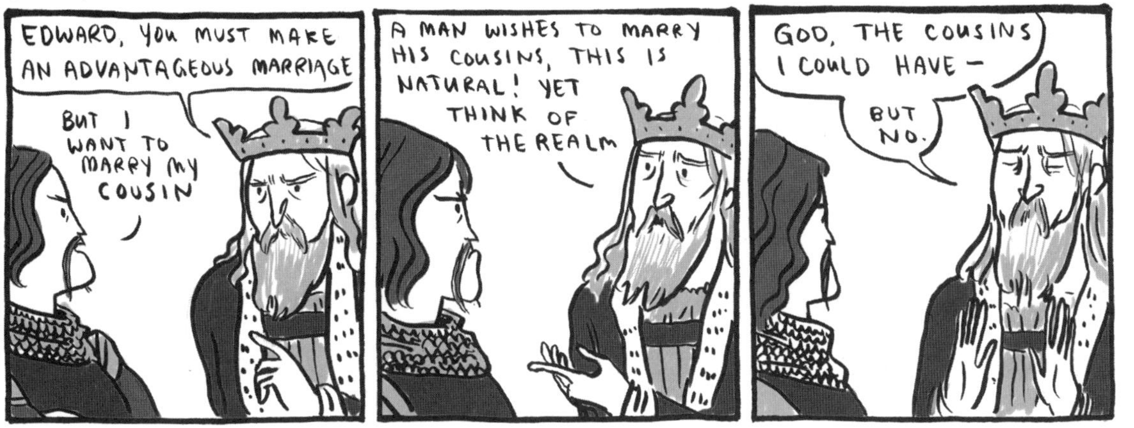
EDWARD, YOU MUST MAKE AN ADVANTAGEOUS MARRIAGE
BUT I WANT TO MARRY MY COUSIN
A MAN WISHES TO MARRY HIS COUSINS, THIS IS NATURAL! YET THINK OF THE REALM
GOD, THE COUSINS I COULD HAVE—
BUT NO.

DUALITY

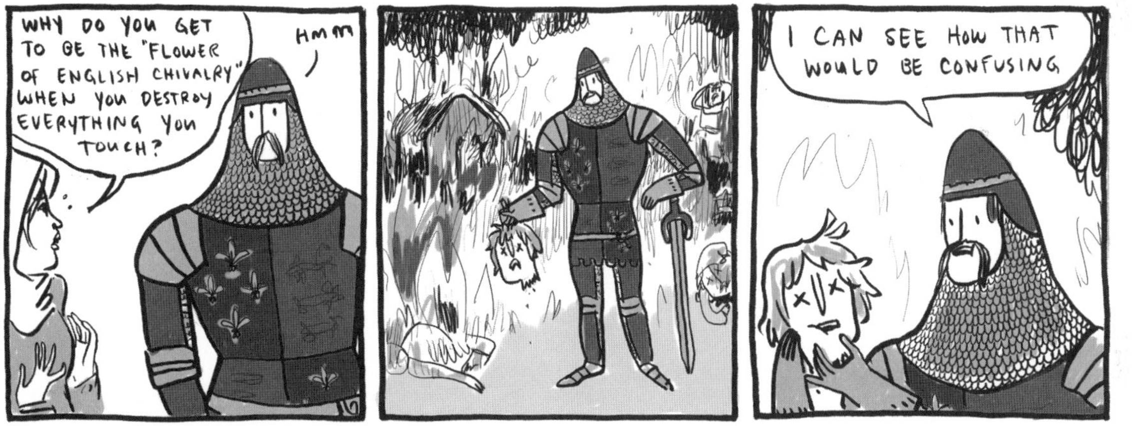
WHY DO YOU GET TO BE THE "FLOWER OF ENGLISH CHIVALRY" WHEN YOU DESTROY EVERYTHING YOU TOUCH?
HMM
I CAN SEE HOW THAT WOULD BE CONFUSING

GONE TOO SOON

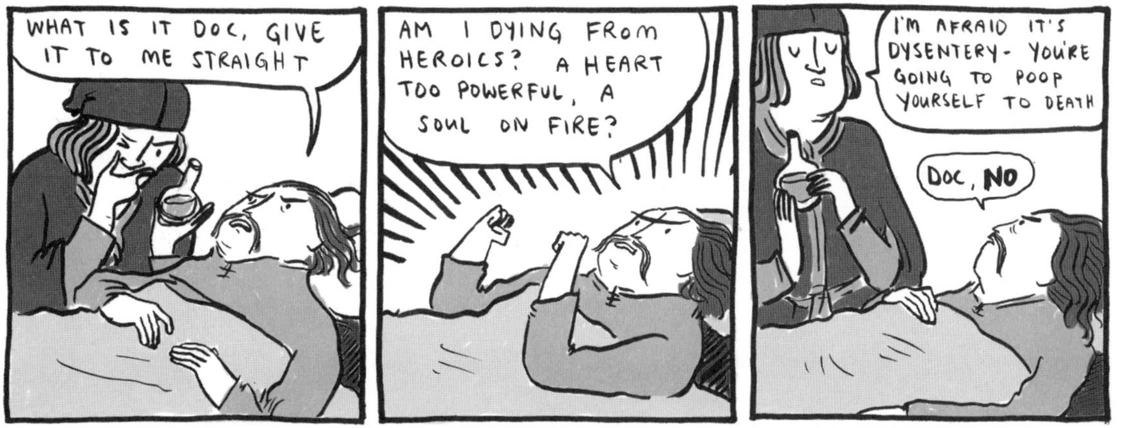
WHAT IS IT DOC, GIVE IT TO ME STRAIGHT
AM I DYING FROM HEROICS? A HEART TOO POWERFUL, A SOUL ON FIRE?
I'M AFRAID IT'S DYSENTERY- YOU'RE GOING TO POOP YOURSELF TO DEATH
DOC, NO

SEXY SCIENCE

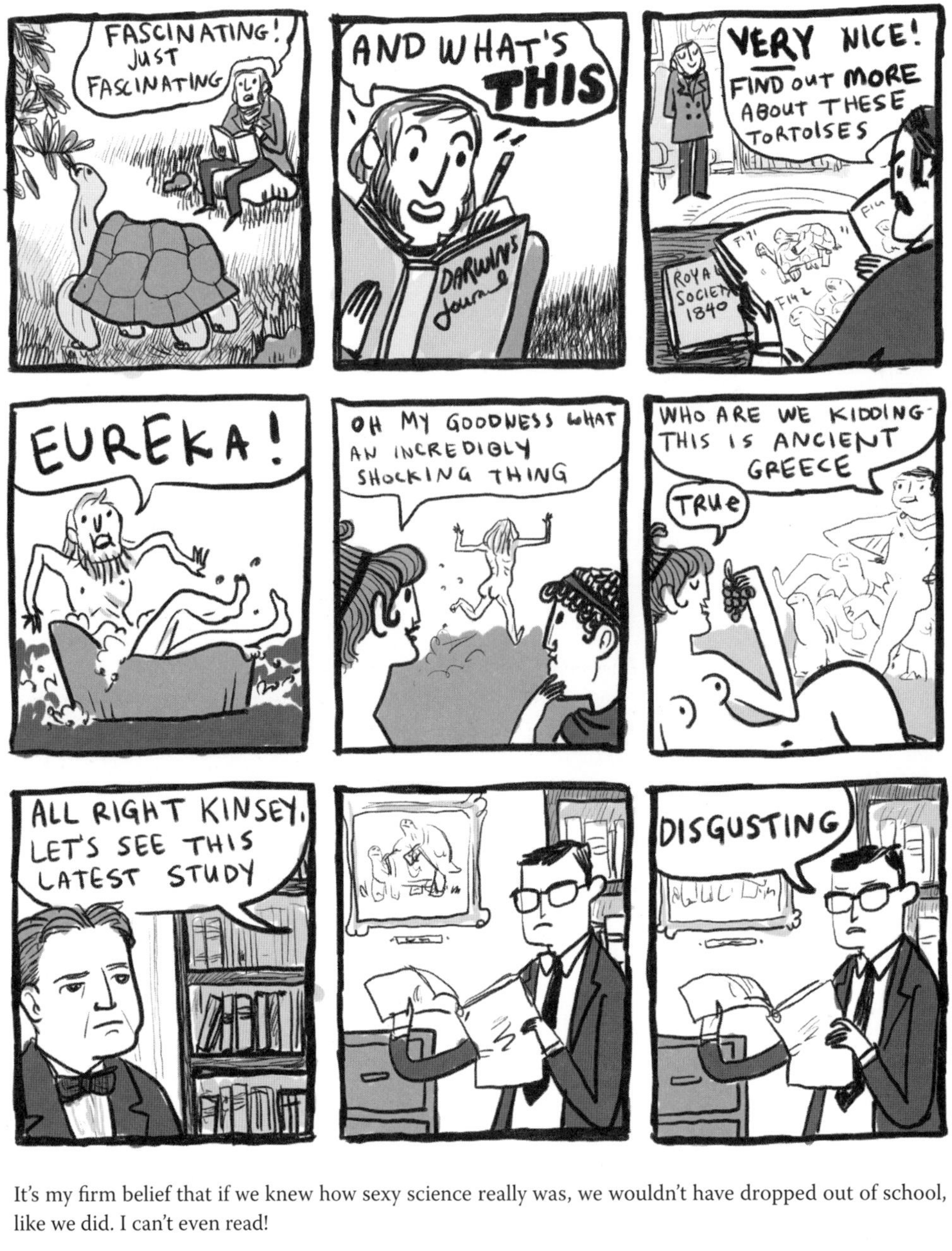
FASCINATING! JUST FASCINATING
AND WHAT'S THIS
DARWIN'S Journal
VERY NICE! FIND OUT MORE ABOUT THESE TORTOISES
ROYAL SOCIETY 1840
EUREKA!
OH MY GOODNESS WHAT AN INCREDIBLY SHOCKING THING
WHO ARE WE KIDDING-THIS IS ANCIENT GREECE
TRUE
ALL RIGHT KINSEY, LET'S SEE THIS LATEST STUDY
DISGUSTING

It's my firm belief that if we knew how sexy science really was, we wouldn't have dropped out of school, like we did. I can't even read!

IDA B. WELLS

CIVIL DISOBEDIENCE

MA'AM YOU'LL HAVE TO LEAVE THE WHITE CAR

IT'S A LADY'S CAR AND I'M A LADY

MA'AM GET OFF

YOU GET OFF

WELL I DON'T KNOW WHAT ANYONE THINKS THEY'RE GOING TO PROVE BY MAKING A FUSS ABOUT GIVING UP SEATS ON PUBLIC TRANSIT

SHE **BIT ME**

THE PEOPLE'S GROCERY

I CAN'T BELIEVE

OUR FRIENDS HAVE BEEN MURDERED

I CAN'T BELIEVE WE NEED THREE COFFINS

I'M GOING TO WRITE ABOUT IT

I CAN'T BELIEVE WE NEED FOUR COFFINS?

FIND A PEN

If Ida isn't your hero, maybe you just don't know enough about her. She's mine. A statue of Ida in every home, or the world isn't fair.

RADICAL OF THE RADICALS

WE ALL APPRECIATE WHAT YOU'RE DOING

BUT?

BUT YOU ARE **LOUD** AND YOU SAY UNCOMFORTABLE THINGS AND IT IS VICTORIAN TIMES

SO WHAT MAKES PEOPLE UNCOMFORTABLE IN VICTORIAN TIMES?

I DON'T KNOW, BEING ALIVE?

THE NEW YORK TIMES

THANK YOU SO MUCH FOR COMING TO ENGLAND!

I'VE READ ALL ABOUT YOU!

ALL GOOD THINGS, I HOPE!

WELL... THEY WERE AMERICAN NEWSPAPERS

OH—JUST HORRIBLE, HORRIBLE THINGS THEN

COMPLETELY INSANE

MARCH ON WASHINGTON
YOU CAN JOIN THE SUFFRAGE PARADE, BUT LIKE, IN THE BACK
VOTES
THE VERY BACK. OR THE NEXT DAY? OR NOT AT ALL? IT'S JUST THAT IT'S A VOTES FOR WOMEN THING, WE DON'T WANT TO MAKE IT A RACE THING
BUT
THANKS FOR YOUR support
YEAH IT SOUNDS LIKE A RACE THING
IT'S NAAWT A RACE THING

SWORD AMONG LIONS
GRANDMA IDA, YOU FOUGHT ALL YOUR LIFE, IS IT GOOD TO BE OLD AND RESTING NOW?
AW, AREN'T YOU NICE DEAR BUT GRANDMA IS RUNNING FOR SENATOR
HAND THESE OUT
SLAP
IDA

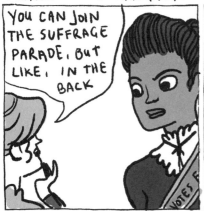

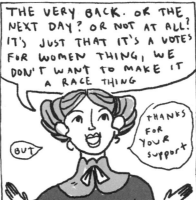

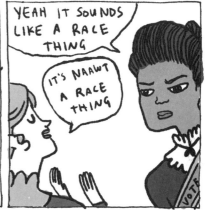

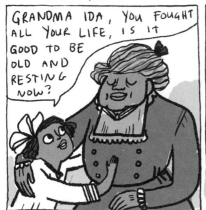

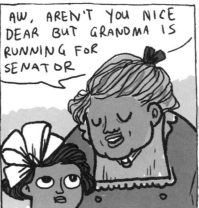

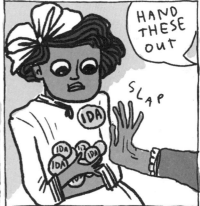

COMIC SOUP

SPACE BABES

WE ARE THE SPACE BABES COME TO TAKE OVER YOUR PLANET
WE NEED TO FIGHT BACK
SURRENDER
WAIT, WAIT- LET'S HEAR THESE GUYS OUT

CLICKBAIT

OH HUN, WAIT
NEW YORK NEW
15 PHOTOS OF HOW THE OTHER HALF LIVES THAT WILL MAKE YOUR HEAD EXPLODE
#12 ESPECIALLY
Jacob Riis
I HATE IT WHEN THEY DO THAT
LET'S BUY IT THOUGH

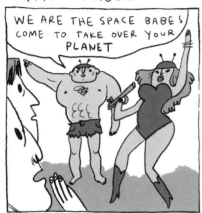

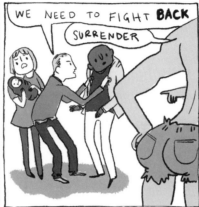

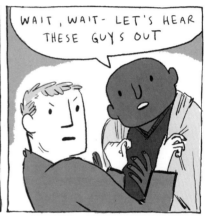

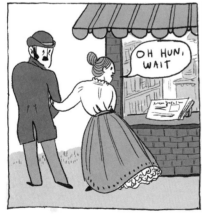

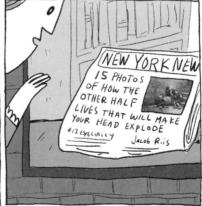

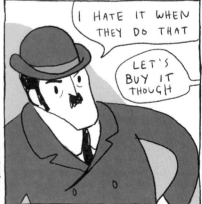

PERVERT CLUB

WELCOME TO PERVERT CLUB

THE FIRST RULE OF PERVERT CLUB IS THAT YOU DON'T TALK ABOUT PERVERT CLUB

AND SO

WHAT'S **WRONG** WITH YOU

IT'S A SECRET

DREAMS COME TRUE

I WILL ALWAYS BE THE **UGLY DUCKLING**

MY **CARD**

BOB DOCTOR NU·YU PLASTIC SURGERY

THANK YOU DOCTOR

SO BEAUTIFUL

THE ONLY COOL GIRL

IT'S JUST, ALL MY BEST FRIENDS ARE GUYS, YOU KNOW?

FOR SURE

GIRLS ARE LIKE, "OMG MY HAIR, BLUH I ONLY EAT SALAD," AND I'M LIKE — **NO.**

YAH YOU'RE COOL

LITERALLY EVERY OTHER GIRL ALIVE

YOU ALONE WALK THIS PATH

REGINALD

REGINALD, YOU'RE MY BEST KNIGHT, I CAN'T USE YOU FOR AN UNIMPORTANT BATTLE

I MUST DEPLOY YOU STRATEGICALLY

I SHALL BE HERE UNTIL MY LORD REQUIRES MY SERVICES

OH REGINALD I DID THAT THING WHERE YOU WAIT TOO LONG AND IT BECOMES A WHOLE **THING,** THE WAITING, AND—

AVIARY

THIS MESSAGE IS URGENT AND VERY IMPORTANT

TO THE AVIARY

AVIARY

I'M SORRY, ALL WE HAVE LEFT IS CRAIG

AW NOT CRAIG

·CRAIG·

FIRST DATE

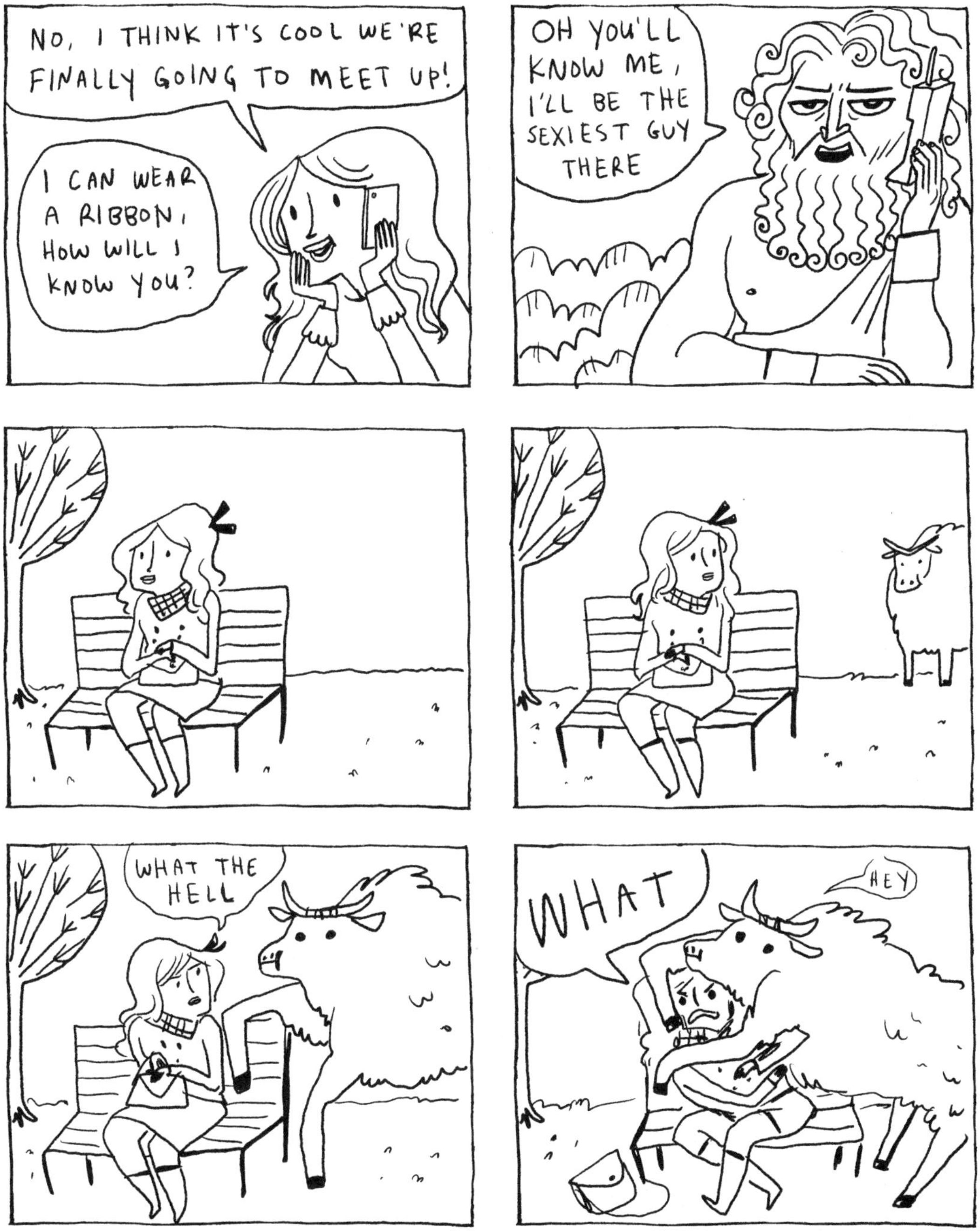

NO, I THINK IT'S COOL WE'RE FINALLY GOING TO MEET UP!
I CAN WEAR A RIBBON, HOW WILL I KNOW YOU?
OH YOU'LL KNOW ME, I'LL BE THE SEXIEST GUY THERE
WHAT THE HELL
WHAT
HEY

CAR GAMES

I LOVE ROAD TRIPS
YOUR TURN ALLEN
OK!
HMM
GOT ONE

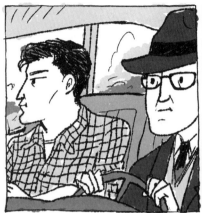

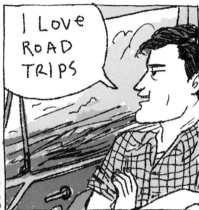

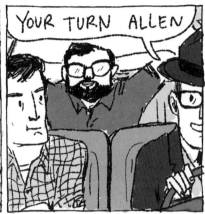

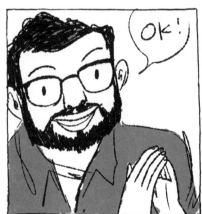

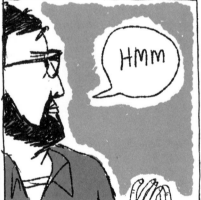

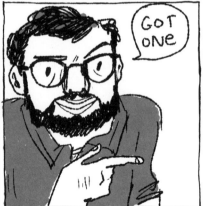

Is that low hanging fruit? Don't mind if I do.

I SPY
WITH MY LITTLE EYE
THE BEST MINDS OF MY GENERATION
DESTROYED BY MADNESS, STARVING
HYSTERICAL
DAWN
TOUGH

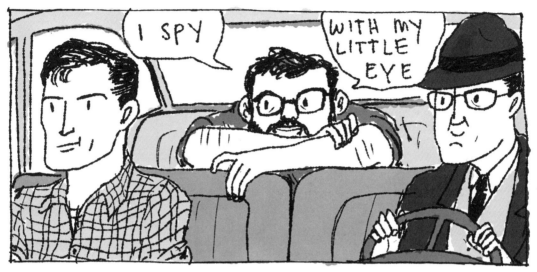

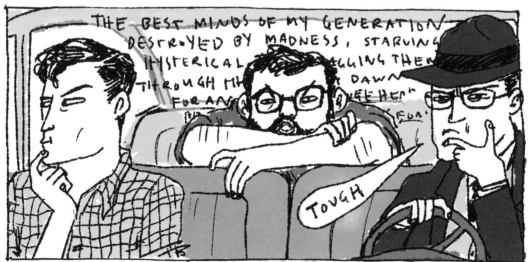

KOKORO
(PART ONE)

LESSON #1

SENSEI! TEACH ME ABOUT **LIFE**

LIFE! WHAT LIFE! TO LOVE IS A SIN, AND THERE IS NO ONE ON THIS EARTH WHO CAN TRULY BE TRUSTED. ONE DAY YOU WILL CURSE MY NAME, AND IN FACT, I CURSE MY OWN SOUL

COOL THANKS

CHANCE ENCOUNTER

OH SENSEI!! I DIDN'T KNOW YOU'D BE HERE

I LIKE THIS GRAVEYARD. GOOD PLACE TO **CHILL**

NICE GRAVES

AND WHO IS THIS? FRIEND OF YOURS??

I AM HERE TO BE ALONE

Kokoro is one of those books that maybe you have to read in a class, and you think that it's kind of dry, but then somehow it gets under your skin and you can't stop thinking about it. And I guess they call them classics because they stick around like that.

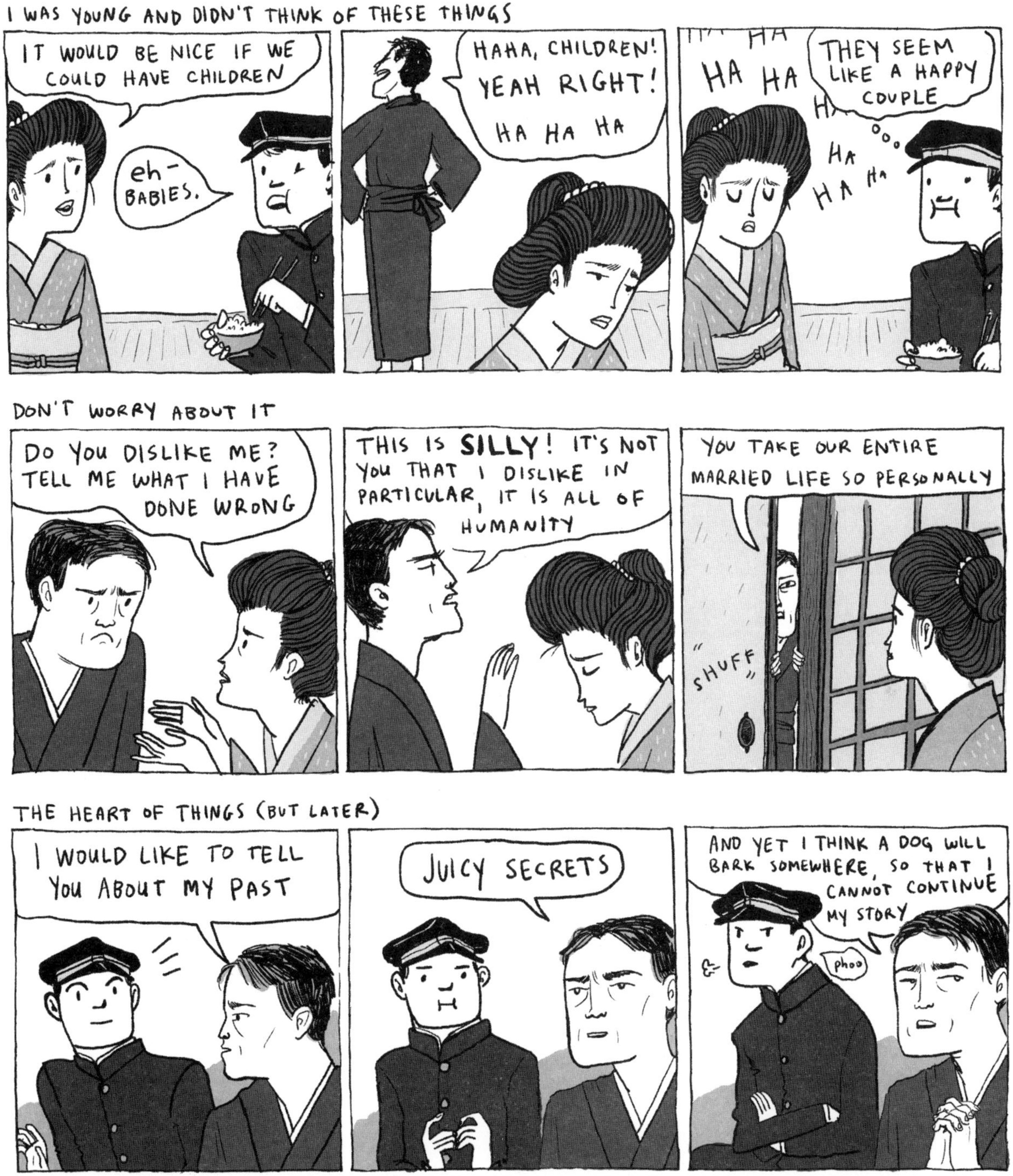
I WAS YOUNG AND DIDN'T THINK OF THESE THINGS
IT WOULD BE NICE IF WE COULD HAVE CHILDREN
eh- BABIES.
HAHA, CHILDREN! YEAH RIGHT!
HA HA HA
HA HA HA HA HA HA
THEY SEEM LIKE A HAPPY COUPLE
DON'T WORRY ABOUT IT
DO YOU DISLIKE ME? TELL ME WHAT I HAVE DONE WRONG
THIS IS SILLY! IT'S NOT YOU THAT I DISLIKE IN PARTICULAR, IT IS ALL OF HUMANITY
YOU TAKE OUR ENTIRE MARRIED LIFE SO PERSONALLY
SHUFF
THE HEART OF THINGS (BUT LATER)
I WOULD LIKE TO TELL YOU ABOUT MY PAST
JUICY SECRETS
AND YET I THINK A DOG WILL BARK SOMEWHERE, SO THAT I CANNOT CONTINUE MY STORY
phoo

CAREERS

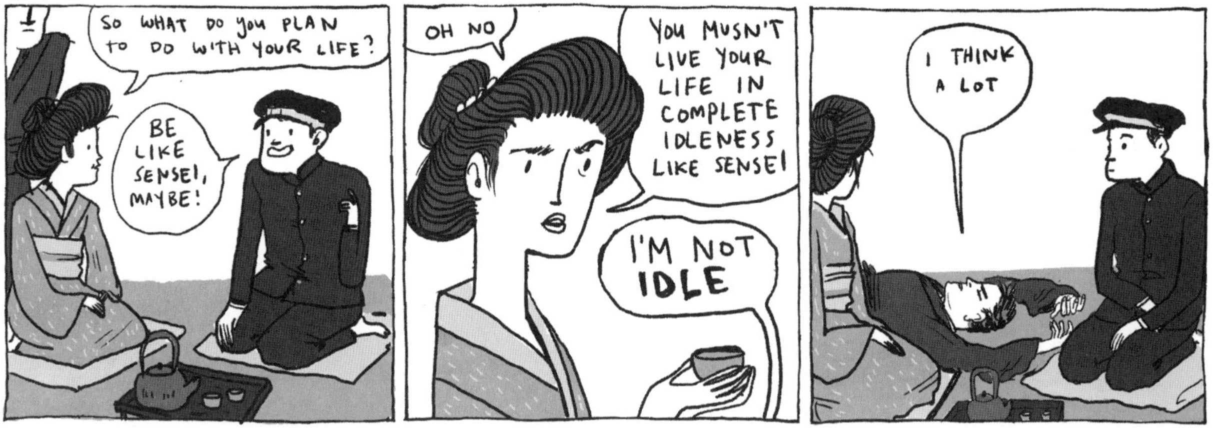
SO WHAT DO YOU PLAN TO DO WITH YOUR LIFE?
BE LIKE SENSEI, MAYBE!
OH NO
YOU MUSN'T LIVE YOUR LIFE IN COMPLETE IDLENESS LIKE SENSEI
I'M NOT **IDLE**
I THINK A LOT

CONFIDENCE BOOST

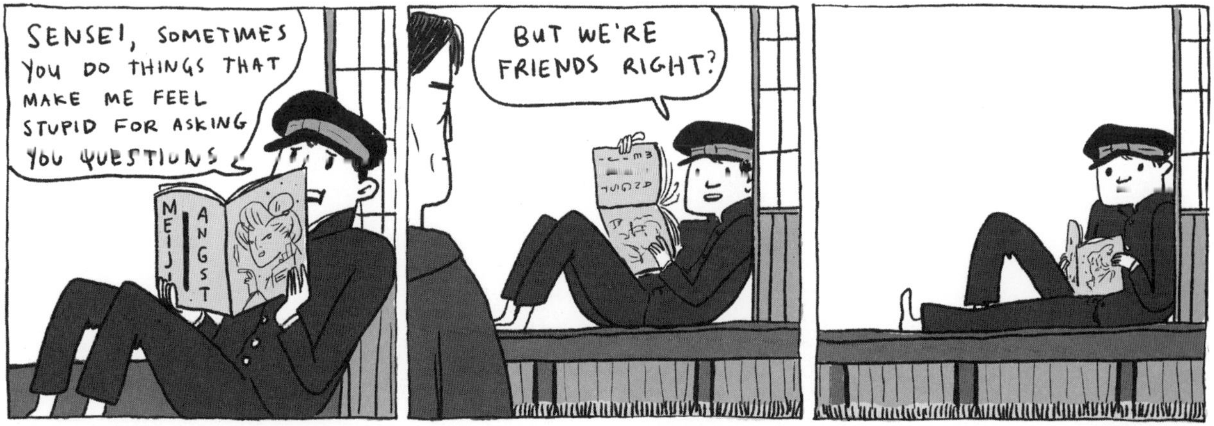
SENSEI, SOMETIMES YOU DO THINGS THAT MAKE ME FEEL STUPID FOR ASKING YOU QUESTIONS
MEIJI
ANGST
BUT WE'RE FRIENDS RIGHT?

DROPPING HINTS

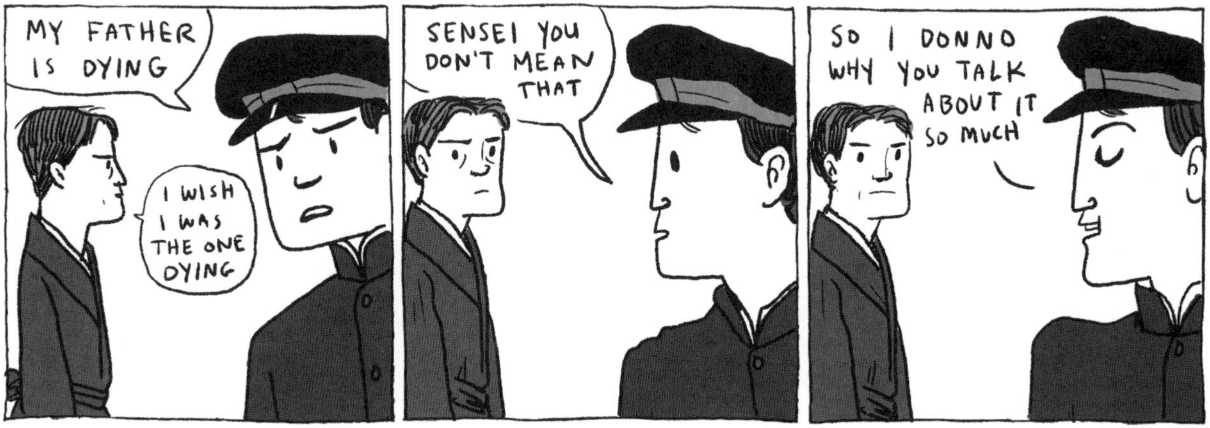
MY FATHER IS DYING
I WISH I WAS THE ONE DYING
SENSEI YOU DON'T MEAN THAT
SO I DONNO WHY YOU TALK ABOUT IT SO MUCH

KOKORO
(PART TWO)

HOME IN THE COUNTRY

MOM! DAD! I'M BACK FROM TOKYO AND I MET THE MOST AMAZING GUY!

HE'S SMART, HE'S COOL, HE'S MYSTERIOUS AND...

HE SURE SOUNDS... GREAT

OH YOU DON'T EVEN KNOW

MEANWHILE BACK AT SENSEI'S

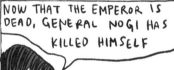

NOW THAT THE EMPEROR IS DEAD, GENERAL NOGI HAS KILLED HIMSELF

HOW INTERESTING THAT IS. ISN'T IT? VERY INTERESTING.

DO WE HAVE SWORDS OR ANYTHING AROUND?

ASKING FOR A FRIEND

GET A JOB

WHAT A NICE DIPLOMA. YOU SHOULDN'T HAVE BENT IT. THE DOG TRIED TO EAT IT BUT I SAVED IT.

PfFt SO

WHAT DID YOU STUDY IN UNIVERSITY?

MOM DON'T BE SO PROVINCIAL

YOU WERE THERE FOR YEARS

WHAT DOES ANYONE STUDY IN UNIVERSITY

AM I NOT MY FATHER'S SON

THE END HAS REALLY COME FOR ME, MY SON
AIN'T THAT THE TRUTH
SON...
A LETTER FROM SENSEI??
"BY the time you read this, I will be dead"
SENSEI NO!
SON...

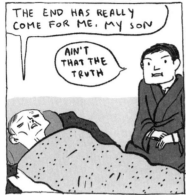

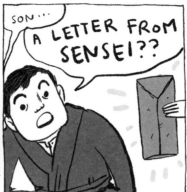

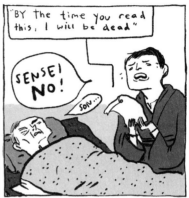

NEXT TIME ON KOKORO

LONELINESS LOOKS GOOD ON YOU! MAKE IT HAPPEN!

HER FLOWER ARRANGEMENTS ARE STUPID! WHY AM I SWEATING?
?
HOLD THE FEELINGS INSIDE!

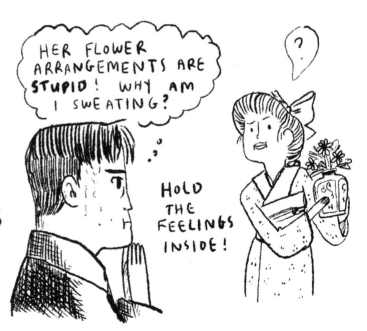

SHALOTT

HANG IN THERE
WHO KNOWS WHAT THE CURSE MAY BE
YEAH
TIRRA
LIRRA

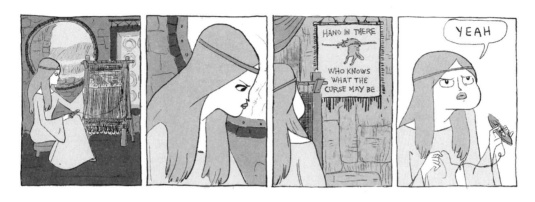

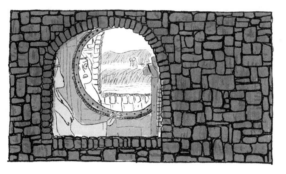

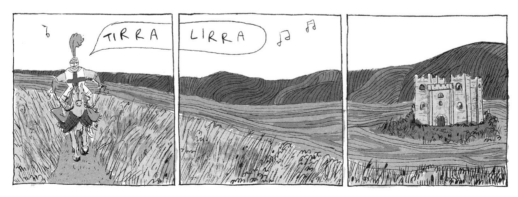

I don't care how hot some random dude is, getting to peek at him is probably not the best reason to invoke a vague curse that takes your life. I'm sure Lancelot was a babe, but still.

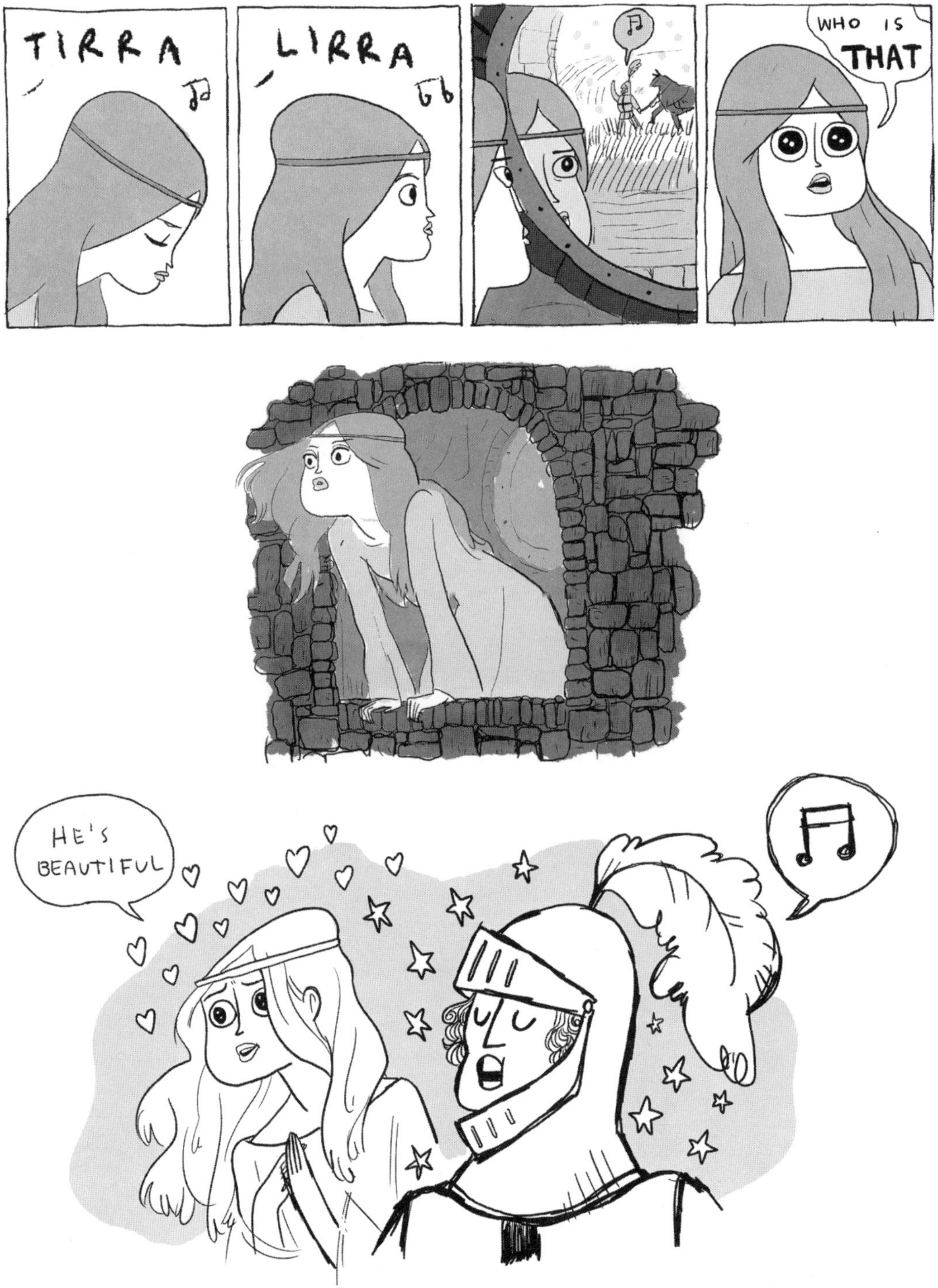
TIRRA
LIRRA
WHO IS THAT
HE'S BEAUTIFUL

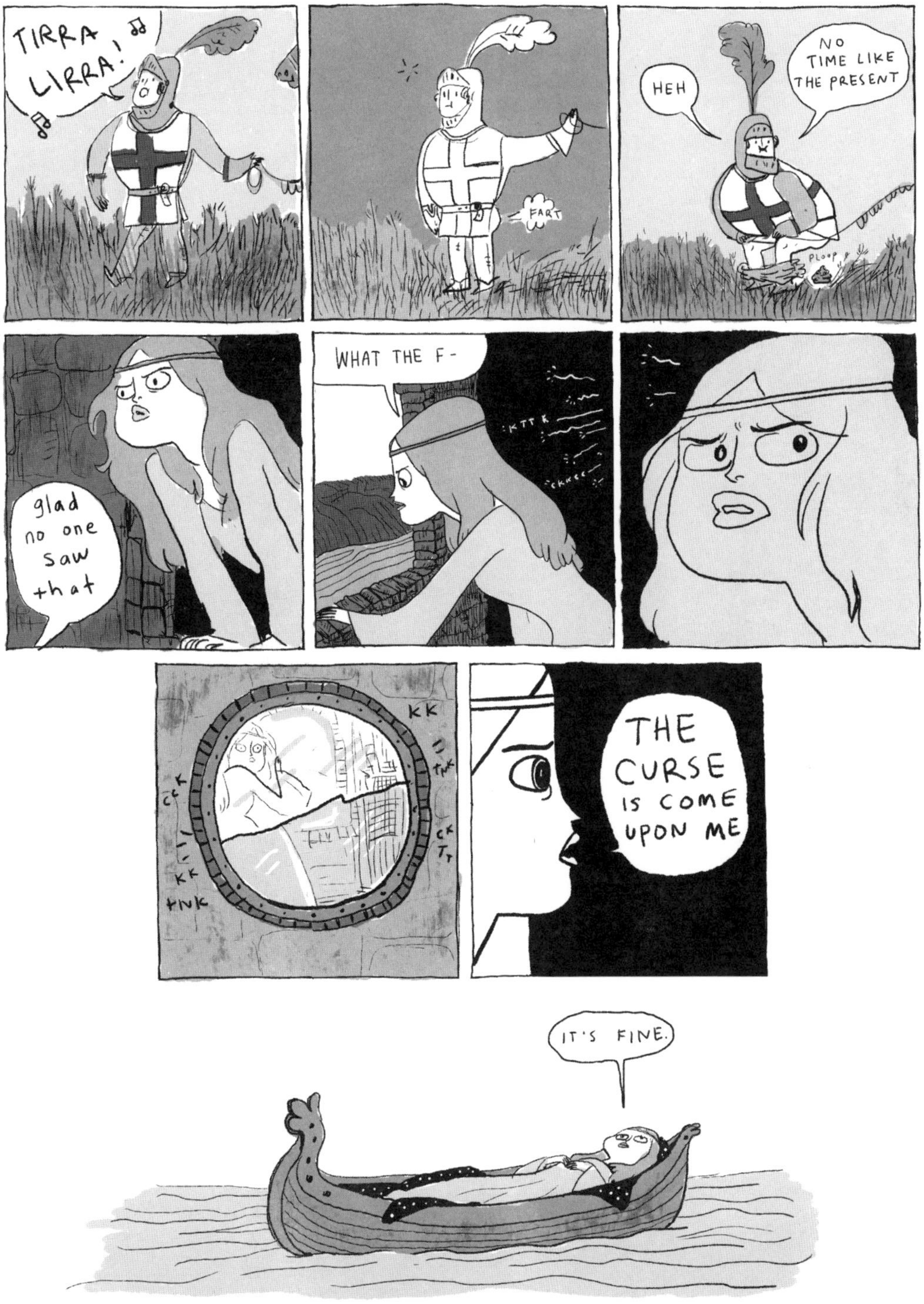
TIRRA LIRRA!
FART
HEH
NO TIME LIKE THE PRESENT
PLOOP
glad no one saw that
WHAT THE F-
KTTK
THE CURSE IS COME UPON ME
IT'S FINE.

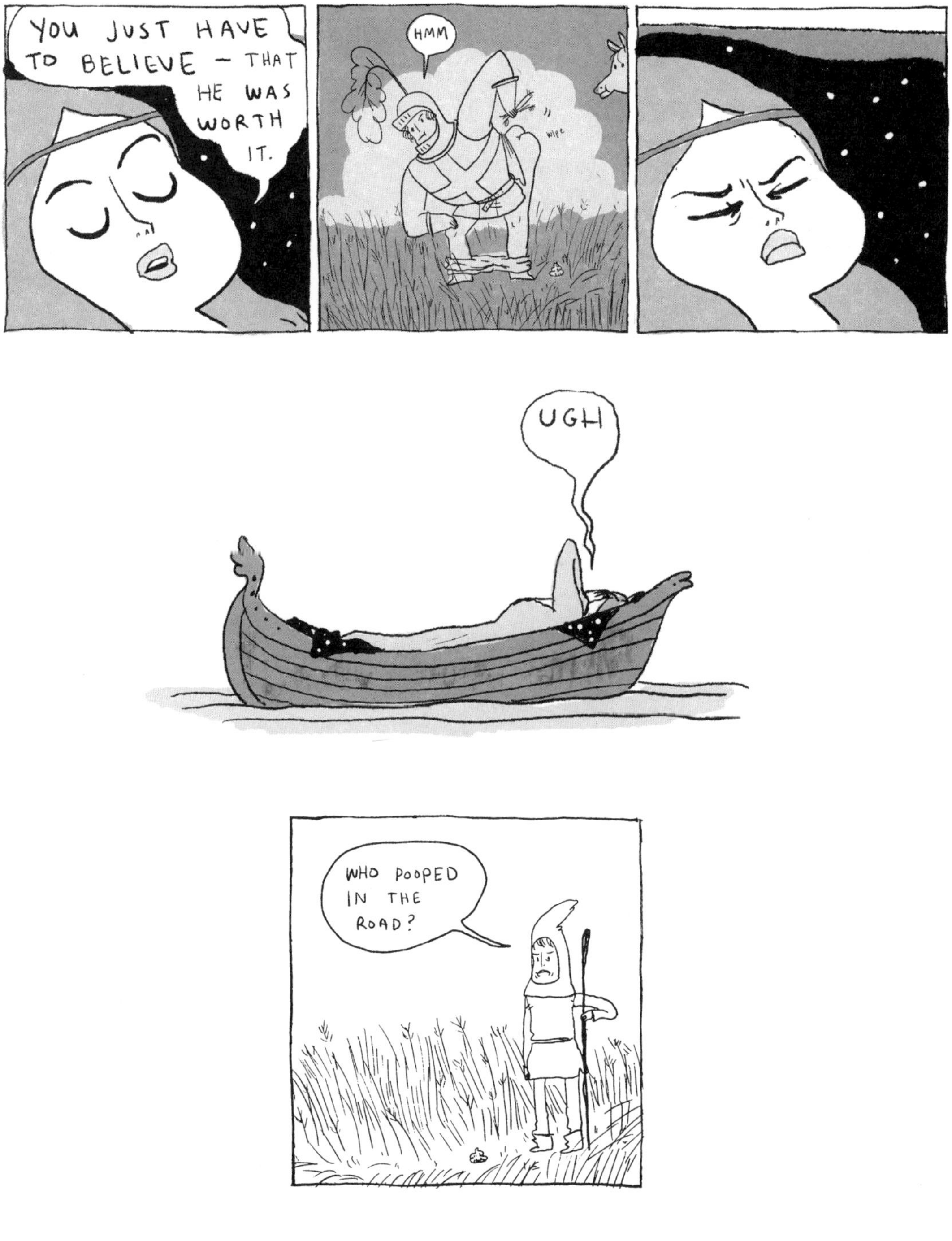
YOU JUST HAVE TO BELIEVE - THAT HE WAS WORTH IT.
HMM
UGH
WHO POOPED IN THE ROAD?

Femme Fatale

TROPE
MY PACKAGE, FINALLY
SIGN PLEASE
IS- IS IT A GUN??
IT'S A KNITTED HAT
I JUST THOUGHT ...
I ENJOY GUNS AND CRAFTS. DON'T BOX ME IN.
OK

MODERN SPY
EVER SINCE I GOT MARRIED ALL MY SOCIAL NETWORK ADS ARE ABOUT BABIES. IT'S CRAZY.
I KNOW - WHEN I LOG ON IT'S JUST A WALL OF ADS LIKE "KILL YOUR LOUSY HUSBAND!"
IT'S LIKE, GET OUT OF MY LIFE, GOOGLE
EXACTLY

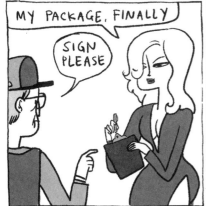

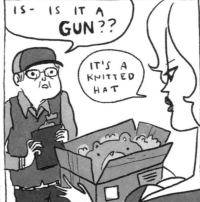

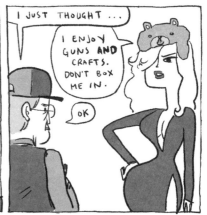

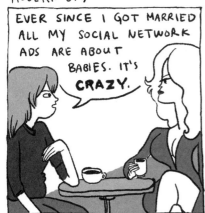

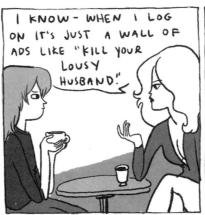

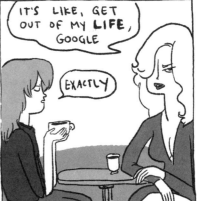

Dames like this are *stranger danger* and you need to watch out. But you know, there's more to their lives than walking through a detective's door in a cloud of fog.

THAT AIN'T RIGHT

DOC YOU GOTTA HELP ME
I GOT LEGS... THAT WON'T QUIT
THAT'S CONTAGIOUS!!

YOU'RE A BUM, I'M A BUM

IF YOU'RE SO SMART, HOW'D YOU END UP WITH A CROOK LIKE ME
CHARLIE YOU KNOW I WAS ALWAYS BAD AT MAKING CHOICES
CHARLIE IS ROTTEN, ROTTEN I TELL YOU
SO DON'T DATE HIM
THAT LEAVES JOHNNY, BUT JOHNNY ... IS TWO BIT
GIRL DON'T DATE HIM EITHER

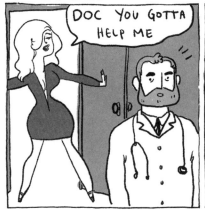

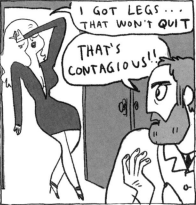

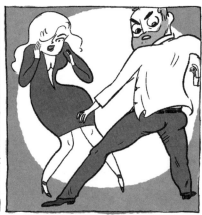

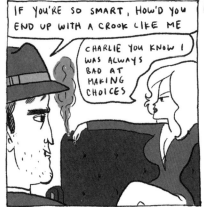

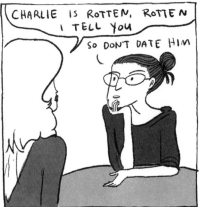

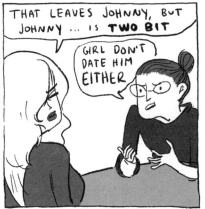

FEMME FATALE 24/7

AIN'T THIS A PRETTY PICTURE. ALL THE OFFICES IN ALL THE WORLD, AND A DAME LIKE YOU WALKS INTO MINE

IT'S NOT LIKE THAT

SURE, I'M NO GOOD. WHY THEY OUGHTA LOCK ME UP AND THROW AWAY THE KEY

BUT THIS IS JUST A REGULAR DENTIST APPOINTMENT NO OFFENCE

YOU ARE **NOT** GETTING A STICKER

SUITS YOU

YOU CROSSED ME, JOHNNY

BABY - NO

I'M SORRY JOHNNY

BROADSIDE BALLADS

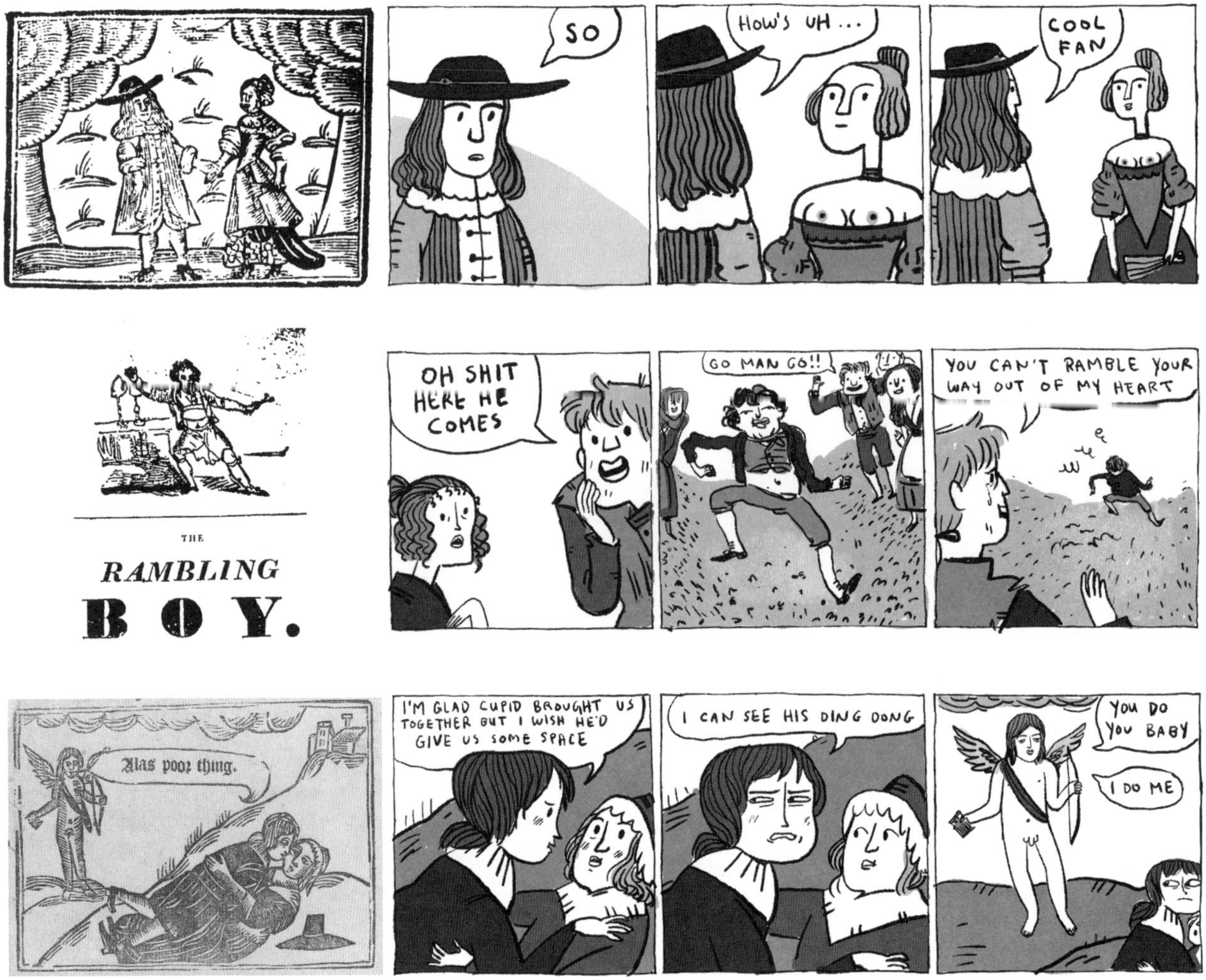
SO
HOW'S UH ...
COOL FAN
THE
RAMBLING
BOY.
OH SHIT HERE HE COMES
GO MAN GO!!
YOU CAN'T RAMBLE YOUR WAY OUT OF MY HEART
Alas poor thing.
I'M GLAD CUPID BROUGHT US TOGETHER BUT I WISH HE'D GIVE US SOME SPACE
I CAN SEE HIS DING DONG
YOU DO YOU BABY
I DO ME

All broadside images were taken from the Bodleian Library (ballads.bodleian.ox.ac.uk). The University of California also has a great collection (ebba.english.ucsb.edu). Please take a look! Broadside illustrations were often used over again for different songs, so it's not unusual to see them pop up in new places, though perhaps comic riffs is a new one.

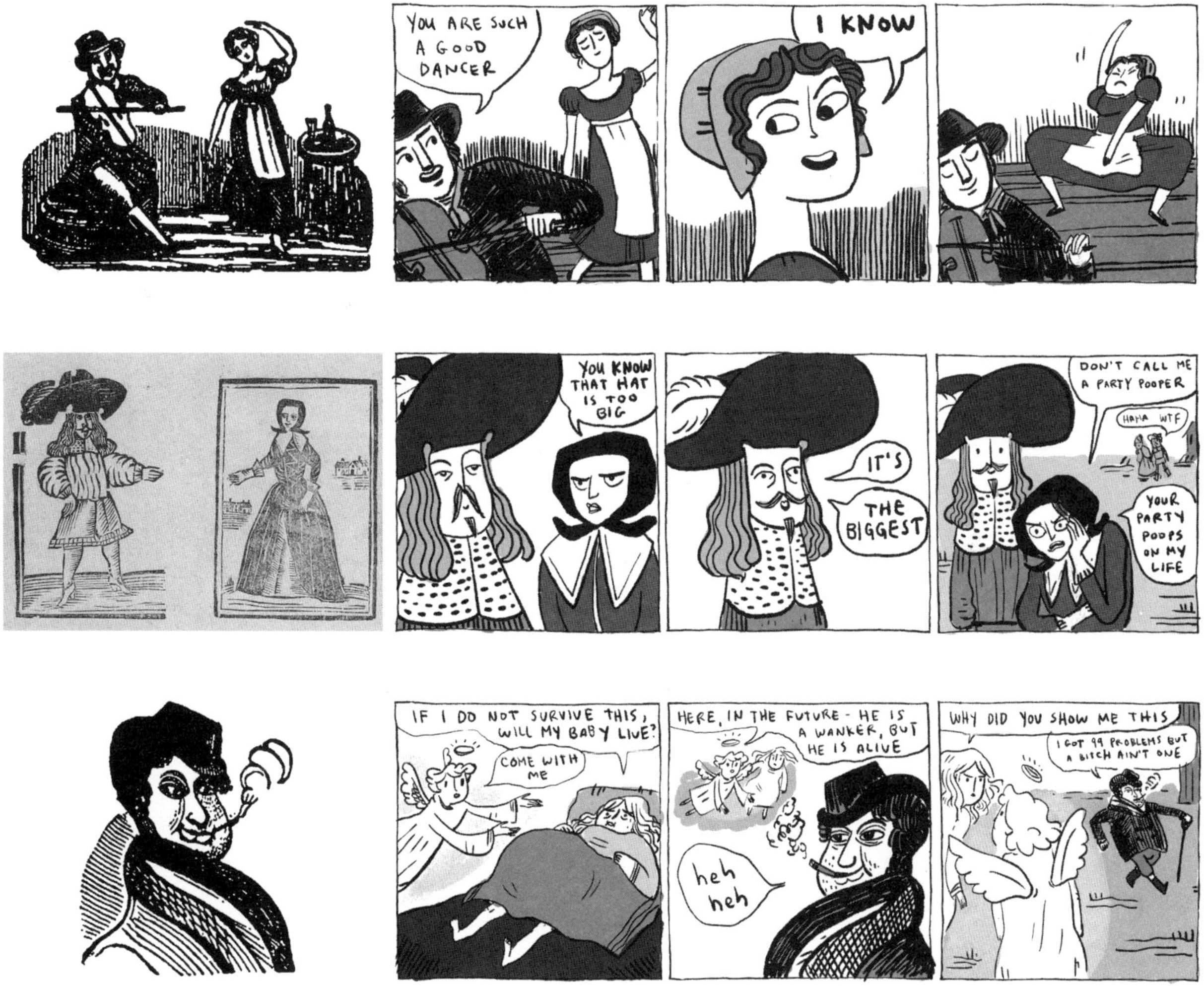
YOU ARE SUCH A GOOD DANCER
I KNOW
YOU KNOW THAT HAT IS TOO BIG
IT'S
THE BIGGEST
DON'T CALL ME A PARTY POOPER
HAHA WTF
YOUR PARTY POOPS ON MY LIFE
IF I DO NOT SURVIVE THIS, WILL MY BABY LIVE?
COME WITH ME
HERE, IN THE FUTURE - HE IS A WANKER, BUT HE IS ALIVE
heh heh
WHY DID YOU SHOW ME THIS
I GOT 99 PROBLEMS BUT A BITCH AIN'T ONE

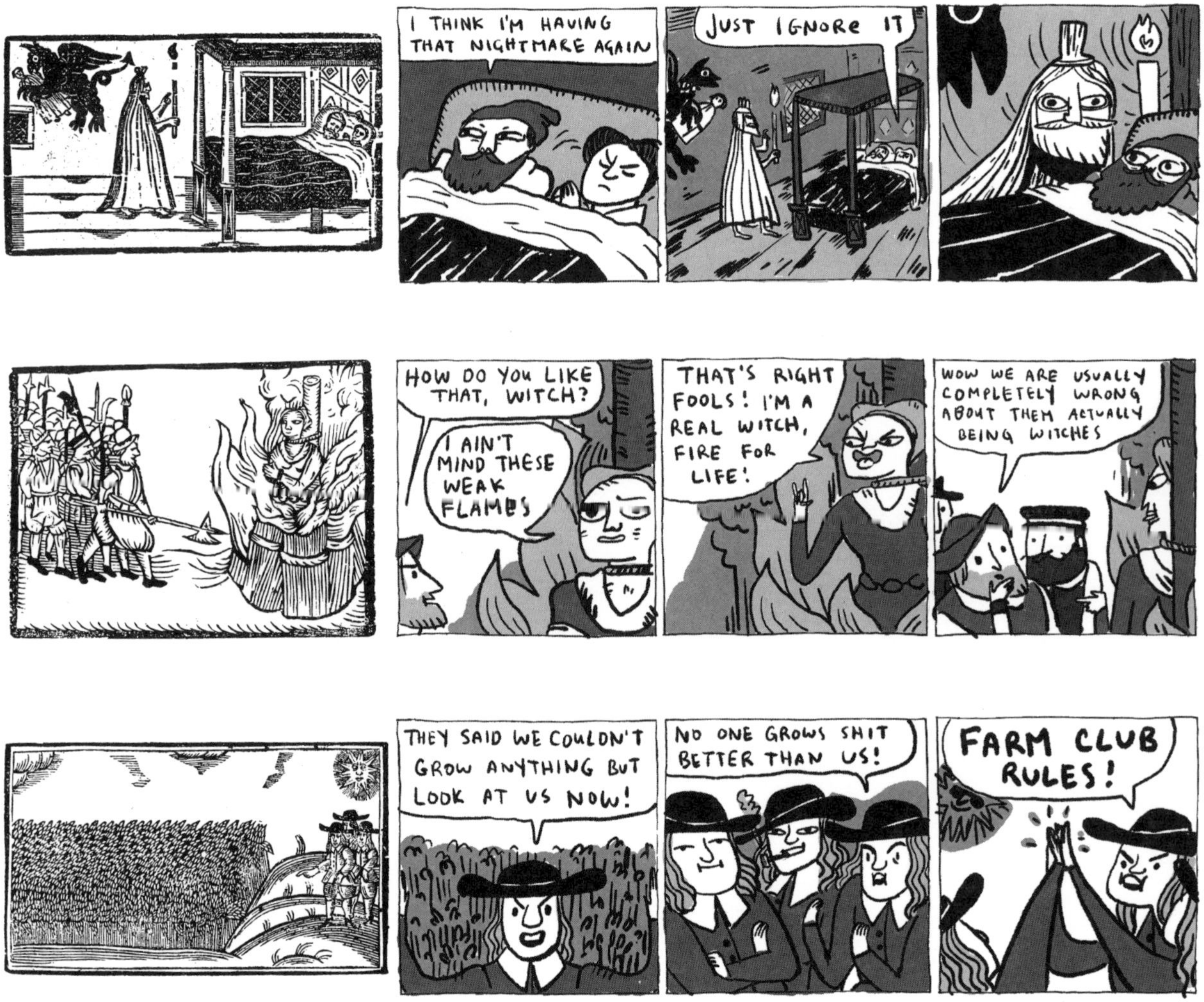
I THINK I'M HAVING THAT NIGHTMARE AGAIN
JUST IGNORE IT
HOW DO YOU LIKE THAT, WITCH?
I AIN'T MIND THESE WEAK FLAMES
THAT'S RIGHT FOOLS! I'M A REAL WITCH, FIRE FOR LIFE!
WOW WE ARE USUALLY COMPLETELY WRONG ABOUT THEM ACTUALLY BEING WITCHES
THEY SAID WE COULDN'T GROW ANYTHING BUT LOOK AT US NOW!
NO ONE GROWS SHIT BETTER THAN US!
FARM CLUB RULES!

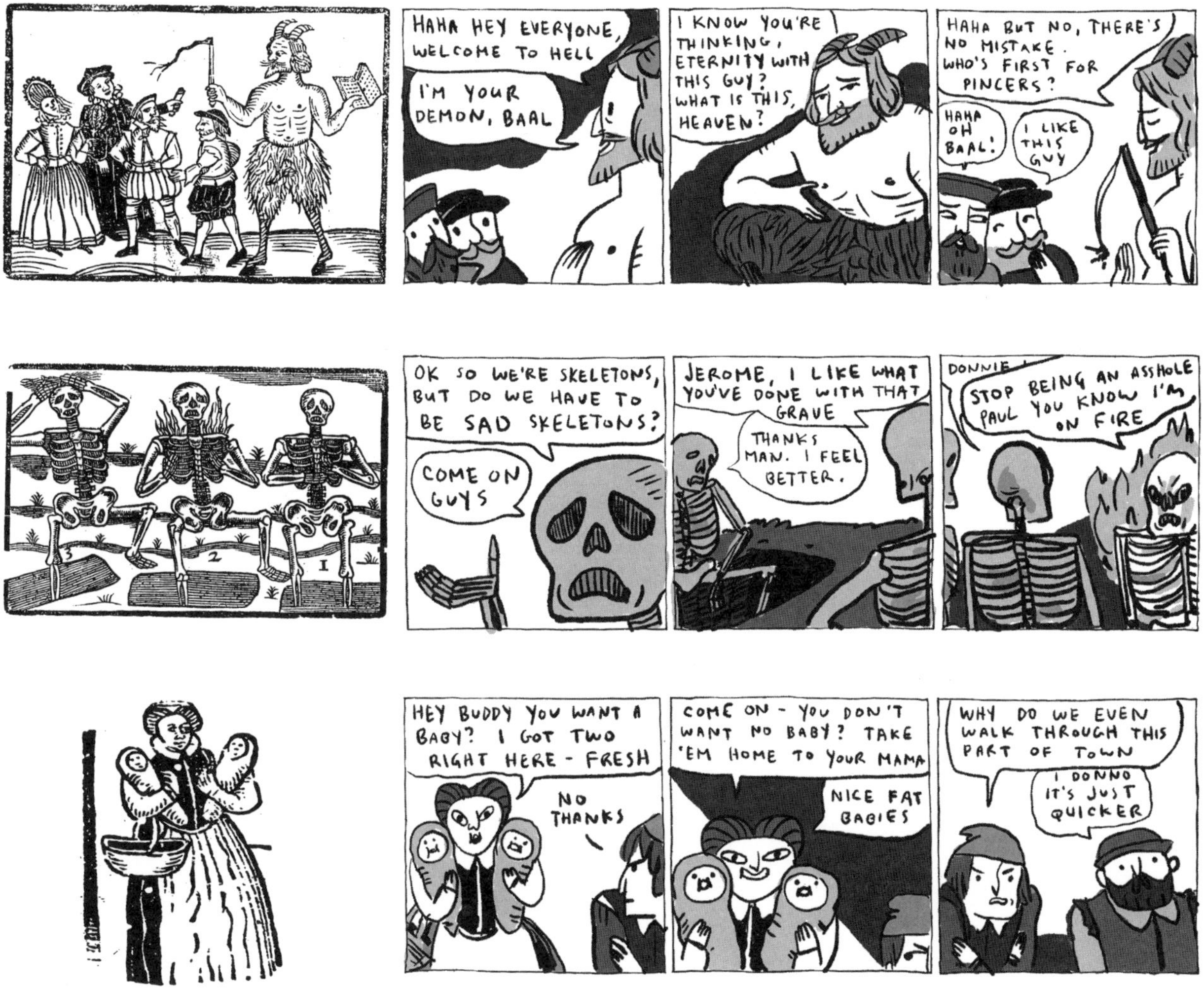
HAHA HEY EVERYONE, WELCOME TO HELL
I'M YOUR DEMON, BAAL
I KNOW YOU'RE THINKING, ETERNITY WITH THIS GUY? WHAT IS THIS, HEAVEN?
HAHA BUT NO, THERE'S NO MISTAKE. WHO'S FIRST FOR PINCERS?
HAHA OH BAAL!
I LIKE THIS GUY
OK SO WE'RE SKELETONS, BUT DO WE HAVE TO BE SAD SKELETONS?
COME ON GUYS
JEROME, I LIKE WHAT YOU'VE DONE WITH THAT GRAVE
THANKS MAN. I FEEL BETTER.
DONNIE!
STOP BEING AN ASSHOLE PAUL YOU KNOW I'M ON FIRE
HEY BUDDY YOU WANT A BABY? I GOT TWO RIGHT HERE - FRESH
NO THANKS
COME ON - YOU DON'T WANT NO BABY? TAKE 'EM HOME TO YOUR MAMA
NICE FAT BABIES
WHY DO WE EVEN WALK THROUGH THIS PART OF TOWN
I DONNO IT'S JUST QUICKER

HEY EVERYONE - LET'S MAKE THIS THE BEST TURTLE CLUB PARTY YET
JUST A BUNCH OF COOL GUYS WHO LIKE TO GET DOWN WITH TURTLES
COOL
WAIT, HOLD UP - WTF
OH YEAH MAN, THOMAS BROUGHT A SNAKE
I DONNO, IT'S HIS FIRST TIME
YEAH OK - BUT IT'S LIKE, DID HE EVEN **READ** THE INVITATION

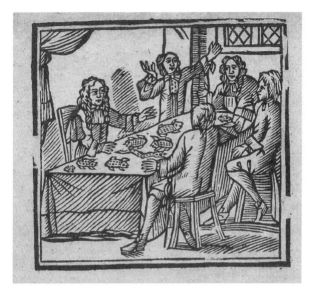

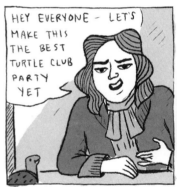

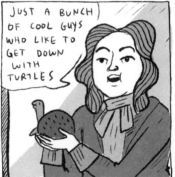

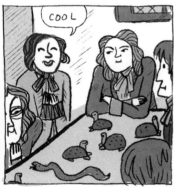

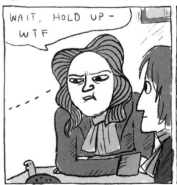

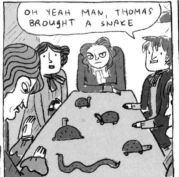

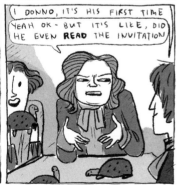

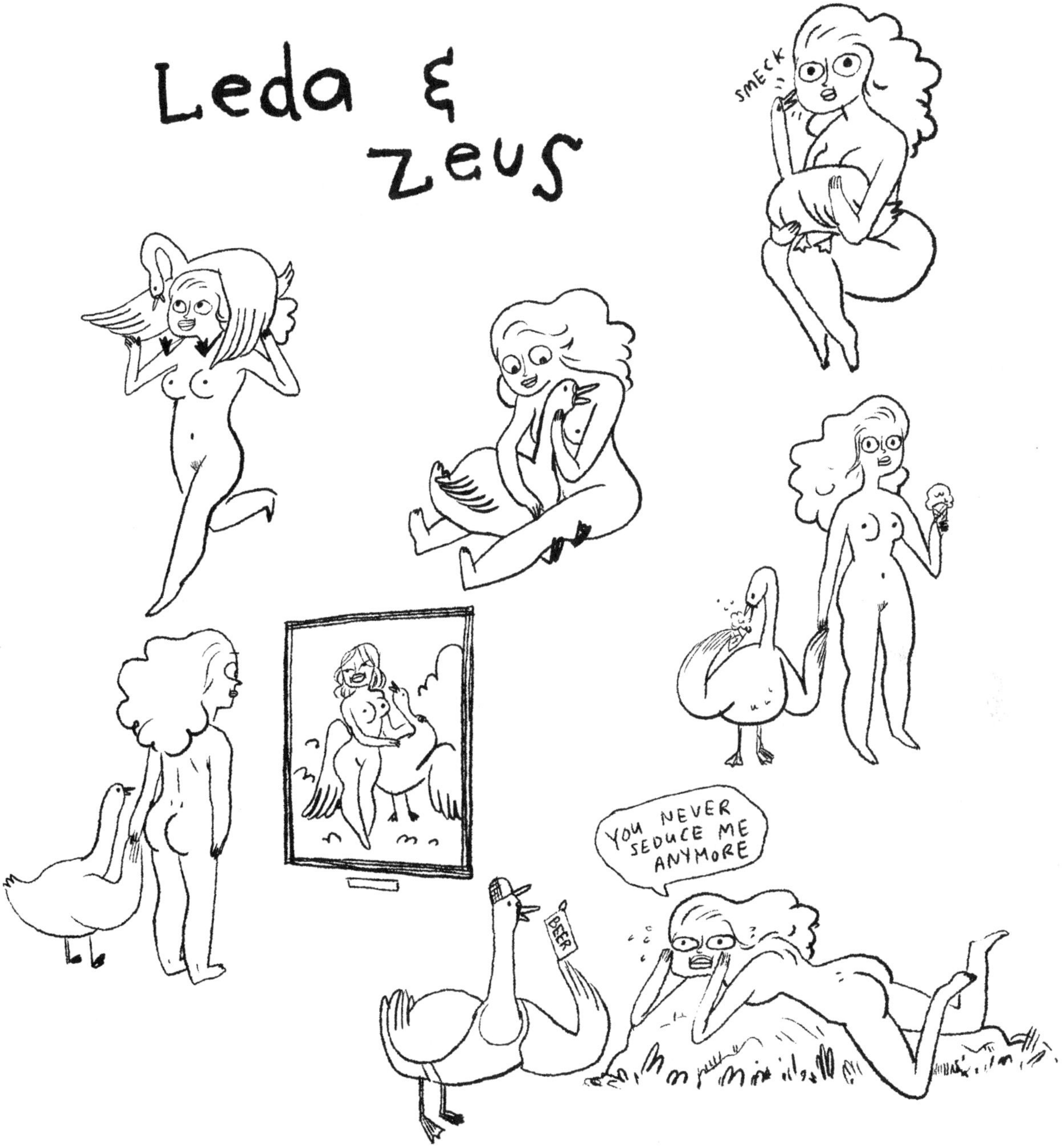
Leda & Zeus
SMECK
BEER
YOU NEVER SEDUCE ME ANYMORE

IT IS A TRUTH UNIVERSALLY ACKNOWLEDGED
THAT A SINGLE SKEPTIC IN POSSESSION OF A LOGICAL MIND
MUST BE IN WANT OF A TRUE BELIEVER

HOUSE FULL OF MULDERS

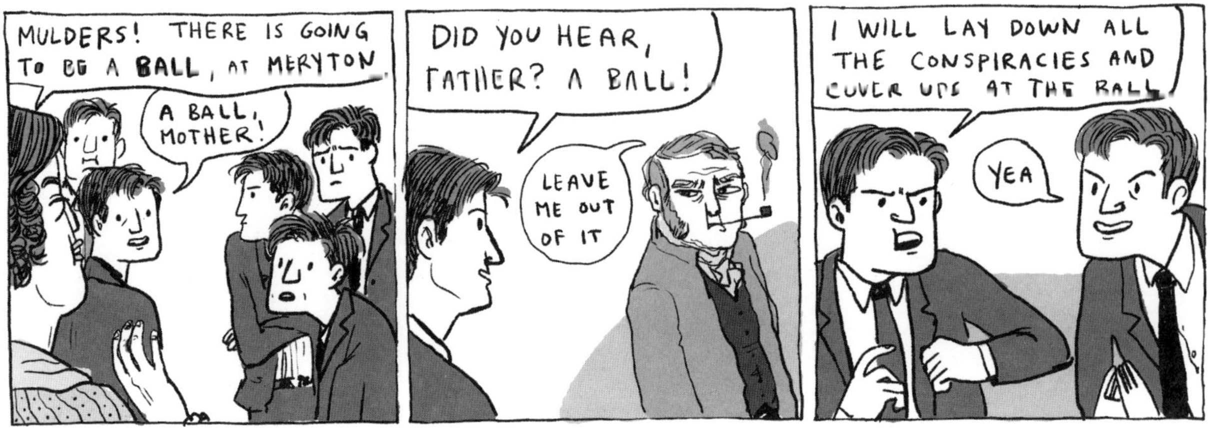

MULDERS! THERE IS GOING TO BE A BALL, AT MERYTON
A BALL, MOTHER!
DID YOU HEAR, FATHER? A BALL!
LEAVE ME OUT OF IT
I WILL LAY DOWN ALL THE CONSPIRACIES AND COVER UPS AT THE BALL
YEA

In a world
With a million *Pride and Prejudice* jokes and revamps
Here is another one of those

BUT WHAT SHALL I WEAR?
I'M ON IT
THIS METAL BONNET WILL KEEP THE ALIENS OUT
EXCEPT FOR IMPLANTED CHIPS
YOU WILL MAKE SUCH A MATCH IN YOUR METAL BONNETS! LET US VISIT THE HABERDASHERY!
sigh

AND SO

WILL YOU NOT DANCE WITH A MULDER, MISS SCULLY?
I DETEST DANCING
BUT ARE THEY NOT HANDSOME? I DARESAY THEY ARE UNCOMMONLY PRETTY
grunt
I CAN'T BELIEVE I'VE BEEN ASSIGNED HERE

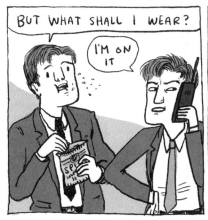

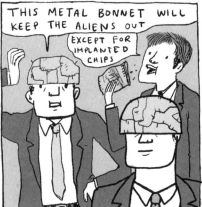

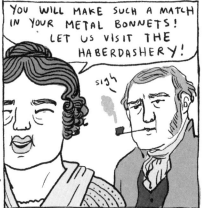

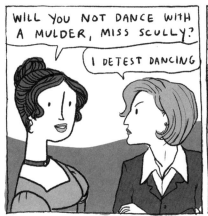

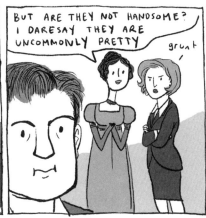

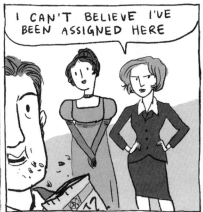

THE INVASION OF CANADA

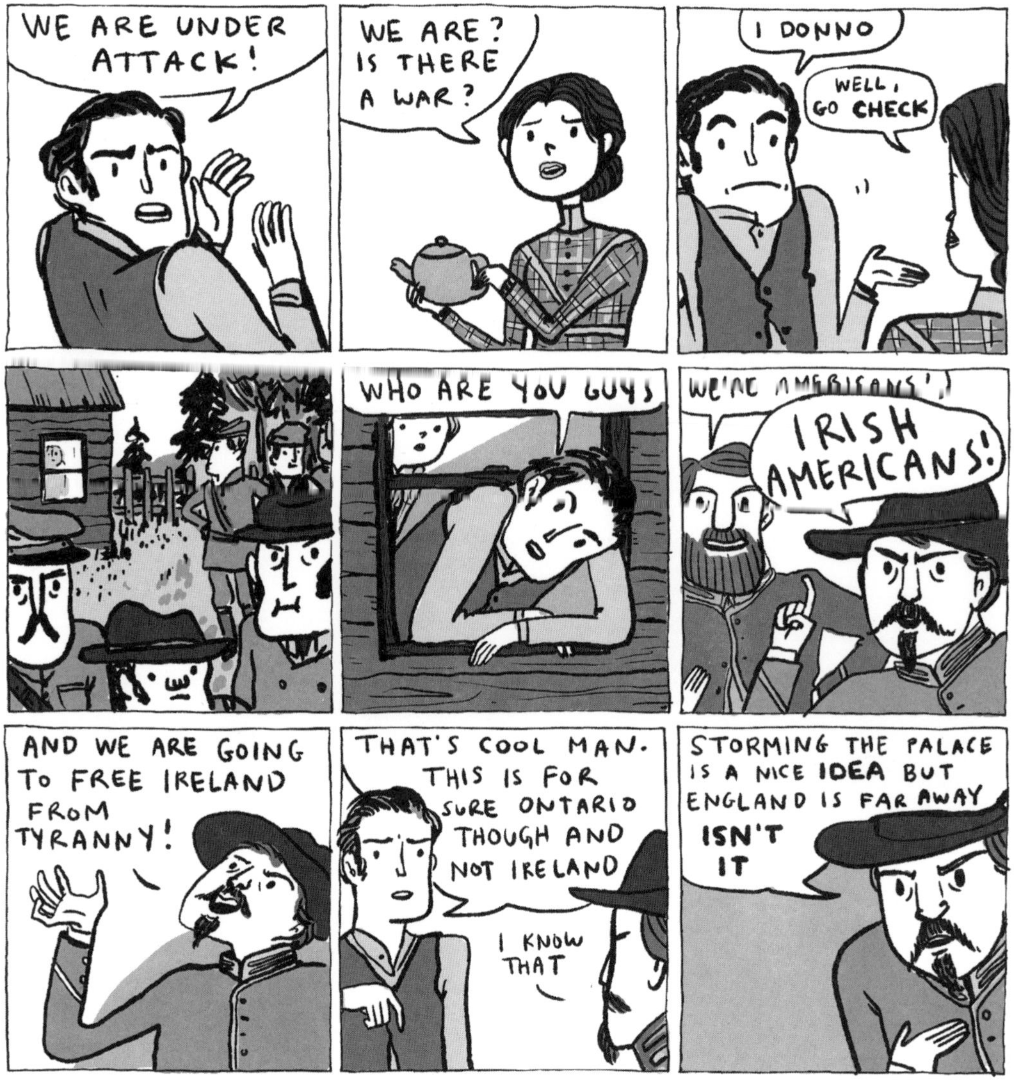

WE ARE UNDER ATTACK!
WE ARE? IS THERE A WAR?
I DONNO
WELL, GO **CHECK**
WHO ARE YOU GUYS
WE'RE AMERICANS!
IRISH AMERICANS!
AND WE ARE GOING TO FREE IRELAND FROM TYRANNY!
THAT'S COOL MAN. THIS IS FOR SURE ONTARIO THOUGH AND NOT IRELAND
I KNOW THAT
STORMING THE PALACE IS A NICE **IDEA** BUT ENGLAND IS FAR AWAY **ISN'T IT**

In Canada, we learn that the Irish American raids of the 1870s provided us with a high horse we like to use even today! Why is America always picking on us? Stop invading us with bad plans to trade us for Ireland. Maybe we don't like to be treated that way, you ever think of that? How *rude*.

WHO WOULD SUSPECT IRISHMEN COMING FROM BUFFALO TO TAKE CANADA HOSTAGE IN EXCHANGE FOR IRELAND!
YEAH PROLLY NO ONE EVER
CANADA IS GIGANTIC THOUGH - NO OFFENSE - AND LIKE, ENGLAND FORGETS WE'RE HERE SOMETIMES I THINK.
- I FEEL LIKE THERE ARE A LOT OF HOLES IN THIS PLAN
NO - THIS PLAN MAKES SENSE OK
YEAH OK
OK THEN
IF ANY OF YOU BURN DOWN MY HOUSE FOR IRELAND I'M GOING TO BE UPSET
MR. PRESIDENT, OUR OWN MEN ARE INVADING CANADA! RIGHT NOW!
GOOD LORD! WHAT FOR?
TO FREE IRELAND!
TO FREE...
SURE, OK
I FEEL LIKE THERE ARE A LOT OF HOLES IN THAT PLAN

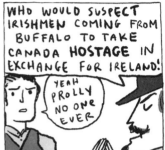

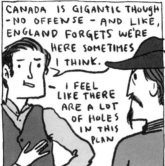

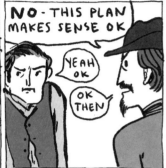

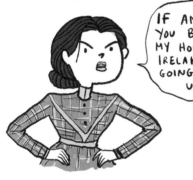

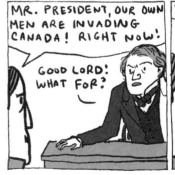

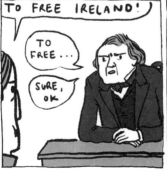

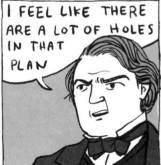

Lady's Favor

I'LL TAKE IT

MY LADY LOVE THREW ME HER HANDKERCHIEF!
BOOGS ON THAT.
DUDE- NO
sniff

TIME TO GO

I'M GOING TO WAR. I NEED A LOCK OF YOUR HAIR
OF COURSE
THANKS BABE
SHHNK
I'M OUT
REMEMBER ME!

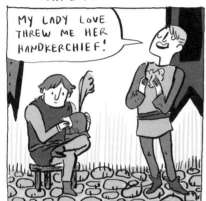

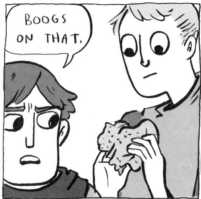

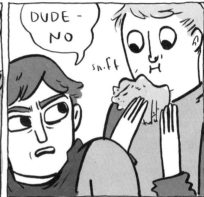

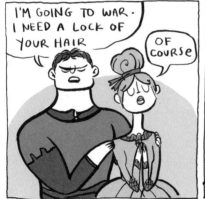

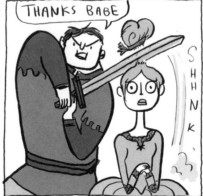

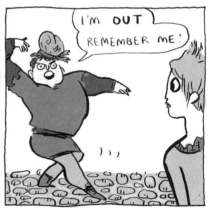

It's always Stupid Medieval Joke Day at my house!

DEMURE

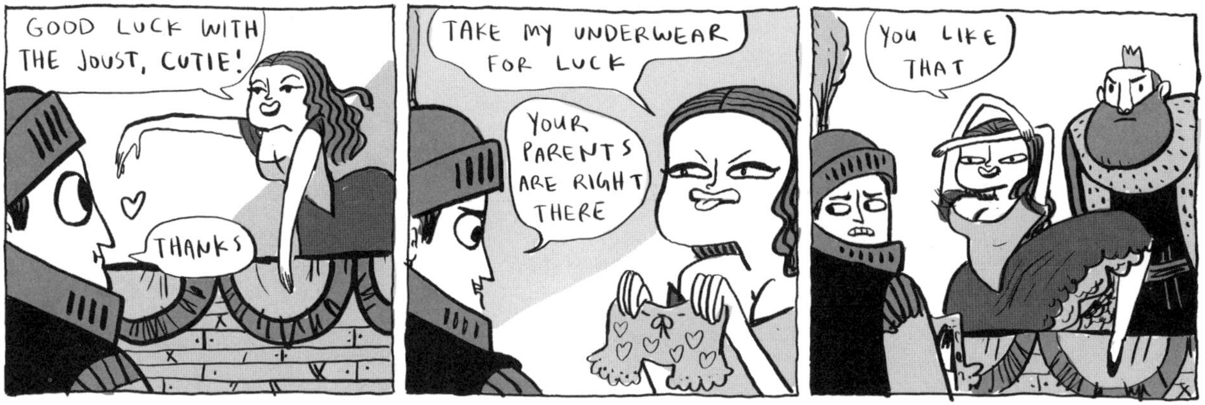
GOOD LUCK WITH THE JOUST, CUTIE!
THANKS
TAKE MY UNDERWEAR FOR LUCK
YOUR PARENTS ARE RIGHT THERE
YOU LIKE THAT

I Need A TOKEN OF LOVE

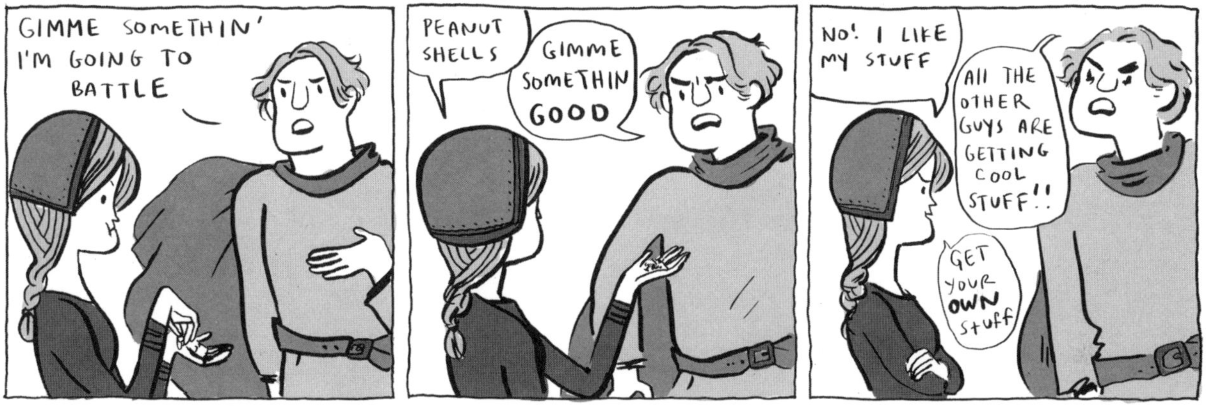
GIMME SOMETHIN' I'M GOING TO BATTLE
PEANUT SHELLS
GIMME SOMETHIN GOOD
NO! I LIKE MY STUFF
ALL THE OTHER GUYS ARE GETTING COOL STUFF!!
GET YOUR OWN STUFF

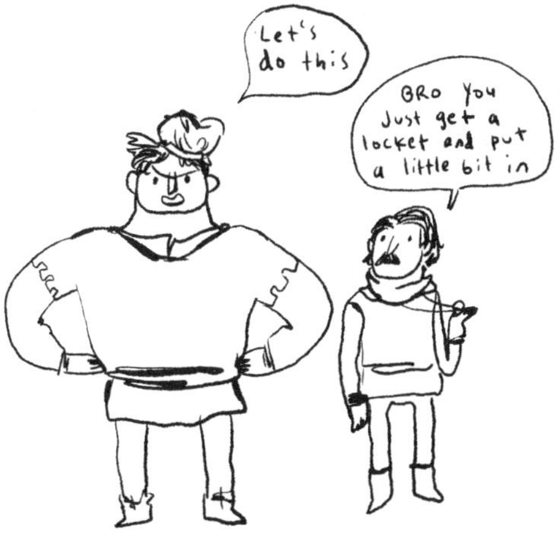
Let's do this
BRO you just get a locket and put a little bit in

TOM LONGBOAT

WOULDN'T SEND MY DOG THERE

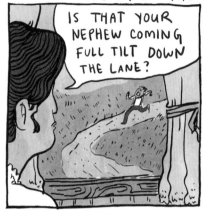

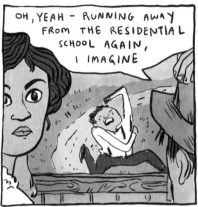

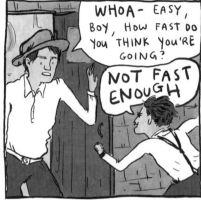

IS THAT YOUR NEPHEW COMING FULL TILT DOWN THE LANE?
OH, YEAH - RUNNING AWAY FROM THE RESIDENTIAL SCHOOL AGAIN, I IMAGINE
WHOA- EASY, BOY, HOW FAST DO YOU THINK YOU'RE GOING?
NOT FAST ENOUGH

TROPHIES PLEASE

HEY HEY! WHAT'S ALL THE HUBUB?
BIG RACE!
YOU DON'T SAY! WHO'S WINNING THE THING?
ME!
SAY WHAT
OH SORRY- I MEANT I WON IT FIVE MINUTES AGO
WOULD HAVE BEEN SIX BUT A HORSE FELL ON ME

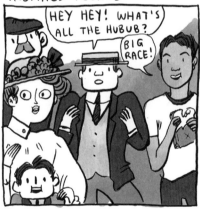

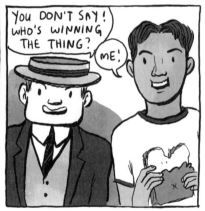

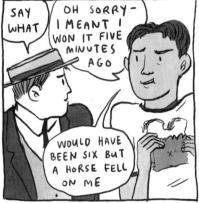

Tom Longboat, Onondaga champion. For a while his name was shorthand for "fast," as in, "you want me to run *that far*? Who do you think I am, Tom Longboat?" I'd like to see you turn your name into shorthand for anything, let alone a living version of the Flash.

TRAINING TECHNIQUES

LOOK AT MY BOY THERE, RUNNING EVERY DAY TILL HE DROPS, A MAN'S WAY TO TRAIN
!
HE LOOKS NEAR DEATH! HIS BODY NEEDS A RECOVERY DAY
THAT'S STUPID AND LAZY AND WHO ASKED **YOU**
WINNING EVERY RACE DOESN'T MAKE YOU AN EXPERT -
PUKE IT OUT BOY
YES, IT DOES
BLEUGGH

TOUGH CALL

HOW'S THE BIG SPORTS EXCLUSIVE GOING?
WELL...
HE'S TALL, PHOTOGENIC
- FRONT PAGE STUFF
RUNS FASTER THAN ANYONE, VERY MODEST
- HELL OF A GUY
LADIES LOVE HIM
- ALL KINDS OF LADIES
SO I'M HAVING A HARD TIME COMING UP WITH A PROPERLY RACIST HEADLINE
YET I BELIEVE YOU CAN DO IT

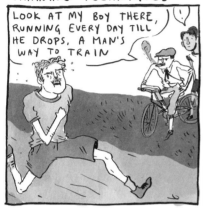

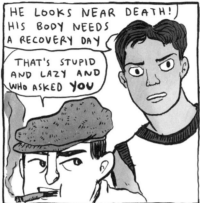

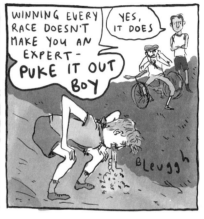

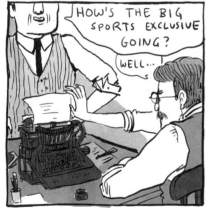

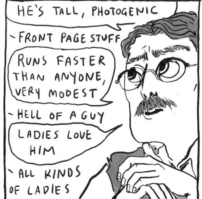

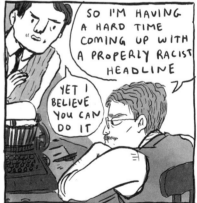

TWICE WOUNDED IN WWI

LONGBOAT! GLAD YOU'RE NOT DEAD LIKE THE RUMOURS SAID, I NEED A TOP RUNNER FOR THIS MESSAGE

YES SIR

GREAT- SO I MAPPED OUT WHERE YOU NEED TO GO. THIS AREA.

ARE THE SKULLS HELPFUL? ANYWAY THIS IS YOUR ROUTE

HAPPY RETIREMENT

SAY- YOU'RE TOM LONGBOAT, THE RUNNER! I HEAR YOU'RE HANGING AROUND BARS THESE DAYS, FOR SHAME

OH COME ON, THAT'S SOME GUY WHO'S BEEN IMPERSONATING ME, HAVE A LITTLE IMAGINATION

PFF

OK JUST KIDDING, I'M NOT TOM LONGBOAT, I'M BABE RUTH

ARE YOU REALLY BABE RUTH THOUGH

MONTURIOL'S AMAZING SUBMARINE

ICTINEO I

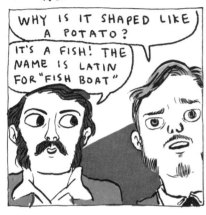

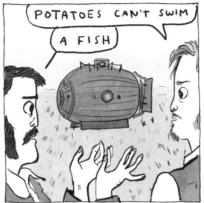

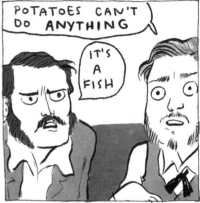

WHY IS IT SHAPED LIKE A POTATO?
IT'S A FISH! THE NAME IS LATIN FOR "FISH BOAT"
POTATOES CAN'T SWIM
A FISH
POTATOES CAN'T DO ANYTHING
IT'S A FISH

ROOM FOR FOUR

BEEP BEEP HERE COMES THE FUTURE AM I RIGHT
OH MY GOD IT'S SO CUTE
UM NO IT'S NOT CUTE
IT'S WICKED
IT'S SO LITTLE AND FAT
STOP THAT
I'M GOING TO LOOK AT CORAL WITHOUT YOU
FWOOM

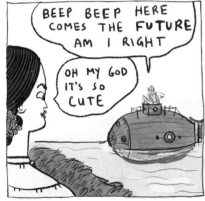

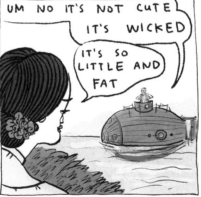

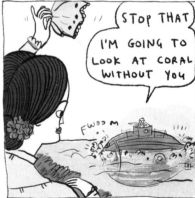

Narcís Monturiol i Estarriol might not have been the first person to think up a submarine, but he was the first to put a lot of things together to make it work. Come with me, under the sea, in my little fat submarine! Toot toot!

ONE MILE AN HOUR

SO YOU WANT THE SPANISH NAVY, IN ALL SERIOUSNESS, TO RIDE AROUND

IN FRONT OF EVERYONE

IN SLOW MOVING SUNKEN JUGS

I CAN ADD STEAM PROPULSION!

FARTING JUGS

DRAWING UNDER PRESSURE IS HARD OK

SCRAP METAL

HOW'S THE INVENTING BUSINESS?

LOUSY

SO NO ONE IS INTERESTED IN YOUR UNDERWATER COMMUNIST BARRELS

SUBMARINE

SHOW ME AN INVENTOR WHO CAN'T SAY THE SAME

UTOPIAN. SUBMARINE.

FOUNDING FATHERS (IN A MALL)

WORTH IT

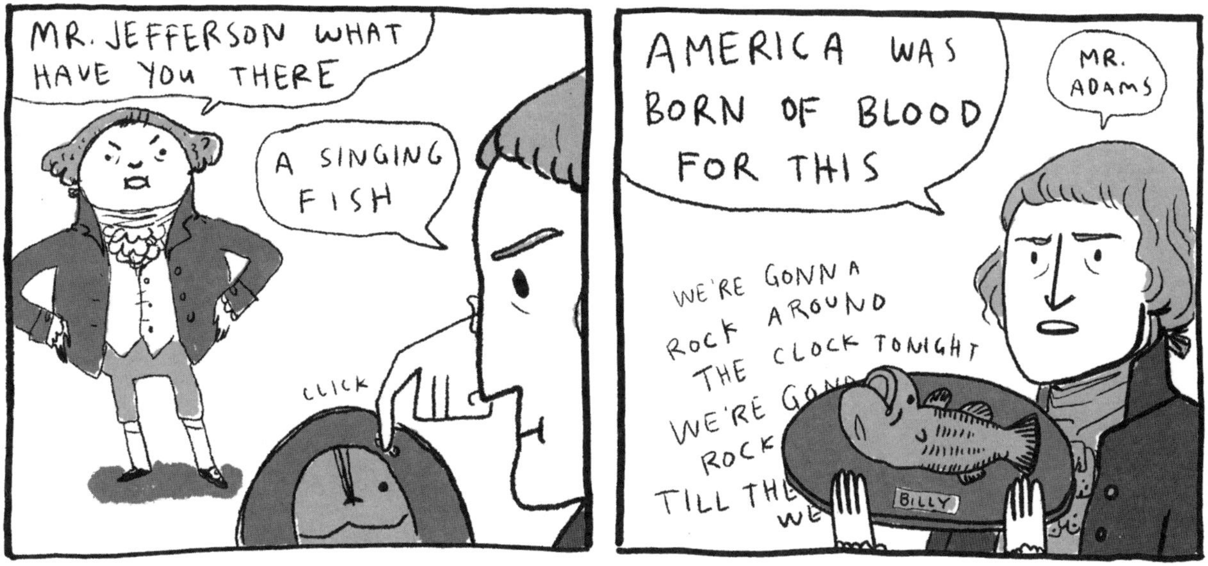
MR. JEFFERSON WHAT HAVE YOU THERE
A SINGING FISH
CLICK
AMERICA WAS BORN OF BLOOD FOR THIS
MR. ADAMS
WE'RE GONNA ROCK AROUND THE CLOCK TONIGHT
BILLY

STUCK

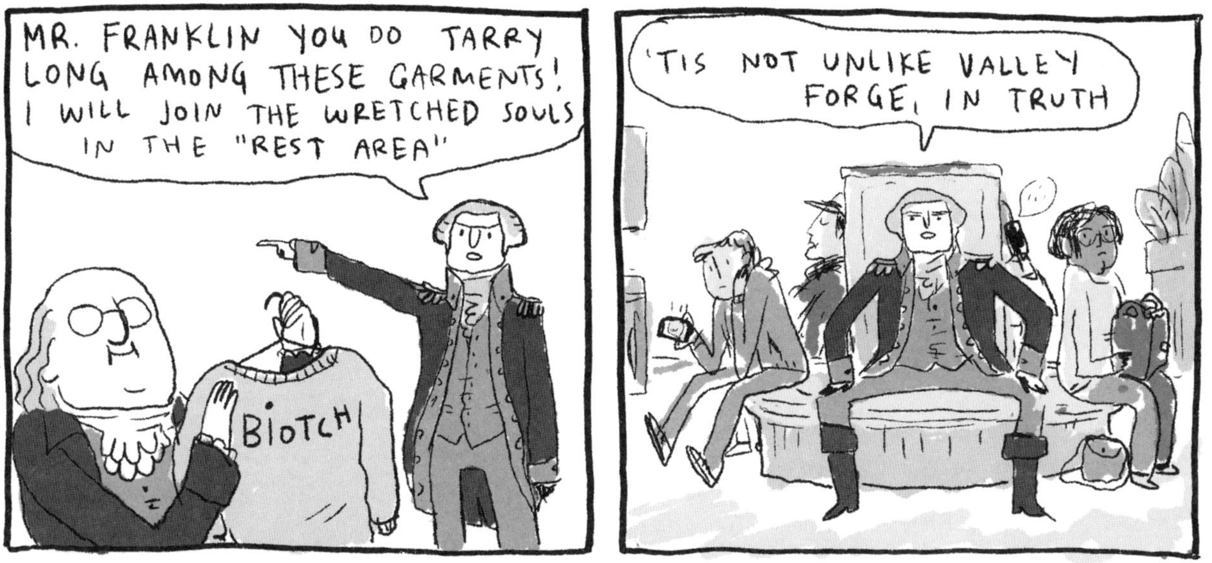
MR. FRANKLIN YOU DO TARRY LONG AMONG THESE GARMENTS! I WILL JOIN THE WRETCHED SOULS IN THE "REST AREA"
BIOTCH
'TIS NOT UNLIKE VALLEY FORGE, IN TRUTH

TOO MANY FLIES

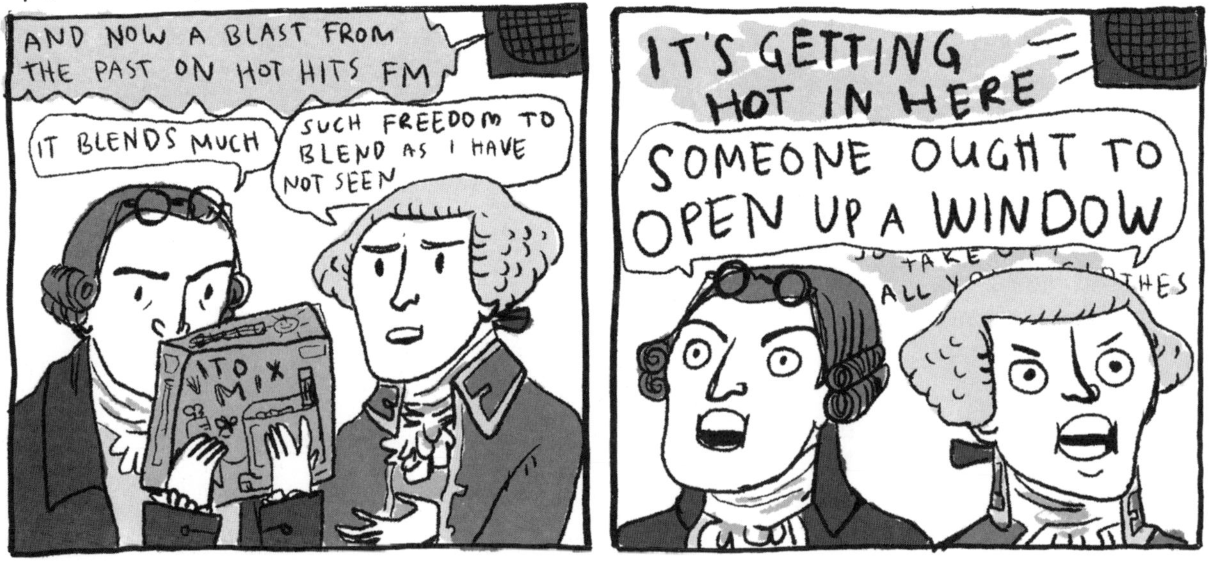
AND NOW A BLAST FROM THE PAST ON HOT HITS FM
IT BLENDS MUCH
SUCH FREEDOM TO BLEND AS I HAVE NOT SEEN
VITO MIX
IT'S GETTING HOT IN HERE
SOMEONE OUGHT TO OPEN UP A WINDOW

SALTPETER, JOHN

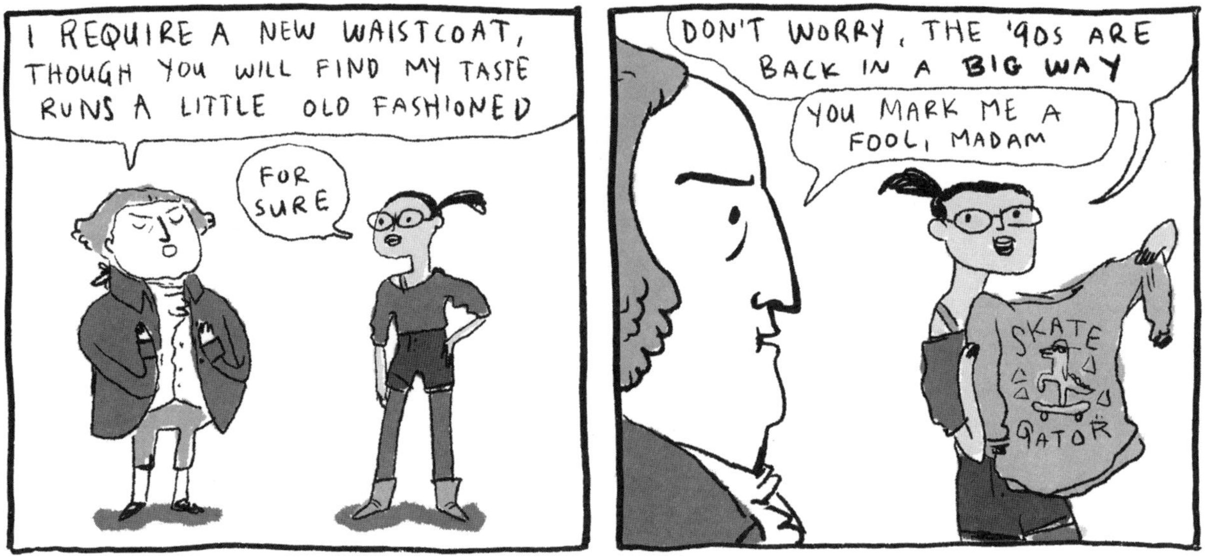
I REQUIRE A NEW WAISTCOAT, THOUGH YOU WILL FIND MY TASTE RUNS A LITTLE OLD FASHIONED
FOR SURE
DON'T WORRY, THE '90S ARE BACK IN A BIG WAY
YOU MARK ME A FOOL, MADAM
SKATE GATOR

SHOE LACES

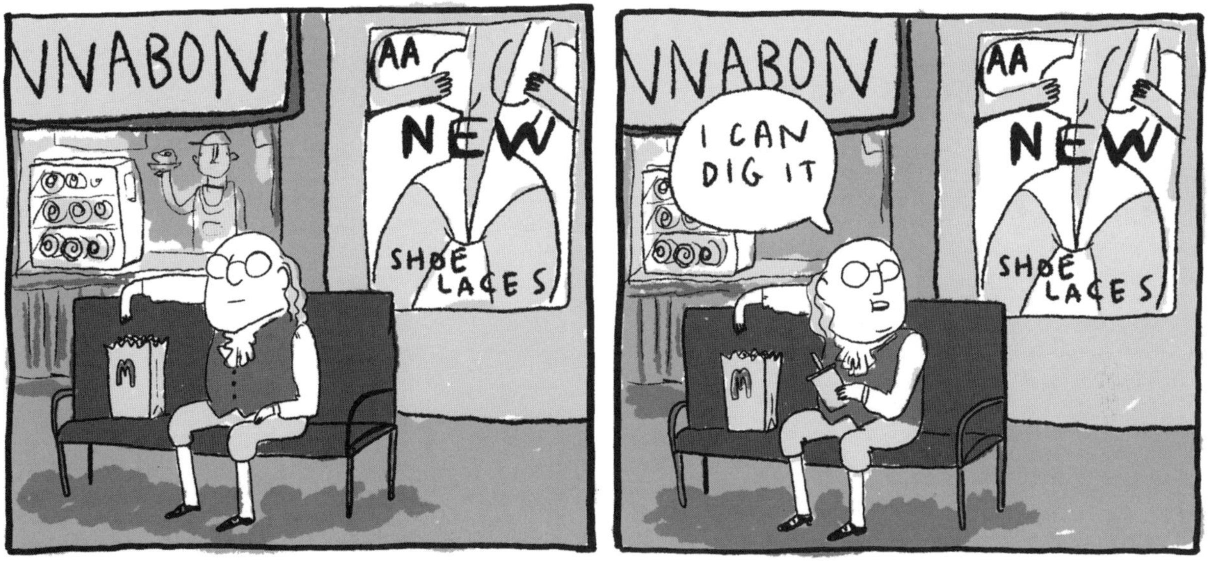
VNABON
AA
NEW
SHOE LACES
M
I CAN DIG IT

I'LL BE HERE ALL NIGHT

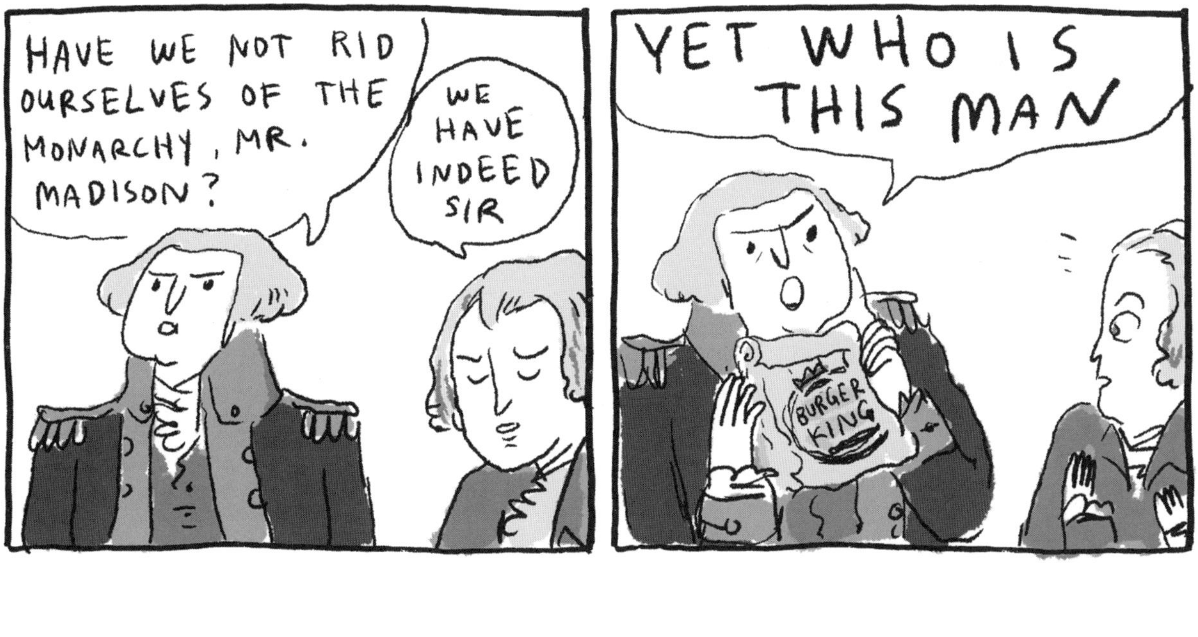
HAVE WE NOT RID OURSELVES OF THE MONARCHY, MR. MADISON?
WE HAVE INDEED SIR
YET WHO IS THIS MAN
BURGER KING

FOUNDING FATHERS

(STUCK IN AN AMUSEMENT PARK)

INFINITY

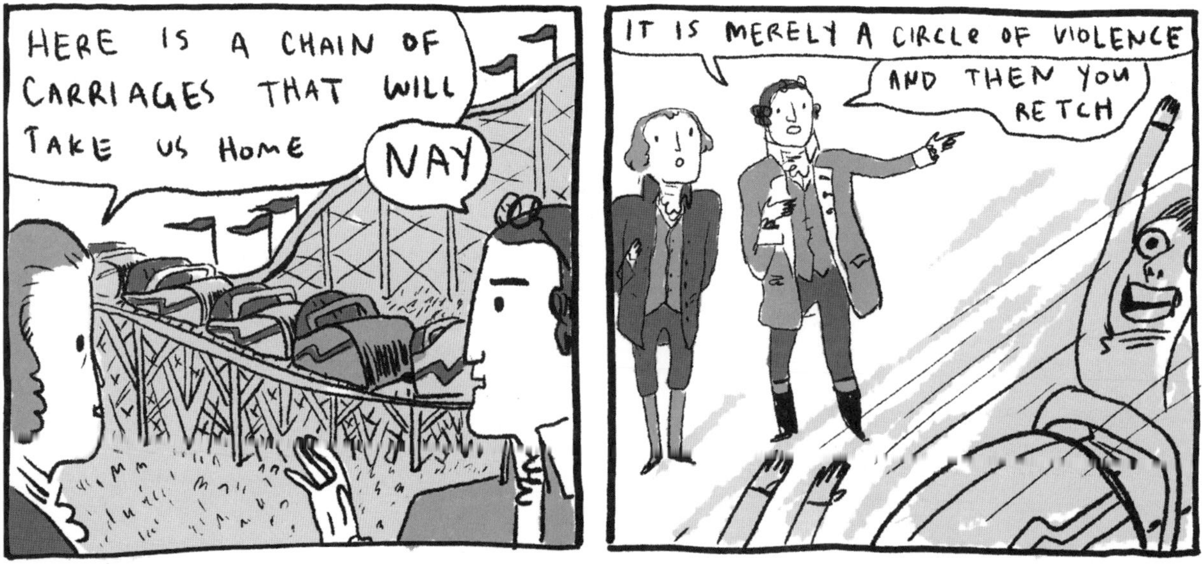
HERE IS A CHAIN OF CARRIAGES THAT WILL TAKE US HOME
NAY
IT IS MERELY A CIRCLE OF VIOLENCE
AND THEN YOU RETCH

THE THOMAS PAINE RIDE

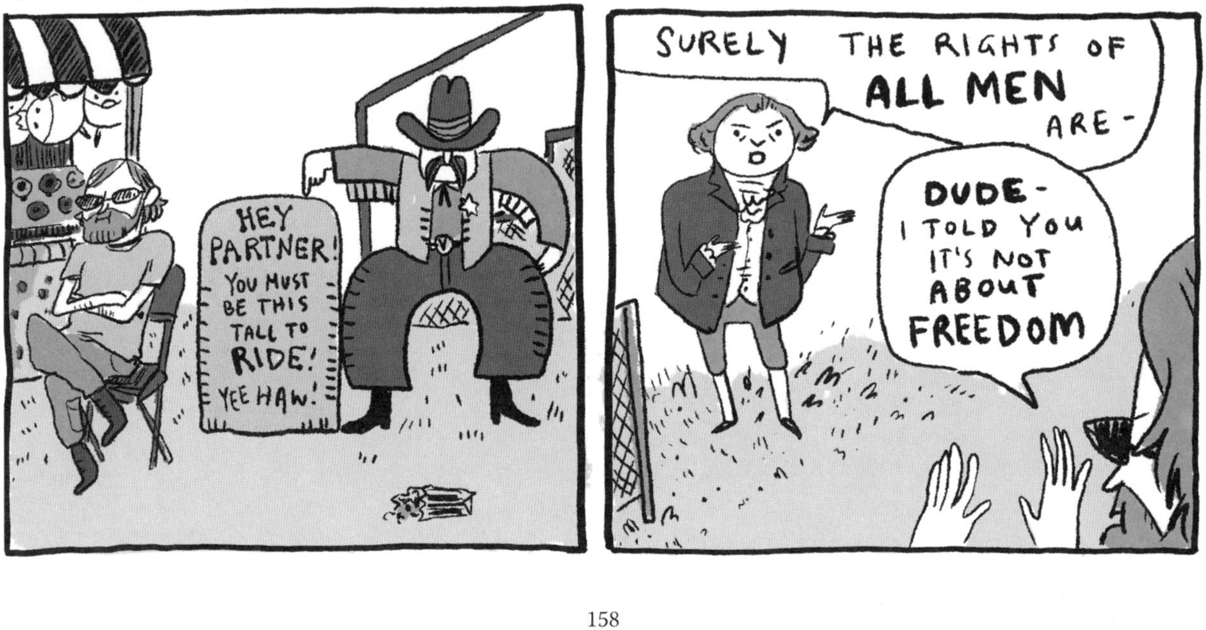
HEY PARTNER! YOU MUST BE THIS TALL TO RIDE! YEE HAW!
SURELY THE RIGHTS OF ALL MEN ARE-
DUDE- I TOLD YOU IT'S NOT ABOUT FREEDOM

SUSTENANCE

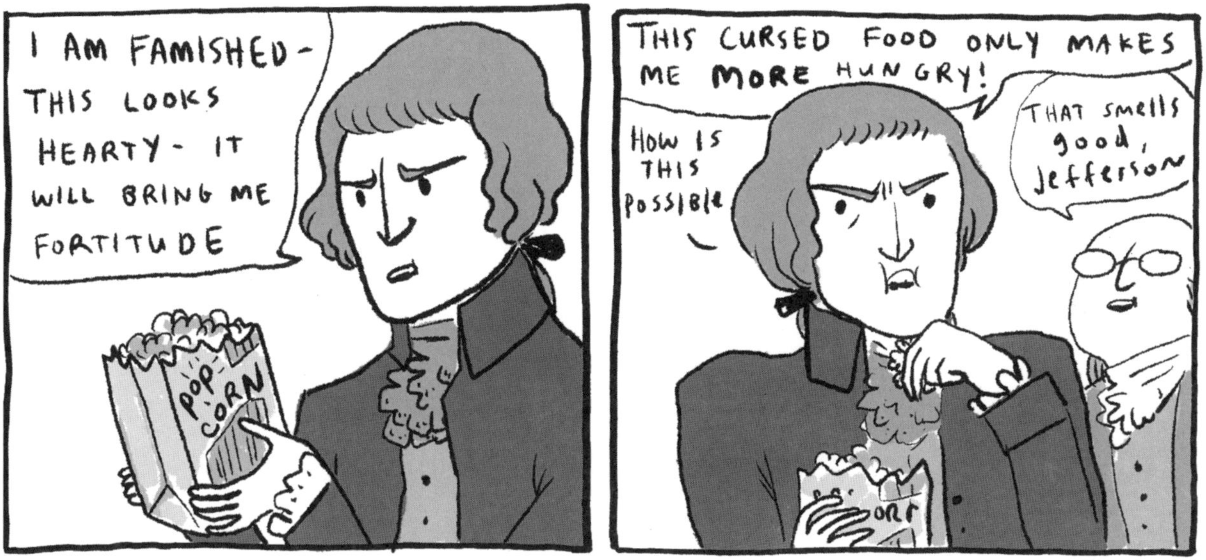
I AM FAMISHED - THIS LOOKS HEARTY - IT WILL BRING ME FORTITUDE
POP CORN
THIS CURSED FOOD ONLY MAKES ME MORE HUNGRY!
HOW IS THIS POSSIBLE
THAT smells good, Jefferson

BEWARE

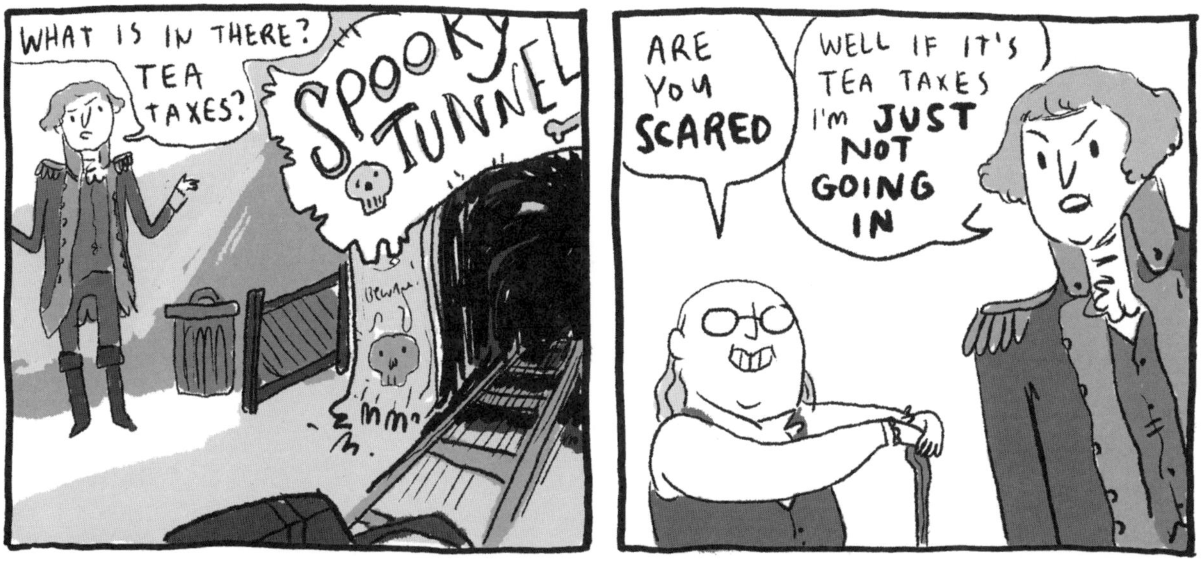
WHAT IS IN THERE? TEA TAXES?
SPOOKY TUNNEL
ARE YOU SCARED
WELL IF IT'S TEA TAXES I'M JUST NOT GOING IN

ABIGAIL WILL ENJOY IT

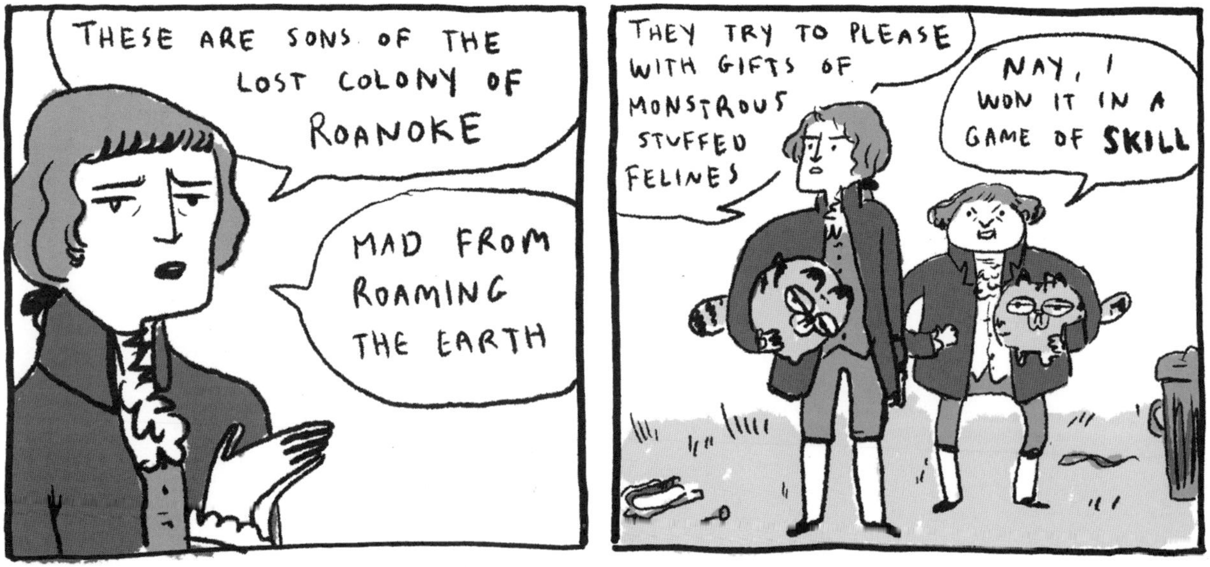
THESE ARE SONS OF THE LOST COLONY OF ROANOKE
MAD FROM ROAMING THE EARTH
THEY TRY TO PLEASE WITH GIFTS OF MONSTROUS STUFFED FELINES
NAY, I WON IT IN A GAME OF SKILL

OH FRANKLIN

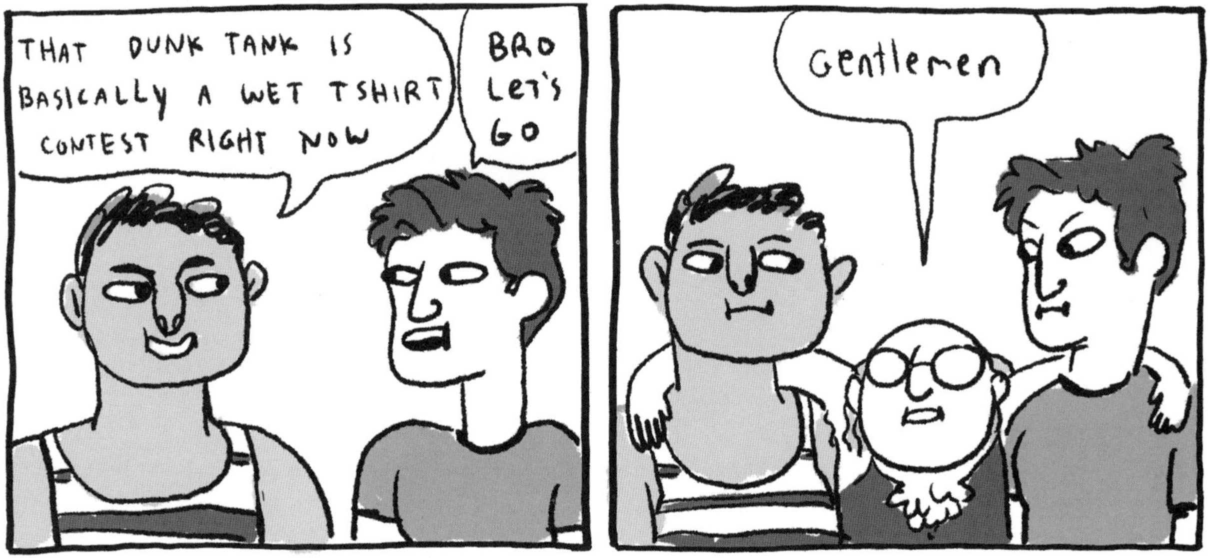
THAT DUNK TANK IS BASICALLY A WET TSHIRT CONTEST RIGHT NOW
BRO LET'S GO
Gentlemen

RAGE OF ACHILLES

TROJANS!
YOU WILL PAY

I FEAR WE WILL NOT CROSS THE RIVER BEFORE ACHILLES IS UPON US IN ALL HIS WRATH
TOO LATE!
RR
IPP
OH SHIT

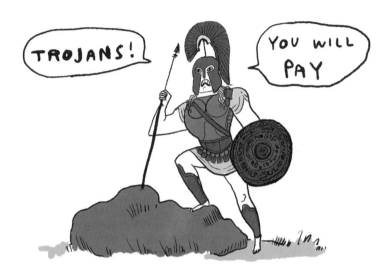

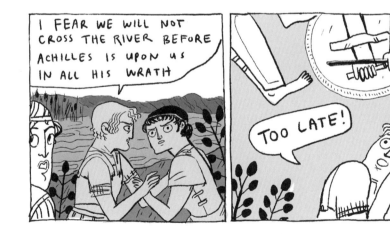

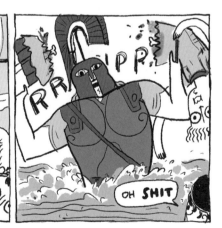

Achilles maybe needs some counselling, like, it's not as though I come to your house and fill it with slaughtered Trojans, why would you do that to mine? You know? Common courtesy.

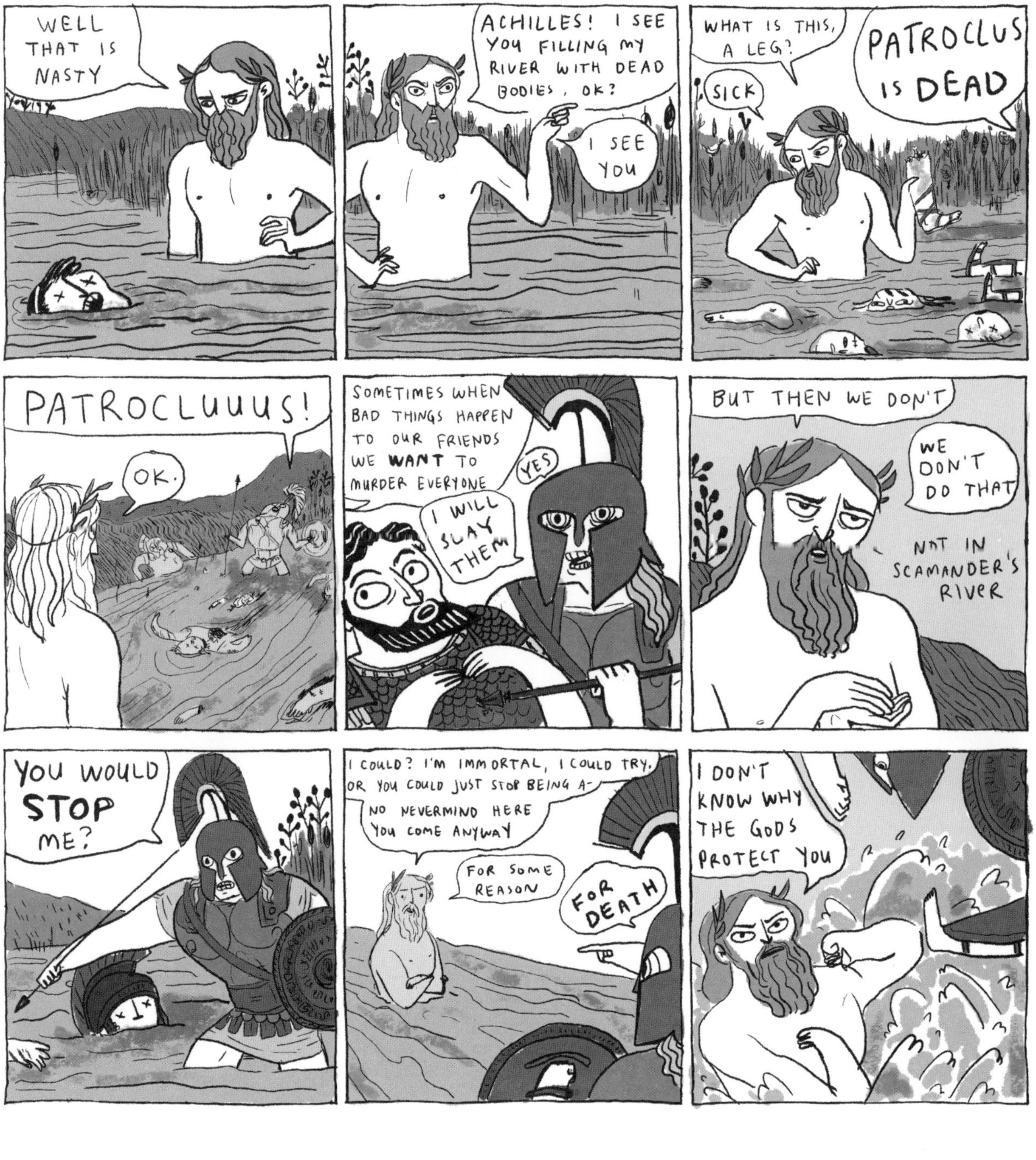
WELL THAT IS NASTY
ACHILLES! I SEE YOU FILLING MY RIVER WITH DEAD BODIES, OK?
I SEE YOU
WHAT IS THIS, A LEG?
SICK
PATROCLUS IS DEAD
PATROCLUUUS!
OK.
SOMETIMES WHEN BAD THINGS HAPPEN TO OUR FRIENDS WE **WANT** TO MURDER EVERYONE
YES
I WILL SLAY THEM
BUT THEN WE DON'T
WE DON'T DO THAT
NOT IN SCAMANDER'S RIVER
YOU WOULD **STOP** ME?
I COULD? I'M IMMORTAL, I COULD TRY. OR YOU COULD JUST STOP BEING A-
NO NEVERMIND HERE YOU COME ANYWAY
FOR SOME REASON
FOR DEATH
I DON'T KNOW WHY THE GODS PROTECT YOU

THE ENCHANTRESS

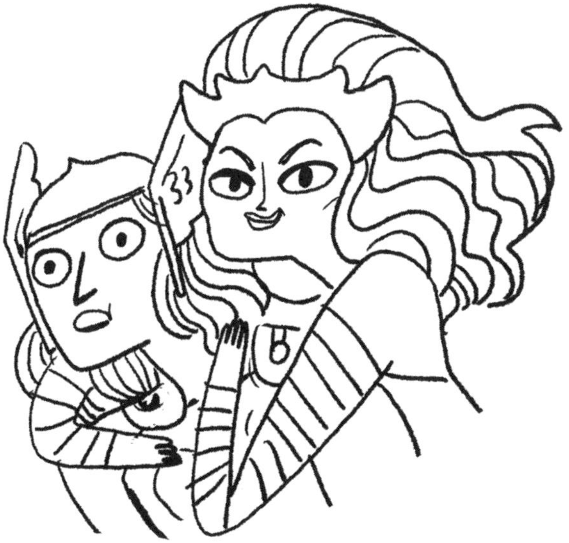

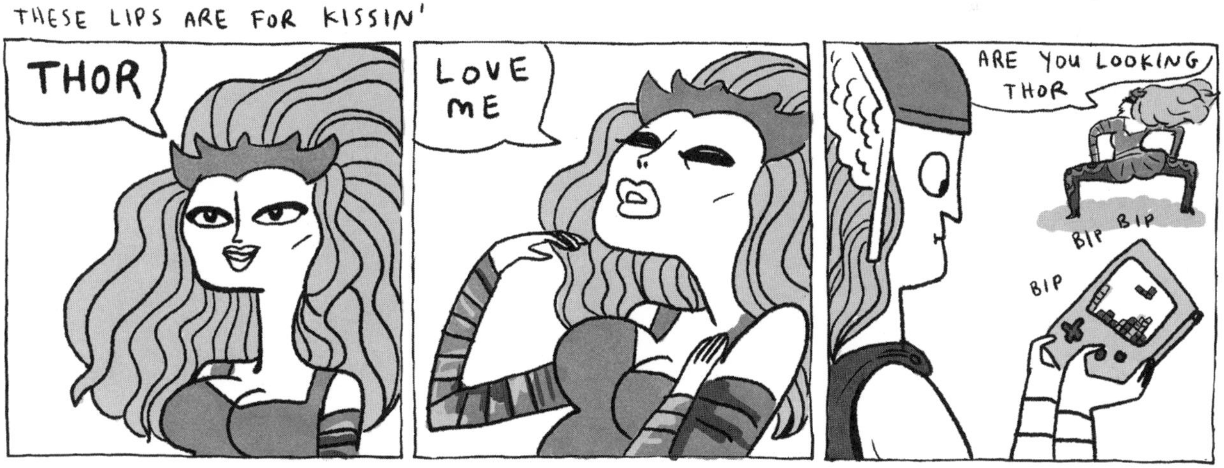
THESE LIPS ARE FOR KISSIN'
THOR
LOVE ME
ARE YOU LOOKING THOR
BIP BIP
BIP

Thor, Thor, Thor, hey Thor, it's me. Thor, are you looking, Thor?

HOW DID YOU GET IN WHY ARE YOU HERE

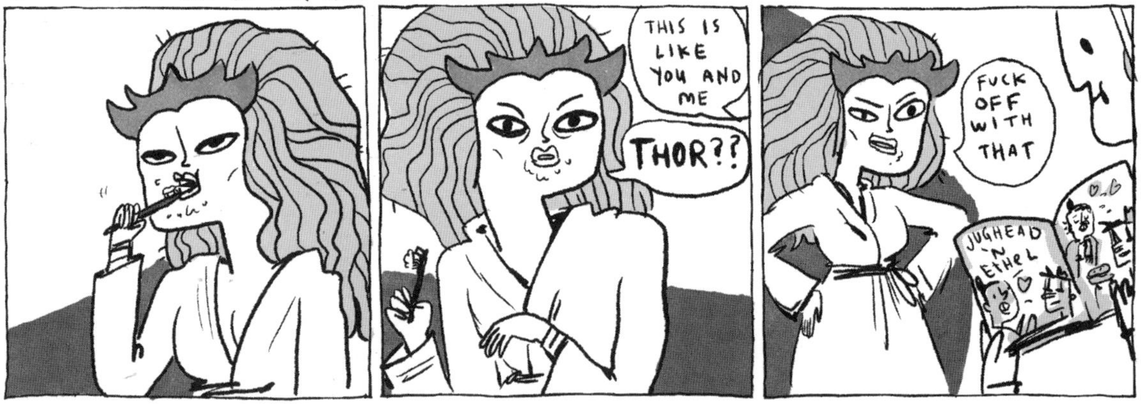
THIS IS LIKE YOU AND ME
THOR??
FUCK OFF WITH THAT
JUGHEAD 'N ETHEL

THAT'S THE TICKET

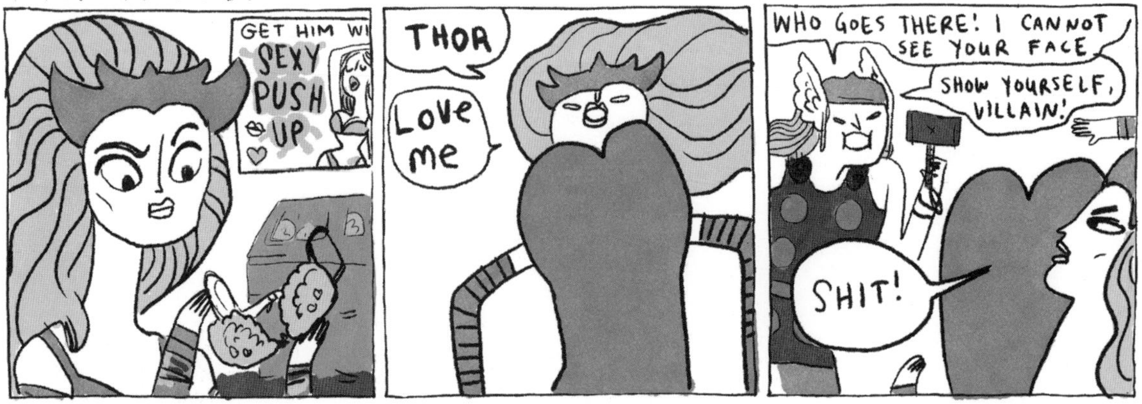
GET HIM WI
SEXY PUSH UP
THOR
Love me
WHO GOES THERE! I CANNOT SEE YOUR FACE
SHOW YOURSELF, VILLAIN!
SHIT!

HEART'S DESIRE

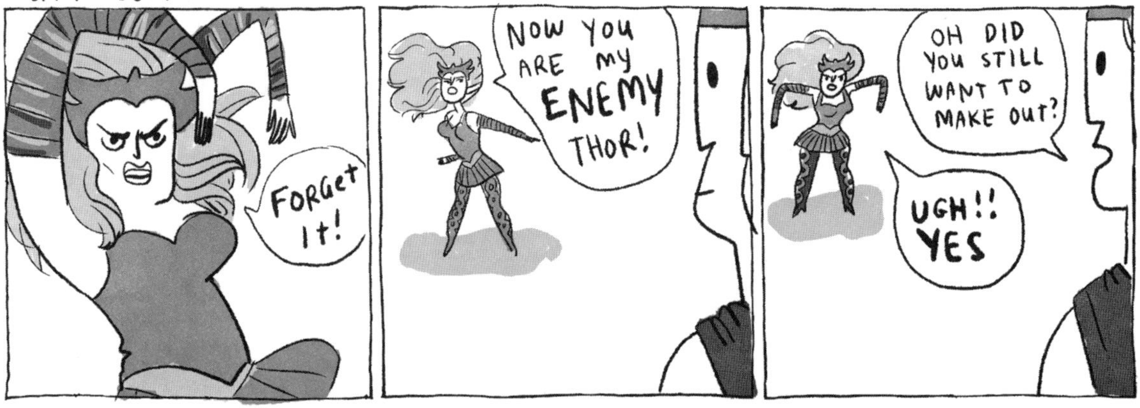
ForGet It!
NOW YOU ARE MY ENEMY THOR!
OH DID YOU STILL WANT TO MAKE OUT?
UGH!! YES

KATHERINE SUI FUN CHEUNG

WHAT BARRIERS

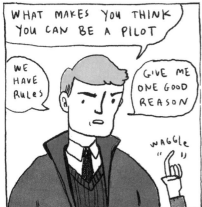

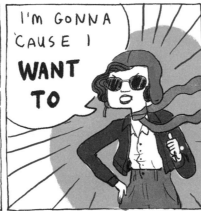

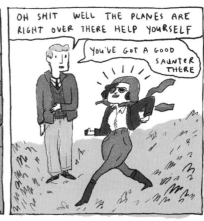

WHAT MAKES YOU THINK YOU CAN BE A PILOT
WE HAVE RULES
GIVE ME ONE GOOD REASON
WAGGLE
I'M GONNA 'CAUSE I WANT TO
OH SHIT WELL THE PLANES ARE RIGHT OVER THERE HELP YOURSELF
YOU'VE GOT A GOOD SAUNTER THERE

PRO SHOW

FIRST FEW HOURS OF LESSONS AND I HAVE TO SAY - YOU'RE A NATURAL
SO I HAVE A COUPLE OF THINGS IN MIND BEFORE ANY SOLO FLIGHTS,
THE USUAL
...
OR YOU COULD JUST GO, OK THEN
COOL - TIME FOR STUNTS

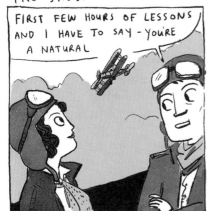

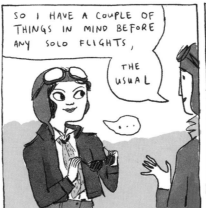

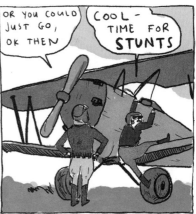

Katherine had this inspiring attitude she shared with a lot of early aviatrices. Aviation was brand new, and she thought, "That looks cool. I'd like to do that. So I will." Like it was that easy. Side note, not too much time goes by before Top Gun washes up once again on these shores.

BRIGHT STAR

SO, TODAY'S SCHEDULE, AS YOU CAN SEE-
AHEM- YOU'RE GOING TO HAVE TO TONE DOWN THAT THING WHERE YOU ARE COOLER AND MORE DARING THAN EVERYONE ELSE, IT'S DISTRACTING
WE ARE ALL COOL AND DARING HERE OK
CAN'T HELP IT SIR

TAKE MY BREATH AWAY

WHO IS TOP GUN
I AM
TOP GUN
YOU ARE NOT IN THIS MOVIE
STOP FLEXING
NO
TOP GUN

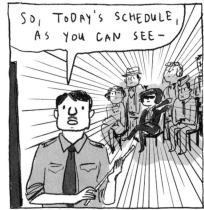

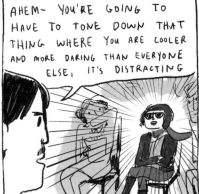

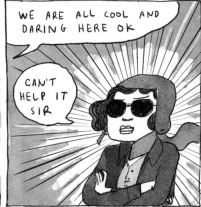

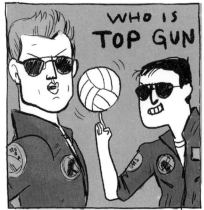

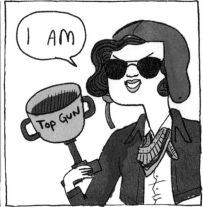

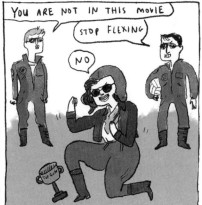

INDEX

Hailing from Cape Breton, Nova Scotia, Kate Beaton is the award-winning cartoonist of *Hark! A Vagrant*, the wildly popular webcomic, published as a bestselling book that was translated into French, Spanish, and German. She is also the author of the children's book *The Princess and the Pony* (Scholastic, 2015). Beaton earned a bachelor's degree in history and anthropology at Mount Allison University where she developed her lifelong obsessions with literature, history, and drawing, and began turning them into very funny comics. Her work has appeared in the *New Yorker*, *Harpers*, the *National Post*, and *The Best American Comics* anthology. Her website is harkavagrant.com.